Library of
Davidson College

Sainte-Beuve and Greco-Roman Antiquity

Sainte-Beuve
and
Greco-Roman
Antiquity

❖

Ruth E. Mulhauser

The Press of Case Western Reserve University
Cleveland and London • 1969

Copyright © 1969 by The Press of Case Western Reserve
University, Cleveland, Ohio 44106. All rights reserved.
Printed in the United States of America.
Standard Book Number: 8295–0158–4.
Library of Congress Catalogue Card Number: 69–17684.

❖

"L'écueil à éviter, ce
serait de voir l'Hellénisme
là où il n'y en a pas,
d'abuser de ce genre d'influence,
et de la trop étendre."

Causeries du lundi XII, 81

Preface

The twentieth century has witnessed a tremendous leap in cultural as well as in technological information. New means of instant communication by sight as well as by sound have impelled occidental man to investigate more thoroughly than ever before cultural traditions which had remained, except for sporadic encounters, insulated from his daily preoccupations. Artistic creativity in all its forms has sought and found new material and inspiration in the diverse traditions recently opened to it as well as in modern scientific technology. Historically, any period of forceful innovation has been accompanied by an apparently complete rejection of the prevailing culture, but with time the innovations seem to blend into a harmonious whole with the traditional culture and to enrich it.

The past hundred years in literary criticism have not been dissimilar to the more general cultural explosion: its history has been characterized by ferment, new directions, increased precision in methods and functions; a new science of aesthetics has attained its maturity. In such a context any consideration of Sainte-Beuve's vast critical production must inevitably be historic and analytic rather than directly relevant to our own time. And yet, certain parallels do appear, certain attitudes maintain a general validity. In fact, there is a curious analogy in the explosion of knowledge in the nineteenth century, the result of faster communication by railroads, broader dissemination of printed material through newspapers and the industrial production of books, as well as through contacts with new cultural areas as a result of colonization, to the explosion of knowledge in our own century. France, in particular, knew war and revolution, but the obverse sides of these coins were foreign experience and democratization at home. Even the traditional sources of her culture, Greece and ancient Italy, "made the headlines" as modern nations seeking independence and nationhood. Sainte-Beuve (1804–69) lived entirely within this period of change. Rarely absent from Paris after his arrival in 1818, he was keenly aware of, reflected, and even took a limited leadership in contemporary movements. His interest in Greco-Roman antiquity reflects, therefore, neither a reactionary attitude nor any alienation from his world; rather, it was a dynamic, pragmatic answer to intellectual problems of his day.

The very nature of the critic's Hellenism, circumstantially and designedly free from the traditional discipline of university study and continuing long after the completion of all formal education, gives an imprecise quality to any attempt at a factual exposition of his preparation or, indeed, of the level of his knowledge at any particular period. It is, nevertheless, possible to isolate certain pieces of the mosaic, as it were, to examine them individually, and, with new perception of the parts, to make some evaluation of the whole. Sainte-Beuve's knowledge of Latin, both the language and the literature, is obvious even to the most casual reader of his works: in the first part of the study, I have therefore concentrated more on his contacts with Greece, both ancient and modern, hoping thereby to bring balance to the evidence for the second part of the work and support for its general title. No picture of Sainte-Beuve's positions on certain questions related to this antiquity could claim any accuracy, moreover, if it did not take into account his personal reading, not only of Greek and Roman authors and the commentary on them but also of French humanistic literature, for this latter proved to be a rich source of inspiration and direction toward antiquity. Finally, the critic never lost sight of his own contemporary world. As a journalist and a Parisian, he perceived and charted its intellectual currents; often he was well acquainted with the men who were reponsible for new or changing ideas. His knowledge of things Greek was broadened and refined by the intellectual give-and-take of conversation with specialists, travellers, and native Greeks. He had a living contact with Greek civilization.

In a study such as this one it would be highly satisfying to be able to say with assurance, "This particular fact, Sainte-Beuve learned from that particular book," but in the end, such exactness is not nearly so important as his resultant attitudes. Sainte-Beuve never considered himself a "professional" classicist; he took great pains to disclaim any pretention in that field except as an amateur. He was an "adorateur d'Homère" rather than a savant. Whatever the source of his knowledge, it oriented his mind in certain ways, and the very heterogeneity of his knowledge gives a rather special character to his attitudes toward antiquity. A note of undue modesty on the subject characterizes all his public writings like a recurring refrain and has all too frequently been taken at face value by both his contemporaries and his subsequent critics.

A partial explanation of this modesty lies in the critic's own definition of a Hellenist. It is a definition fulfilled by few men of his generation, and even then only at the sacrifice of certain other aspects of Sainte-Beuve's own broad, humanistic Hellenism. This rigorous definition led Sainte-Beuve quite naturally to criticize French education in this area. He admired the English system, but even more apparent is his outspoken praise for the new German scientific method. Toward the end of his life, when French classicists had accepted the philological method, Sainte-Beuve felt obliged to warn against its exaggeration. For almost forty years, however, his active interest as an amateur provided a certain stimulus to his professional colleagues.

A further clarification of the critic's apparent ambivalence comes if one examines it from the point of view of the form in which he wrote, for literary criticism is inevitably a paraliterature dependent on a work of art before it. Various social and political pressures must be assumed to have played a role in the choice of the *lundi* to be written. It would be wrong, however, to negate entirely the critic's freedom of choice for his articles from among the hundreds of books published each year. If he returned again and again to books on antiquity, this fact is not solely a reflection of nineteenth-century production. It must also reflect some quality of Sainte-Beuve's critical mind. The individual judgments result from particular circumstances, but the continued choice of subject presents ample evidence of his constant preoccupation with Greco-Roman antiquity.

One pleasant duty remains to be fulfilled. This study has been long in preparation, for many extraneous reasons. I should be presumptuous if I said that it is a better work for the lapse of time, but I can, in all simplicity, say that it is a maturer study. It is a pleasure to acknowledge the kindness and generosity of two Conservateurs de la Collection Spoelberch de Lovenjoul, M. Marcel Bouteron and M. Jean Pommier, for permission to work there and to have microfilm made. I am particularly grateful to M. and Mme. Jean Bonnerot for their exemplary scholarship, suggestions and many kindnesses. Professor Lander MacClintock gave encouragement and helpful advice at an early stage of this study. I also thank Miss Nancy Devine for her expert aid in reference and bibliographic problems. Professor Frances Guille of the College of Wooster patiently read the manuscript at two different stages. My colleagues, Professors Rubén Benítez, Catherine Bill Osborn, and Francis Bliss read the manuscript and made valuable suggestions. I am particularly indebted to my colleague, Professor Lester G. Crocker and to my brother, Professor Frederick Mulhauser of Pomona College, for their encouragement and cogent advice in the preparation of this work. It is a pleasure to express my gratitude to the American Association of University Women for the faith in my project, expressed by a grant which allowed me time to read, reflect, and organize this study. I am also particularly glad to recognize a continuing debt to Case Western Reserve University and its administrative officers for two sabbatical leaves and much other aid. The entire responsibility, nevertheless, for the inadequacies and shortcomings is mine.

R. E. M.
Cleveland, Ohio

Note on Abbreviations

and Index Volumes for the Work of Sainte-Beuve

I. All editions and printings of Sainte-Beuve's works from his death until the present Pléiade editing have conformed to the pagination given in the two index volumes. I have given an identifying abbreviation, the volume and the page in the notes. I have, however, used the following editions in my own work.

Tab.   *Tableau historique et critique de la poésie française et du Théâtre français au XVIe siècle* (Paris: Charpentier, 1843).

Poésies complètes (Paris: Alphonse Lemerre, 1879), 2 vols.

P.L.   *Portraits littéraires* (Paris: Garnier Frères, n.d.), 3 vols.

P.C.   *Portraits contemporains* (Paris: Calmann-Lévy, 1881), 5 vols.

P.F.   *Portraits de femmes* (Paris: Garnier Frères, 1870).

Pr.L.   *Premiers Lundis* (Paris: Michel Lévy Frères, 1875), 3 vols.

Chat.   *Chateaubriand et son groupe littéraire sous l'Empire*, ed. M. Allem (Paris: Garnier Frères, 1948), 2 vols.

xiv • *Note on Abbreviations*

    C.L.   *Causeries du lundi* 3⁰ édition (Paris: Garnier Frères, n.d.), 15 vols.
    N.L.   *Nouveaux lundis* 5⁰ édition revue (Paris: Calmann-Lévy, 1879), 13 vols.
    EsV   *Etude sur Virgile* suivie d'une Etude sur Quintus de Smyrne 2⁰ édition (Paris: Michel Lévy Frères, 1870).
    Oeuvres   *Oeuvres* ed. Maxine Leroy. Bibliothèque de la Pléiade (Paris: Gallimard, 1949), 2 vols. I have used these volumes only for articles not collected elsewhere.

II. The index volumes are precious in any study of Sainte-Beuve:

    Charles Pierrot *Causeries du lundi, Portraits de femmes, et Portraits littéraires: Table générale et analytique* (Paris: Garnier Frères, 1926).

    Victor Giraud *Table alphabétique et analytique des "Premiers lundis" "Nouveaux lundis" et "Portraits contemporains"* (Paris: Calmann-Lévy, n.d.).

III. I have also abbreviated the following works of Jean Bonnerot to facilitate the constant use made of them.

    Bibliog. *Bibliographie de l'Oeuvre de Sainte-Beuve* (Paris: L. Giraud-Badin, 1937–52), 3 parts in 4 vols.

    C.g. *Correspondance générale de Sainte-Beuve* (Paris: Stock [Vols. 1–6]; Privat-Didier [Vols. 7–16], 1935–).

    Un Demi-Siècle. *Un Demi-Siècle d'études sur Sainte-Beuve 1904–1954* (Paris: "Les Belles Lettres," 1957).

IV. One other bibliography of Sainte-Beuve criticism which is very helpful is:

    Bruce H. Mainous and Hensley G. Woodbridge *A Sainte-Beuve Bibliography 1938–1952* (Rochester: University of Rochester Press, 1954).

Contents

PART I LANGUAGE AND READINGS
  1. Introduction   3
  2. Study and Readings   16
  3. The Activist   42
  4. Library and General View   74

PART II IMPLICATIONS FOR CRITICISM
  1. Historians and Historiography   97
  2. Homer and Erudition   116
  3. The *Greek Anthology* and Translation   147
  4. The Bucolic Poets and Poetic Theory   181
  5. The Active Campaign for Tradition   212

APPENDIX
List of Publications by Sainte-Beuve concerning Antiquity   243

BIBLIOGRAPHY   247

INDEX   255

PART I
❖
Language and Readings
❖

Ah! savoir le grec . . . c'est l'apprendre sans cesse . . .

Nouveaux lundis VI, 93, 94

Chapter 1

Introduction

At first sight the Empire seemed to have found both a new enthusiasm for the ancient cultures and a new depth of understanding of them. The Revolutionary and early Empire leaders talked a great deal about Greek democracy and Roman administration. As a consequence there is a Greco-Roman tinge to much of the writing of the period. The French language itself was enriched by numerous learned words from Greek stems and a popular verse of the time read:

> Myriagramme, Panthéon,
> Mètre, kilomètre, oxygène,
> Litre, centilitre, Odéon,
> Prytanée, hectare, hydrogène,
> Les Grecs ont pour nous tant d'attraits
> Que, de nos jours, pour bien entendre
> Et bien comprendre le français
> C'est le grec qu'il faudrait apprendre.[1]

The decorative arts and even ladies' fashions under Napoleon were inspired by ancient Rome. What seems at first to supply abundant evidence of a renaissance in Greco-Roman studies is, however, only a popular, superficial fashion, arising from an attempt at historic self-justification by the Revolutionaries and the Emperor rather than a genuine reaction of minds penetrated by ancient thought. Almost never was the study of Greek as a language at a lower ebb in France than at the beginning of the nineteenth century. It is common to point out that while English and German classical scholarship discovered new paths, notably in Homeric studies, France dallied in the "esprit antiquisant" of the eighteenth century, either reading *Le Jeune Anacharsis* of the Abbé Barthélemy or listening to La Harpe pay lip service to Greek literature, which he really could not read in the original. The Empire poets and men of letters were, for the most part, survivors from the *ancien régime*, creating polished didactic verse or translating Virgil, Horace, and Ovid into elegant French prose. But all of this was being done in a very traditional neoclassic fashion, and almost unquestioningly. Madame de Staël, however, raised something of an issue.

Committed to her belief in the continual progress of mankind, Madame de Staël interpreted Greek literature and civilization as inevitably inferior to Christian civilizations. Under this interpretation, Rome fared somewhat better in her esteem: and, it may be added, she knew Rome and Latin better. But the northern literatures profited both from Christianity and melancholy in her scale of values. She was not really interested in the Mediterranean civilizations, although she always bowed ceremoniously in the direction of Greece. Her trip to Germany also brought her into contact with some of the outstanding German scholars and intellectuals, with the result that she became aware of the new perspectives in Greek studies. After her visit to Italy with Schlegel she cast a veil of Romantic melancholy over the Roman ruins. It may well be suggested that Corinne's relegation of Mediterranean culture to secondary importance provoked a more articulate defense of the Greco-Roman tradition by new champions, who attempted to base their defense on something more than the neoclassic stock answers.

One of the curious points in the study of Empire literature is the seeming rivalry or antagonism between its two greatest writers, Madame de Staël and Chateaubriand, for it now appears that such a rivalry was more the doing of their friends than of the writers themselves.[2] The publication of *De la littérature* in 1800 was soon followed by that of *Le Génie du Christianisme* in 1802. Chateaubriand too believed that Christianity added an element of truth that had been lacking in even the greatest pagan literatures, but was tempted into areas that Madame de Staël had no desire to explore. Chateaubriand, like so many French writers before him, was bewitched by the idea of producing the great French epic. Already, in *Le Génie*, he had confronted Homeric texts with Biblical parallels, and although, by the dogma of his criticism, the Biblical text was always superior, the author was, upon occasions at least, more eloquent about the Homeric passage.[3] This critical preparation resulted in *Les Natchez*, and then in *Les Martyrs*, but, as Sainte-Beuve pointed out much later, Chateaubriand had tried to write an epic by prescription, and such an undertaking could only produce a kind of pastiche, an overintellectualized work of art. On the other hand, although his Homer was not completely freed from the insipidity of late eighteenth-century taste, Chateaubriand did infuse into the Greek poet a melancholy which he expressed in a magnificent, sonorous style, one which would lead Sainte-Beuve to remark about Chateaubriand repeatedly, "c'est l'Homère de nôtre siècle."[4] In the end, whether Chateaubriand's descriptions are accurate or not, whether his Homer is our poet or not, are secondary details. The important point is that he lent his sonorous style and descriptive imagination to create a picture of Hellenic lands such that, for the new generation of 1827, the true Greece, with its landscapes, was the Greece of *Les Martyrs* and *L'Itinéraire*.

To Boissonade must go the credit for beginning the reaction against La Harpe's doctrinaire and, all too frequently, mistaken views of ancient literatures. This was not a labor to be accomplished single-handed nor overnight, but Boissonade was not alone. In 1814, Villemain wrote: "M. de La Harpe n'avait pas assez médité les Anciens."[5] At the Athénée, in 1815, Lermercier attacked the doctrinaire critic, though somewhat abortively, for he began from an axiom that in poetry and eloquence Greece was recognized as the absolute model of perfection. The return to antiquity inherent in such a concept was neither critical nor scientific. The historian Sismondi brought the public nearer to a new concept of Greece in order to explain his ideas on the isolation of seventeenth-century French Classicism. By 1820 Villemain and Cousin were both teaching at the Sorbonne, and Daunou was at the Collège de France. The new spirit found an exponent in the publishing business too: Firmin Didot dreamed of a family reputation equal to that of the Estiennes in the sixteenth century. With the collaboration of Adamantios Coray, the Greek patriot and scholar, and later with the help of the Greek Dr. Nicolas Piccolos, and of Boissonade, Courrier, and Chardon de la Rochette, Didot published new texts of Greek classics as well as new translations. Courrier's idea of translation into popular language created a stir and much criticism, but it posed squarely again the question: "What constitutes a good translation?" Burnouf's new grammar of classical Greek appeared in 1813, and in 1816 Hase began to teach modern Greek at the Sorbonne. The creation of a chair in modern Greek emphasizes the new dual role of Greece in nineteenth-century France.

The most important name in poetry for the Romantic generation of 1827, curiously enough, just barely escaped oblivion. At his death André Chénier had published only a few poems and none of his more important works, which, even today after careful editing, remain unfinished and fragmentary but demonstrate the great talent and thoughtful artistry of this "martyr-poet." Chateaubriand, who saw some manuscript poems of Chénier, was struck by a note of melancholy similar to that he was trying to express in *René*. It was not until 1819, however, than an edition of the Chénier poems was published, thus assuring the poet immortality almost thirty years after his death. Chénier's work was received with enthusiasm by the public and especially by the youthful generation of poets. Lamartine recognized explicitly Chénier's influence at this formative stage of his own talent. Hugo announced that the book would be either tossed aside or read many times. Musset, too, often recalled Chénier's verse. But for Sainte-Beuve the effect was more profound, for as G. Walter wrote, "Il poursuivra toute sa vie durant, la défense et l'illustration de l'oeuvre d'André Chénier."[6] It is therefore important to understand Chénier's concept of poetry and to grasp Sainte-Beuve's understanding of Chénier, who was of fundamental importance in the critic's Romantic universe.

The key to Chénier's aesthetic is to be found in his concept of "invention," or poetic creation as we should call it today. "Ce n'est qu'aux inventeurs que la terre est promise," he wrote at the very beginning of his poem "L'Invention." He soon seemed to be aware, however, of a paradox in his thinking, for how was he to imitate the ancients but at the same time dare to be new and original? In order to dispose of this paradox, the poet was forced to redefine the terms "invention" and "imitation." In addition to describing what all men experience and understand, the true poet, according to Chénier, has also the power to see true analogies and to make a synthesis. In fact, what constitutes the poet's originality is his power to express by means of "des noeuds certains, imprévus et nouveaux" the analogies he has perceived. Chénier thus clearly comprehended the basic metaphoric nature of poetic language, and a great part of his further discussion logically becomes a theory of style.[7] The poet further understood, moreover, that style and thought are inseparable and personal; from this point he logically moved to stress the right of individuality.[8] What Chénier sought to restore to poetry from the ancients was their emotional impact. He found the Greek poets open and unspoiled by the complexities of modern civilization, which he repeatedly taxed with being harmful to the poet's true expression. The rich expression of the Greek poets derived from their quality of being "natural." "Eux seuls, dans les égarements de l'enthousiasme, suivaient la nature et la vérité. . . . " Compared to the Greeks, Shakespeare and the northern authors produce "convulsions barbares," according to Chénier, whereas the Greeks are gay, laughing even in the face of death. The point of perfection for Chénier is personal simplicity, naïveté:

> C'est donc la naïveté seule qui produit en nous des émotions vives, profondes et rapides. Un peintre, un auteur seulement pompeux et noble sera copié par tout le monde: celui qui est naïf est à jamais inimitable; sa naïveté est le sceau qu'il imprime à toutes ses pensées, à toutes ses expressions, qui fait que son ouvrage est le sien et ne saurait être celui d'un autre. Vingt autres peuvent être aussi naïfs, aussi excellents que lui; ils ne le seront pas comme lui; ce seront de nouveaux originaux.

This definition of style as a very personal expression set Chénier apart from his contemporaries, but it also implies the answer to the question of his imitation of ancient writers. There was no hesitation on his part in borrowing from ancient authors whatever seized his poetic imagination. His own poetic image is that of a gardener grafting the ancients onto a fresh stem:

> De ce mélange heureux l'insensible douceur
> Donne à mes fruits nouveaux une antique saveur.[10]

This creative imitation which guarantees originality led Chénier to emphasize the importance of tradition, for the aggregate of ideas and true emotions resulting from the observation of human nature form the patrimony of all men and generations. The heritage changes and increases as it passes through the individual mind. Customs and circumstances choose the appropriate facets to be developed in one period or another, in one form or another, until they finally become meaningful to mankind and rejoin the patrimony in new and original expression.

It would be difficult to exaggerate the importance of Chénier's ideas on poetic creation, originality, and tradition to the comprehension of Sainte-Beuve's thought. The critic openly proclaimed in the *Tableau historique et critique de la poésie française . . . au XVIe siècle,* and in *Vie, Poésies et Pensées de Joseph Delorme,* that the Romantic school derived from Chénier. Both as a poet and later as a critic he returned again and again to interpret for himself and his readers Chénier's importance in the renaissance of French lyric poetry. Sainte-Beuve wrote no less than six articles on André Chénier, in addition to the important considerations incorporated into the *Tableau,* and especially into the *Joseph Delorme.* The first article dated from 1829, and the last from 1862, so that there can be no doubt about the fidelity of this admiration or of the central position given to Chénier and his poetics. In the course of all these articles Sainte-Beuve looked at Chénier and his work from several vantage points: he viewed the poet as a political writer during the Revolution; he analyzed the difference of impact that the mature production of the poet, had he lived, would probably have had, and that which the late publication of his work in 1819 actually did have; he reviewed Becq de Fouquières' edition of Chénier's poetry. Perhaps the most germane work other than the *Pensées de Joseph Delorme* is an article comparing Chénier and Régnier, who stand independent at either end of French Classicism: Régnier looking back to a freedom which had passed away, Chénier looking ahead to a new poetics.[11] Sainte-Beuve returned many times to the statement that Chénier brought a new quality, a veritable renovation, to the insipid poetry of the eighteenth century. The critic never really used one of the oversimplified categorical epithets for Chénier; rather, he saw Chénier as a poet of transition, one of the rare artists who can combine into one whole the best of past and future.

In 1855 the critic looked in retrospect to the year 1827, when a group of young poets was searching for a truly contemporary and personal manner of expression. In feelings and ideas they felt an affinity for Chateaubriand, but in poetic form "ils aimaient à se réclamer d'André Chénier, non pas tant pour l'imiter directement que par instinct de fraîcheur, de renouvellement et par amour pour cette beauté grecque dont il nous rendait les vives élégances et les grâces."[12] The point is delicately complex, in that Sainte-Beuve eagerly accepted Chénier as a teacher of poetic form for his generation, but explicitly rejected any idea of direct imitation. It is also important that this statement of 1855 repeated in essence a part of the third pensée that he had published under the alias of Joseph Delorme in 1829,[13] in which he analyzed the influence of Chateaubriand, Madame de Staël, and Chénier. "Joseph Delorme" placed Chateaubriand "hors de cause" as an accepted general influence on the whole generation. The followers of the other two authors, he said, tended to quarrel among themselves over the importance of style and form. (Already, for the young Sainte-Beuve, careful poetic expression was not incompatible with the expression of spontaneous emotion which was sought by Madame de Staël's followers.) After this general statement follow nine consecutive pensées on the technical analysis of Chénier's alexandrine verses before the critic turns to the question of Chénier's physical imagery. "Le mot propre et pittoresque," relieved occasionally by a more abstract epithet which implies rather than states its thought, is the new ideal, more telling and poetic than the metaphysical abstractions so traditional in French poetry.[14] After considering the renewal of the elegy by Chénier and noting its use since that time, quoting among other examples his own efforts in the elegiac form, Sainte-Beuve devotes the last pensée to the subject of artistic feeling or inspiration. The passage is an important definition of Sainte-Beuve's concept of poetry, but it also clearly echoes Chénier in "L'Invention."

Some fifteen years later, Sainte-Beuve was moved to defend Chénier against the unimaginative pedantic criticism of Arnould Frémy, who saw the poet as a mere copier, a superficial disciple and plagiarist of the ancients. In a tone of controlled urbanity, which scarcely covered his impatient anger at Frémy's incomprehension of Chénier's particular poetic gift, Sainte-Beuve quoted Chénier's own description of his borrowings and named this procedure "cet art libre, ce procédé vivant."[15] He further defined Chénier's legacy to the younger poets as "color"; he set the tone somewhat like a classic and poetic Walter Scott. Chénier had, both in his own time and for later generations, that quality highly prized by the Greeks, "la jeunesse, la fraîcheur et la fleur, le θαλερόν si l'on me permet de l'appeler par son nom, le *novitas floridas* de Lucrèce." The final point in Sainte-Beuve's defense was an attempt to assign to Chénier a truer literary rank than that implied by the negative "not of first importance" of Frémy. Perhaps, suggested the critic, some place between Propertius and Theocritus, some role approaching that of Meleager in the first *Anthology*—Meleager, who synthesized the poetic heritage of the Greeks for his contemporary public. The full extent of meaning in this analogy is not completely clear if this article of defense and justification is read separately, but it does indicate that the limitations of Chénier's talent were not hidden from Sainte-Beuve. Indeed, he had pointed them out in the 1829 comparison of Régnier and Chénier. The two talents complement each other in many ways, but especially in the fact that Chénier was a more conscious artist than Régnier, though Régnier's poetry sprang more directly from life experience. This centrality of Chénier is all-important to the understanding of Sainte-Beuve's romanticism as well as his concept of poetry, but at no time did Sainte-Beuve become a blind disciple or imitator of the Byzantine poet.

Second only to Chénier in the critic's faithful admiration were the Pléiade poets. From his first full-length work, *Tableau historique et critique de la poésie française . . . au XVIe siècle*, to the last triple article on Du Bellay in 1867, Sainte-Beuve maintained a predilection and admiration for these poets. Though it can be only conjecture, it is very reasonable to think that it was Ronsard and Belleau who led Sainte-Beuve back to Anacreon and the Anacreontic poets. It might well have been Ronsard's admiration and imitation of Pindar that caused Sainte-Beuve to try to read the Greek poet.

As with Chénier, however, Sainte-Beuve was not blind to the limitations of the Pléiade poets in their attempts to adapt Greek models to French verse. The important point here in both cases is the clear predilection for the most hellenizing poets in the French tradition.

What seems at first sight to be a thin veneer of fashionable Greco-Roman style during the First Empire proves on closer observation to have another aspect among the outstanding literary figures who display a more profound, direct and influential interest in this same Greco-Roman antiquity. If Madame de Staël challenged Mediterranean supremacy, Chateaubriand made Greek landscapes and Homer's poetry real and dynamic. New approaches in criticism began to question La Harpe's doctrinaire pronouncements. Boissonade and his fellow scholars, critics, and teachers introduced new views on ancient literature resulting from their research. Texts were made easily available for direct study. It is hardly surprising to find that Chénier's poetry and poetic theory created such an impact in 1819. He seemed to have a peculiarly modern note for the generation that had been born with the First Empire. For Sainte-Beuve, the literary climate of the First Empire and the impact of Chénier were formative and directing experiences during his adolescent years.

Notes

1. *Revue de l'an VIII*. Quoted in: Maurice Badolle, *L'Abbé Barthélemy et l'hellénsime en France dans la seconde moitié du XVIII⁰ siècle* (Paris: Presses universitaires, 1928), p. 386.
2. *P.F.*, pp. 116–17.
3. Blaise Briod, *L'Homérisme de Chateaubriand* (Paris: Anc. H. Champion, 1928), p. 83. See also Louis Bertrand, *La Fin du Classicisme et le Retour à l'Antique* (Paris: Arthème Fayard et Cie., n.d.), p. 32.
4. *P.C.* III, 321, etc.
5. René Canat, *L'Hellénisme des Romantiques* (Paris: Didier, 1951–55), 3 vols., I, 76. Much of my general introduction is taken from Professor Canat's admirable synthesis, to which I refer all those who are interested in this subject. Despite the separate titles for the individual volumes of Canat's work, all future references will be abbreviated to Canat, I, II and III, with the page number.
6. André Chénier, *Oeuvres complètes,* ed. G. Walter (Paris: Editions de la Pléiade, 1958), p. xxxiii.
7. Francis Scarfe, *André Chénier His Life and Work 1762–1794* (Oxford: Clarendon Press, 1965), p. 96. The entirety of Chapter 5, "His Views on Poetry," has been very helpful.
8. O qu'ainsi parmi nous des esprits inventeurs
   De Virgile et d'Homère atteignent les hauteurs,
   Sachent dans la mémoire avoir comme eux un temple,
   Et sans suivre leurs pas imiter leur exemple;
   Faire, en s'éloignant d'eux, avec un soin jaloux,

Ce qu'eux-mêmes ils feraient s'ils vivaient parmi nous!
Chénier, p. 130.
9. Chénier, p. 681.
10. This phrase, "antique saveur," will be important for Sainte-Beuve.
11. *P.L.* I, 159–75.
12. *C.L.* XII, 59.
13. Charles Augustin Sainte-Beuve, *Vie, poésies et pensées de Joseph Delorme*, ed. G. Antoine (Paris: Nouvelles Editions latines, 1956), pp. 131–34. Even here Sainte-Beuve corrected himself on the word "disciple," saying: "c'est entre les disciples ou plutôt les successeurs de ce jeune poète. . . ."
Henceforth this volume will be referred to as Antoine.
14. Antoine, pp. 146–47.
15. *P.C.* V, 313–14. Sainte-Beuve quoted Chénier's "Epître sur ses ouvrages" (*Oeuvres*, pp. 156–60).

Chapter 2
Study and Readings

The generation of 1827, as Sainte-Beuve called himself and his contemporaries, was initiated into literature through the works of Madame de Staël, Chateaubriand, and Chénier; in these authors they found exalted art, aesthetic religion, liberty, and most especially, a fervent or dynamic attitude toward life. In the meantime, however, their formal education was less contemporary and showed few signs of a renewed vision of the world. After the disruption of the revolutionary years and the new orientation of the *écoles centrales*, Napoleon re-established in 1802 the primacy of Latin in the lycée education, with the persisting conviction that the study of Latin was the best initiation to intellectual discipline.[1]

This philosophy marked the return to the pre-Revolutionary theory, with the emphasis not only on understanding and reading Latin, but also on writing Latin prose and verse, and on speaking the ancient tongue.[2] The rapid succession of changes in the organization and the programs of the schools had been more specious than real during the Revolution and early Empire. The philosophy of French public education in 1800 was still that formulated in 1598 and published in 1600. It said in part: "Les collèges sont des établissements littéraires et par éducation littéraire, il faut entendre culture gréco-latine."[3] The Revolution brought some changes, however, and especially a new organization. The *écoles centrales* replaced the Latin-Greek orientation by an emphasis on utilitarian social and physical sciences. The subject of the Concours de l'an V was: "rechercher les moyens de donner parmi nous une nouvelle activité à l'étude de la langue grecque et de la langue latine."[4] The report of Roger Martin (19 brumaire de l'an VII, or November 10, 1798) suggested the desirability of an organized study of French language and literature, and deplored the small amounts of time devoted to Latin and Greek culture in the *écoles centrales*.[5] Such discussions led to the creation of the lycées, in 1801, as secondary schools where "les lettres redevenaient l'axe et la moëlle du système." Any emphasis on French language and literature was dropped, and Latin became once again the central point of general instruction.[6]

The French university managed to weather the storm of the Revolution and the Hundred Days, but since mere existence was the most important problem of the day, there was little time for new constructive planning. In 1818, at the distribution of prizes for the general competitive exmainations, M. Andrieux, professor of the Collège Bourbon, treated in Latin the following subject: "Non metuendum esse ne juvenes in tractandis veterum scriptis concipiant insanum status popularis amorem aut regni odium legibus temperate."[7] The statement of 1821 by the professors reflects the atmosphere of the period; they took as the basis for their teaching "la religion, la monarchie, la légitimité et la charte."[8] The decade of 1820 was violent with student riots, the suppression of the Faculty of Paris and its re-creation under different men, the suppression of the Ecole Normale, and finally the creation of a Ministry of Public Education. By 1828, however, Cousin and Guizot had been restored to their chairs, and Villemain appointed. A new and brilliant period in French higher education opened under these three exceptional thinkers and talented orators.

Secondary education under the Empire and Restoration presents a somewhat more complex picture, for one of the functions of the newly created lycées was to provide general cultural studies at their highest level. According to this plan, "la maîtrise ès arts doit être la prérogative des lycées comme elle était autrefois celle des grands collèges."[9] Henceforth, no French literature was to be taught at the university level. Literature professors, therefore, composed Latin and French essays at the *licence* level, and, at the doctoral level, two theses: one on rhetoric or logic, and the other on classical literature. At the lycée level the program of studies allotted a certain proportion of time generally to "literary studies," but within this general grouping were included philosophy, history, and geography, as well as what today would be called literature. Furthermore, the heading of "literature" grouped together French, Latin, and Greek in the large Paris lycées. The teaching of Greek in the provinces was by no means universal during this period. As we shall see, Sainte-Beuve testified that there was no Greek taught in Boulogne-sur-mer. Almost inevitably Latin assumed the central position. Dupont-Ferrier, in his history of the great Lycée Louis-le-Grand described the situation thus:

> En 3°, en 2°, en Rhétorique, il s'agissait d'étudier la littérature de trois langues. Le temps réservé à chacune est impossible à préciser exactement, car on les confondait volontiers dans les programmes et sur les horaires. Ainsi en septembre 1814, sur 29 h. ½ de

classes, on consacrait aux "langues française, latine et grecque" 13 h. ½ en 3°, 15 h. ½ en 2°, et 13 h. ½ en Rhétorique. En 1837 Salvandy accordait aux "langues anciennes et française" 7 classes sur 11, en 3° et en seconde; et 10 sur 11 en Rhétorique. C'était ensuite à chaque professeur de distribuer harmonieusement, entre les trois littératures, le temps dont il pouvait disposer. . . . Comme dans les classes de grammaire, les latins l'emportaient sur les français et sur les grecs.[10]

During the Restoration even this admirable institution felt the financial pinch, and although the head of the school recognized that Greek was the basis of all education he was forced to eliminate three Greek professors, with the result of further weakening the study of that language. The education of the generation of 1827, then, was Latin-centered at the expense, not only of Greek studies, but even of the students' own national heritage, both historic and literary. Even as a youth, however, Sainte-Beuve supplemented some of the weaknesses of the formal system of the time by independent methods and by intellectual contact with some of the most active minds of the day.

In *Volupté*, Sainte-Beuve makes Amaury recount his introduction to the Greek language. He tells how, after reading the books on Greece of Daguesseau and Rollin, he conceived the desire to learn Greek, and since no one around him could decipher the Greek alphabet, he began alone and unaided, stubbornly, lulling himself with the dream that soon he would go to Paris where people knew Greek. Paris, to the young boy, seemed to be the city where it would be easiest to learn Greek. There were moments, at that time, when Amaury centered all his future ambition and happiness on being able some day to read Aesop fluently, alone on a grey day after his learned classes were over, under a poor little roof that would remind him of his present abode, in one of those deserted streets where Descartes had remained hidden for three years.[11] A mixture of Romantic revery and stout intellectual curiosity, recounted with a touch of gentle irony, characterized this retrospective picture, drawn by the author almost fifteen years after his own arrival in Paris. It was probably taken in large measure from his own boyhood experience. It also quite aptly characterized the fundamental duality in the critic's attitude toward antiquity, particularly Greek antiquity. Though this duality of sentiment and intellect was never completely resolved, it evolved, in the critic's maturity, into a strong intellectual conviction. Meanwhile Sainte-Beuve's characteristic intellectual curiosity is reflected in the turning of young Amaury from Rollin and Daguesseau to the very fundamental instrument, the Greek language itself, and with sufficient force to make him begin his studies unaided. This curiosity was reinforced by an active imagination, conjuring up future happiness as a result of knowing Greek. Madame Sainte-Beuve was probably very little moved by this kind of motivation for studying in Paris, if indeed her son ever tried to convince her by such arguments to send him there to finish his studies. She did, however, find the financial means in 1818 for him to study in the capital even before his baccalaureate degree. One of his first acts in Paris was to appeal to his uncle for help in finding a tutor of Greek. In the summer of 1818 Sainte-Beuve studied Greek privately with a former priest, Michel Chasles, a strict teacher who was also the father of the critic Philarète Chasles, who was later to be Sainte-Beuve's colleague at the Mazarin Library.[12]

In the fall of that year, Sainte-Beuve was studying the *Iliad* and the Gospels in Greek, and by 1822, the year in which he won the first national prize for his original Latin verse, he also won honorable mention in his lycée for Greek-French translation.[13] This latter prize is significant both as a measure of his ability to read Greek and also for the fact that, despite his unorthodox beginning, he had overtaken and surpassed his fellow students in Greek.

His schoolboy journal of readings for this period also contains indications of his interest in Greek as well as Latin literature. Sainte-Beuve's predilection for history was already evident in the quotations from Sallust, Suetonius, and Tacitus, and in his perceptive comments on Seneca and Augustus. In addition to the historians, the boy was also reading poetry quite widely. One week, for instance, he read Ovid, the eleventh idyl of Theocritus, and some Catullus, according to his journal entries. Occasionally his comments are pointed and mature, as when he wrote that some pedagogues characterized Tacitus for their students by the lines: "Brevis esse laboro/Obscurus fio." He added sharply, "Insensibles, ils critiquent ce qu'ils n'entendent pas."[14] Another entry is a French translation of Sappho's poem in the eighth chapter of Longinus's *On the Sublime*. This text deviates from Boileau's translation, but the variations are hardly important enough to envisage the possibility of a personal translation from Greek. A later notebook for the period, covering roughly the years 1823–29, contains seventeen quotations in Greek from Epictetus.[15] This number of quotations, their sporadic appearance, would seem to indicate Sainte-Beuve had in his hands the Greek text of the *Manual*, and was not merely copying quotations from a secondary source. Notes from other Greco-Roman writers or commentaries include Plato, Plutarch, Aristotle, Homer, Apuleius, Virgil, Xenophon, Anacron, Suetonius, Tacitus, Cicero, Ovid, and Seneca. A note such as Number 730 gives some idea of the program of the young journalist: "Lire *De vita beata. De tranquillitate animi*, de

Sénèque; l'*Ethique* d'Aristote, les *Offices* de Cicéron, Bacon, Charron, *Léviathan* de Hobbes, *Gouvernement civil* de Locke, Shaftesbury." In Note 48 Sainte-Beuve already recognized his limitations as a polyglot, saying, "Je ne suis pas comme les apôtres, et n'ai pas le don des langues; Mithridate en savait vingt-deux; Ennius qui en savait trois, disait qu'il avait trois coeurs." It is clear that at this period Sainte-Beuve read both Latin and Greek authors for his own culture and amusement. While he read the Latin authors in the original, it would seem that during this time he read the Greek authors mostly in French translation.

Sainte-Beuve's study of Greek was not entirely a solitary and classroom affair, for he received much encouragement from several outstanding teachers of the time. If Sainte-Beuve ever did "burn to learn Greek" in Boulogne, he probably received sympathetic understanding and encouragement from M. Clouet, whose own culture, however, was in the traditional Latin pattern. M. Clouet marked the boy's successes as a student with gift copies of Horace and Caesar, and Sainte-Beuve wrote at least one letter from Paris full of affectionate gratitude for his teacher's interest in him.[16] In Paris Sainte-Beuve sat under two teachers of classics notable for their activity in classical erudition of the period: Joseph Planche and Jules-Aimable Pierrot. Planche, by his lexicographic and editorial work, did much to renew the study of Greek in the French schools of the period. Pierrot was more of a Latinist than a Greek scholar, and was later one of the editors of the Panckoucke Latin-French series. He was a liberal thinker in all he did, and was well aware of the new trends of thought about classical antiquity. Less famous than these two men was Théodore Gaillard, about whom Sainte-Beuve wrote affectionately to Eustache Barbe, his Boulonnais friend, saying, "Après M. Clouet, c'est, je crois, celui qui m'a montré le plus d'affection et prodigué [le] plus de soins."[17] Sainte-Beuve remained in contact with Gaillard, and over the years consulted him on Latin subjects and visited with him in Précy. The final teacher who exerted direct influence on the young man's life was, of course, Paul F. Dubois, who became the founder and editor of *Le Globe*, where he gave Sainte-Beuve his first opportunities and lessons in journalism.

In addition to the personal direction of his teachers, Sainte-Beuve had the opportunity during his student years to attend various evening courses of lectures by outstanding scholars. In 1822, with M. Vitet, he attended Jouffroy's course on aesthetics.[18] He also attended Tissot's course on Virgil in 1820.[19] In 1824 Raoul-Rochette lectured on Greek art, and in 1825 Henri Patin, whom Sainte-Beuve knew at *Le Globe*, lectured on Greek tragedy for the group "les Bonnes Lettres." In short, what the curriculum of the schools lacked in the stimulation of the contemporary discoveries and new theories was compensated for by the personality of his teachers and the extracurricular lectures which he attended. One aspect of this manner of learning was inadequate, as Sainte-Beuve was to discover later in life; when he turned seriously again to Greek literature, he felt insufficiently competent in handling the language itself. Despite his own sense of the inadequacy of his classical education, however, Sainte-Beuve, of all the Romantic writers of his generation, was probably the best trained in Greek, and the one most naturally inclined to a real appreciation of both the language and literature. Just as the young critic varied from the norm of his generation by his liberal Jacobin politics, so he did also by his training and active pursuit of knowledge about antiquity.

Although the years 1830–40 are not so rich in precise evidence of the critic's reading and study of antiquity as the previous decade, they do, nevertheless, provide sufficient evidence to allow us to believe with some objective security that Sainte-Beuve maintained contact with ancient civilization, even while attempting to solve the more concrete and circumstantial problems of his own economic future, his political and religious orientation, and his role as a creative artist apart from his critical journalism. Except for the short-lived embarrassing situation created by the rumor that Lamartine, if named ambassador to Greece, would choose the young critic for his secretary, and an equally aborted plan to take a *licence ès lettres* requiring a translation from French into Greek, Sainte-Beuve does not seem to have been actively engaged in advancing his knowledge of the Greek language, ancient or modern, during the first half of this decade.

It is apparent, nevertheless, that from the *Joseph Delorme* in 1829 to the major article on Chénier in 1839 Sainte-Beuve was reading Chénier attentively, and his personal copy of the poet's works is full of marginal notes pointing to Greek sources for the poems.[20] When in 1839 Sainte-Beuve asked for an edition of the poems that would point up all of Chénier's inspiration from ancient poets, it was obviously because he himself had spontaneously engaged in this kind of reading and knew its possibilities, as well as his own limitations to do such an edition.[21] Both the delight and the frustration for Sainte-Beuve in his reading of Chénier during these years must have contributed to his final decision to read Greek with a tutor.

In 1835 Sainte-Beuve again began to keep a notebook of his readings. This notebook carries comments about several Latin poets in the years 1835–40: Catullus, Ovid, Manilius (*Astronomicon*), and Persius. With the possible exception of Manilius, none of these poets was unknown to the critic, and the remarks are too general to be convincing proof of his actual reading during this period. One comment, however, does reveal a motivating force for his frequent thoughts on the Roman elegiac poets and also introduces the name of Theocritus, the Greek poet for whom Sainte-Beuve had a continuing fondness. He wrote:

> —une gloire poétique comme celle de Goldsmith ou de Cowper serait la couronne de mes rêves
> —Goldsmith ou Cowper chez les modernes, Catulle ou Théocrite chez les anciens.[22]

It would be difficult to overestimate this explicit association of his own poetic aspirations in the elegiac vein with those poets, both ancient and modern, whose work he would have liked to equal.

One work of Greek literature also assumes a dual importance in this context, not only because of general commentary on it in the notebook but also because of quotations in Greek with a translation by Sainte-Beuve. This book was the *Greek Anthology*. Since he borrowed the Bosch Grotius Greek-Latin edition of the *Anthology* from the Bibliothèque Nationale, we know that Sainte-Beuve was reading this edition.[23] The poem quoted and translated was one by Choerilus of Samos, a lesser luminary in the collection, who attracted Sainte-Beuve perhaps by the quality of his verse. A personal note provides telling motivation for the careful reading and translation. The critic wrote, "On sait l'esprit de l'Anthologie grecque . . . on en ferait une moderne avec un tout autre genre de beautés et de finesses. Je sais de petites choses charmantes de poètes peu connus. . . ."[24] Clearly, some time before the important decision of 1840 to read Greek again consistently with a tutor, Sainte-Beuve had come to the *Anthology* and to Theocritus, not solely as a critic and interpreter of literature but also as a creative poet seeking and finding inspiration.

In 1839 Sainte-Beuve took one of his rare trips outside the confines of France. Gabriel Faure, who published the notes on this trip, was of the opinion that the principal reason for the trip was to find "le pays des Anciens et les paysages classiques . . . l'Italie de Virgile et d'Horace, dont les noms et les citations reviennent sans cesse sous sa plume."[25] Reading the notes makes it difficult to agree, however, for Sainte-Beuve drove out from Naples to Pompeii and noted only the beautiful landscape and the decadence of man, with no comment on the remains at Pompeii. This curious lacuna in his notebook is somewhat compensated for by the opening lines of the "Eglogue napolitaine":

> Du tombeau de Virgile adorant la colline
> Je m'étais promené jusqu'à la Mergilline,
> Tout plein de ces doux noms que le rêve poursuit.

The poet continues with allusions to the Naples museum and Pompeii which evoke shepherds, Dianas, Bacchantes, and satyrs "qu'André de loin fêtait de sa flute de'ivoire." Of all the ancient authors, only Virgil is explicity named. In the notebook he was of course aware of Tiberius, Virgil, and, in a piquant manner, of Horace: "Je vérifie à tout moment, en Italie, le cabaretier fripon le *caupo malignus* d'Horace; *Le Voyage à Brindès* aura désormais plus de sel pour moi. (Et les disputes des mariniers et des laquais.)"[26]

The museum of Naples evoked Chénier, not Hellenistic Greece. Naples as a whole evoked a line from Statius. Rome had not changed from the time of Sidonius Apollinarius. A happy day's trip to Tivoli with Liszt and Madame d'Agoult resulted in a poem which is much more personal than classical or literary. On the whole, the notes on the trip to Italy are those of the Romantic poet, sensitive to the classical local color of well-known tourist points, but show little perception in depth of the important archaeological sites visited by the critic. It should be added that he was only a mediocre tourist at best, never an archaeologist, and was distracted by poor health and other preoccupations in 1839. It seems almost probable that Italy only confirmed Sainte-Beuve's evolving ideas, and in this manner served the function it was intended for: rest and change, not a "pilgrimage to antiquity."

Greek culture, which was being investigated by archaeologists and studied in its literary texts, attained a kind of climax in its pervasion of French intellectual life as the younger generations of the century reached adulthood. Canat wrote of the 1840s that "rarement une période fut plus hellénisée que celle qui, de 1840–1852, par la science, la critique et l'imitation, met la Grèce dans une place privilégiée, hors concours, et lui offre un encens qui monta longtemps vers de faux dieux."[27] In such a context, Sainte-Beuve's return to the study of Greek takes on a dual aspect of a personal intellectual interest and a representation of his time. It was an active commitment to a deeper understanding and knowledge of a culture with which he had been in constant touch previously but mainly in an indirect fashion.

Sainte-Beuve's resumption of Greek was made possible by the economic stability and leisure time provided, for the first time in his life, by his position at the Mazarin Library. Accordingly, in September 1840 he wrote to his friends in Switzerland: "J'ai des projets d'études, car j'ai toujours eu si peu de temps pour étudier; je veux savoir l'espagnol, me remettre au grec."[28] A year later he wrote to the same friends, "Je lis, j'épèle en grec pour le moment les *Idylles* de Théocrite."[29] While Sainte-Beuve was thus laboriously relearning to read Greek, three of his friends from the *Globe*, Jean-Jacques Ampère, Charles Lenormant, and Prosper Mérimée, were setting out to see Greece itself. Although Sainte-Beuve did not like to travel, he was always interested in the reports of his friends and even more in the literary results of such travels.

28 • *Language and Readings*

Perhaps the most tantalizing and elusive problem in Sainte-Beuve's Greek study is the vital one concerning his Greek teacher. This man has at times seemed almost an illusion, because even the concrete addresses given by Sainte-Beuve at various dates lead inevitably to rooming-houses, which were not required by law at that time to identify roomers. Contemporary scholars have been forced, therefore, to postulate a portrait from two principal sources, a letter by Sainte-Beuve himself recommending Pantasidès to a Madame X ―――― as a tutor, and Jules Troubat's comments in his two books about the critic. Sainte-Beuve's letter is more revelatory about the critic than the tutor, however, for he wrote:

> . . . Mon maître grec s'appelle *Pantasidès;* il est né au Pinde, mais il demeure rue Mazarine 13. Il est très capable, je crains seulement qu'il ne nous quitte dans peu de temps pour aller à Marseille suivre l'éducation des jeunes grecs qui y sont. Pourtant comme ce dernier point n'est pas encore décidé, je vais lui parler demain, car je le vois. Je lui demanderai ses conditions; les miennes seraient un peu trop chères ce me semble. Je lui donne 50 frs. pour 10 leçons. Mais je lui parlerai.[30]

The project to go to Marseilles may not have materialized, for the Archives de Marseilles contain no record of Pantasidès living there. Another letter of Sainte-Beuve, in September 1845, introduced Pantasidès to Dr. Veyne, but contains no more biographic information. Jules Troubat, Sainte-Beuve's last secretary, described him more fully:

> Quelque fois venait s'y joindre le professeur de grec de Sainte-Beuve, Pantasidès, un Epirote, échappé aux massacres des Grecs, élevé chez les moines du mont Athos, et qui avait complété ses études à Naples. Il ne savait pas son âge. Il était venu à Paris donner

des leçons de grec antique, qu'il savait à fond et mieux que personne en France. Il n'y avait avec lui qu'à tourner le robinet pour en faire couler du grec. Sainte-Beuve l'avait pris pour répétiteur, et ils avaient relu ensemble tout Homère, *l'Anthologie* et Thucydide.[31]

Troubat also added that Sainte-Beuve had tried to obtain for Pantasidès a post at the Ecole Normale Supérieure while he was lecturing there, but for some reason Pantasidès was not accepted. The most precise information about this person was given by Félix Duquesnil, but even this precise information has an air of mystification about it which detracts from its plausibility. Duquesnil tells us that the meeting took place in a sort of night club, the Folies Montparnasse, and he also described Pantasidès as "un personnage bizarre, déclassé, un savant oublié dans un beuglant, un Hellène du nom de Pantasidès—on ne saurait mieux dire—lequel, paraît-il, parlait le grec des anciens comme Périclès même."[32] Duquesnil further added that Sainte-Beuve decided to take Greek lessons in order to help Pantasidès financially in a discreet fashion.

One fact, however, does bring Pantasidès out of the illusory into historic reality and may be a helpful key to future knowledge. The death records of Paris show that on July 9, 1886, Jean Pantasidès died. The death certificate on file in the Mairie of the Tenth Arrondissement adds the following information:

> L'an mil huit cent quatre vingt six, le neuf juillet à quatre heures du soir, acte de décès de Jean PANTASIDES; agé de soixante-huit ans, professeur, né à Janino (Turquie) décédé: 200, rue du Faubourg Saint Denis, le huit juillet courant à une heure,—domicilié: avenue du Maine 20, fils de Georges PANTASIDES et de Marie: époux décédés (sans autres renseignements), célibataire.

Sainte-Beuve's lessons, begun in 1840, were doubtless interrupted by the critic's departure for Belgium in 1849. The precise moment for his resumption of Greek studies after his return to Paris is not entirely clear, but a separate *Cahier de notes grecques*, which may be dated 1855–65, leaves no doubt about the critic's active study, probably with Pantasidès. A note in 1860 to the Countess of Circourt says in part "que le Grec par excellence, M. Pantasidès, est de retour." There is no indication, however, of the dates or duration of his absence from Paris. Troubat affirmed that Pantasidès was present at the moment of Sainte-Beuve's death.[33] Troubat also described a regular little hellenizing salon at Sainte-Beuve's house in which Pantasidès was the leading figure.[34]

From these snatches of information, nevertheless, it is apparent that Sainte-Beuve *did* read Greek literature in the original with some regularity from 1840 to his death, and that this avocation was the source of social as well as purely intellectual pleasure for the critic. The exceptional paucity of information about Pantasidès, who was in Paris during a highly philhellene period of activity but seems not to have joined any philhellene group, either political or cultural, would seem to indicate that what he could transmit to the French critic was basic linguistic competence and direct contact, particularly aural contact, with the poetry, unencumbered by erudition or professional pedantry of any sort. It also seems fair to conclude, in the same manner, that by facilitating his direct attention to literature Pantasidès exerted some influence on Sainte-Beuve's taste and judgments. This influence seems never to have been preponderant or decisive, however, for Sainte-Beuve always exercised a personal choice of authors as subjects for his articles, and Pantasidès could not make him truly appreciate Pindar.

The year 1842 found Sainte-Beuve preparing his article on Anacreon (April 15, 1842), for which he borrowed from Victor Cousin *Les Fleurs des Muses grecques et Sapho*. He also turned to Professor Rossignol for the scholarly bibliography on Anacreon, and for help on a problem which had interested him earlier in the *Tableau*, namely, the authenticity of Anacreon's poetry, which some Renaissance and later critics had tried to attribute to Henri Estienne, suspecting the authenticity of his 1554 translation of the poet. Just before the Anacreon article was published the critic borrowed the Heinsius edition of Theocritus from the Arsenal Library. In June he wrote to his friend Juste Olivier that he was going to "me bercer des Dion et des Timoléon, des Armodius et des Aristogitons chrétiens et martyrs." He did not completely forsake pagan antiquity, however, for his library borrowings also show Millet's *La Destruction de Troie* (1544) in July, the *Deipnosophistarum* of Athenaeus (Schweighauser 1807 edition) in August, and Jean Boivin's *Vita Pithoei* in October, as well as Cassianus's *Geoponicorum sive de rustica libri XX* edited by J. N. Niclas, Pontanus's *Opera varia* (1524), Denys of Halicarnassus's *Examen critique des écrivains de la Grèce*, and the first volume of Lefebvre de Villebrune's translation of Athenaeus's *Works* (1789).[35] This whole series of readings was doubtless in preparation for the articles on Homer which appeared in January and February 1843. In October 1842 Sainte-Beuve also published "Stances et sonnets imités d'Ovide" in the *Revue des Deux Mondes*, evidencing once again his literary poetic inspiration. Finally in a letter to Madame Olivier, dated December 28, 1842, he announced that he would write for the *Journal des Débats*, "mais sur l'ancienne littérature seulement, sur Homère et Théocrite; plus un moderne: j'en ai assez."

The year 1843 began auspiciously with the two articles on

Homer and a new enlarged edition of the *Tableau*.[36] In January the critic borrowed Plutarch's *Hommes illustres* (vol. 7), as well as the first volume of his *Oeuvres morales*, Quatremer de Quincy's *Jupiter Olympien*, and Choiseul-Gouffier's *Voyage en Grèce* (vol. 2) from the Mazarin Library for the second Homer article. In May, he again had the *Jupiter Olympien* and Eustathius's *Commentarii*, perhaps to check something in the Homer articles which had already appeared. After his incisive article of July 1, "Quelques vérités," the critic turned again to ancient literature with an article on Euphorion in September. In the same month he thanked a young scholar, Péricaud, for his study on Minutius Felix, and about this same time Jacques Adert, the Swiss Hellenist, sent Sainte-Beuve his study on Theocritus, for which Sainte-Beuve thanked him with his usual excessive modesty.[37] This latter exchange was the beginning of a long friendship based in large measure on the critic's interest in Adert's classical scholarship.

The years 1846 and 1847 bring to light a charming idyll in Sainte-Beuve's busy life. Almost weekly during these years he stopped his professional or mundane occupations to read Horace with Ondine Valmore, the beautiful young daughter of the Marcelline Desbordes-Valmore to whom Sainte-Beuve rendered many services over the years. This reading often resulted in exchanges of "second thoughts" in letters and notes on their interpretations of the poet. The library borrowings continued, generally paralleling Sainte-Beuve's articles. Sainte-Beuve's notebook of reading indicates that in 1847 he was reading the *Palatine Anthology*, for there is a translation of an epigram of Philodemus.[38] He had also quoted Crinagoras in a letter to Pavie dated October 5. He read Egger's *Conclusions homériques* with attention and interest, and he knew Halévy's books on Greek drama (1847).

An evolution in the critic's attitude toward his Greek studies, or, more precisely, a clarification of the motivating force for this exacting study by the busy journalist-librarian, gradually becomes apparent. Several notes in letters to different people during these last years of the decade, when brought together, form a pattern and define the critic's attachment to this sort of study. Quoting Ovid about Virgil, he wrote in 1846 to Ravaisson to thank him for his book on Aristotle, saying that he himself had not had time in his youth to get to know antiquity profoundly, "mais je l'adore et je me prends à ceux qui en savent les avis. Je vous suivrai autant que je le pourrai dans vos sanctuaires."[39] Despite the *précieux* compliment, the sentiment is significant especially when it is read with another note of thanks, to Boissonade this time, in June of the same year. Here, probably answering a compliment from the Hellenist on his reading of Chénier and recognizing the Greek poetic sources of the poet's inspiration, he wrote, "c'est une grande douceur de repasser par ces sentiers, et de sentir surtout qu'on y marche à la suite d'excellents guides. Il est tel vers d'un ancien qui, nous revenant en mémoire, suffit à charmer tout un jour." The significance of the words "douceur" and "charmer" in this letter is more evident after the verb "adorer" in the previous letter, and becomes even clearer when they are set beside a note in *Mes Poisons*, which may be dated early in 1847:

> Et moi aussi, en relisant dernièrement Théocrite j'ai senti se reveiller en moi *mon âme pastorale*, cette âme de l'âge d'or, que tant de couches d'airain, de terre et de plomb recouvrent, et qu'il faut aller chercher tout au fond de soi et de son passé. Voilà les vrais classiques; en les lisant, il semble qu'on retrouve son âme d'autrefois, on se ressouvient.[40]

Finally, in September of the same year he wrote to Pavie, "Je lis toujours du grec de temps en temps, à petites doses; ce que j'en veux avoir, ce n'est pas la connaisance c'est la *saveur*. A cette fin, quelques pages, une petite idylle, une petite épigramme de temps à autre suffit." All of these key words derive from the affective rather than from the intellectual vocabulary and have sometimes been inferred to mean an overdelicate, neoclassic sentimentality on the part of the critic. We shall see later, in defining Sainte-Beuve's concept of tradition, that such was not the case. For the moment it must suffice to note the critic's conscious clarification of his purpose in reading Greek and the terms in which he did it. It was not as a professional classicist, or even as a literary critic, that Sainte-Beuve continued to read Greek literature, but as a poet and a sensitive reader, an *amateur* in the original sense of the word. His contacts with erudite specialists continued to increase and fertilize his own thinking, however, even though his conception of his active role never deviated from that of critic-interpreter to a lay audience.

The revolution of 1848 brought a readjustment in the critic's life that was both immediate, with his resignation as librarian at the Mazarin Library, and long-range, as a result of his realistic view of the political needs of France, which permitted him to support sincerely but not blindly the Second Empire. The events in the spring of 1848 seem to have led Sainte-Beuve back to Greece for at least a moment of solace, guidance, or consolation, for in April he wrote in his notebook, "Je viens de lire quelques pages d'Hérodote. le premier livre, la prise de Sardes, la chute de Crésus: beauté simple, vérité éternelle . . . quelques belles paroles, sur toutes les choses vraies encore après des milliers d'années," and also, about the same time, noted three verses of Lucretius "qui expriment la situation du monde."

> Usque adeo res humanas vis abdita quaedam
> Obterit et pulchros fascis saevasque secures
> Proculcare ac ludibrio sibi habere vedetus
> (De rerum natura, liv. V [1233–35])[41]

By September, however, the critic had left Paris for Liège, where there was little leisure and no friendly tutor to continue his Greek studies. Indeed, he wrote to Des Guerrois in February, 1849, "je suis un manoeuvre et je ne lis plus Léonidas de Tarente."

The statement in *La Constitution* in 1850,[42] that he did not dare treat books on antiquity because of his lack of adequate preparation, is almost amusing in light of the fact that for no other period is there so complete and exact a record of his Greek studies. In addition to the direct references in his notebooks and correspondence, as well as to the allusions in articles, there is for this decade a separate *Cahier de notes grecques*[43] which leaves no doubt about his active engagement in a serious study of Greek language and literature. Although it is probable that the Greek notebook was intended, at least partially, for use with his students at the Collège de France and the Ecole Normale, its value was not restricted to that use. In revising earlier articles for new collected editions, as well as in writing new essays, the critic made abundant use of these notes, either by allusion or by quotation, as a means of clarifying, amplifying, or even correcting various points. It is also clear from the notebook that Sainte-Beuve must have been meditating on several articles, one, for instance, on Agathias Scholasticus and Paul the Silentiary. He also noted the possibility of an article "De la Tragédie de Rhésus, ou de l'emploi des ficelles dramatiques dans l'antiquité," and added, "Je l'ai tout fait dans mon esprit." These articles were probably never written, even in draft form, for there is no further evidence of them among the critic's papers. There is some reason to believe that the critic either had this notebook on his table during his lessons with Pantasidès or jotted down immediately afterwards interesting points of their discussions. Such a custom would account both for the lack of erudite notes and the quantity of purely grammatical and morphological notes. Careful textual reading, even laborious explications at times, are complemented by translations, which the critic enjoyed as a creative art as well as a linguistic technique to insure his complete understanding of an epigram. The diversity of the authors cited is even more striking if one recognizes the relative difficulty the critic had in reading Greek. Anthologies explain this diversity in part, for in addition to the *Greek Anthology*, Sainte-Beuve referred frequently to Stobaeus's *Anthology*. Other authors were old friends: he had even written about several. Naturally, the Latin authors are numerous, for Latin was perhaps the only foreign language that Sainte-Beuve ever really completely mastered by his own standards.

It would probably be a mistake to see this notebook as proof of an orientation different from that defined in the late forties; Sainte-Beuve's distinction between the professional classicist and the amateur still obtained in his own mind, and his definition of "knowing Greek" thus appears overstringent to a layman. This definition, made in 1863, was, he said, the result of his own repeated failures in this effort, for

> Ah! savoir le grec, ce n'est pas comme on pourrait se l'imaginer, comprendre le sens des auteurs, de certains auteurs, en gros, vaille que vaille (ce qui est déjà beaucoup), et les traduire à peu près; savoir le grec, c'est la chose du monde la plus rare, la plus difficile,—j'en puis parler pour l'avoir tenté maintes fois et y avoir toujours échoué;—c'est comprendre non pas seulement les mots, mais toutes les formes de la langue la plus complète, la plus savante, la plus nuancée, en distinguer les dialectes, les âges, en sentir le ton et l'accent,—cette accentuation variable et mobile, sans l'entente de laquelle on reste plus ou moins barbare;—c'est avoir la tête assez ferme pour saisir chez des auteurs tels qu'un Thucydide le jeu de

groupes entiers d'expressions qui n'en font qu'une seule dans la phrase et qui se comportent et se gouvernent comme un seul mot; c'est, tout en embrassant l'ensemble du discours, jouir à chaque instant de ces contrastes continuels et de ces ingénieuses symétries qui en opposent et en balancent les membres; c'est ne pas rester indifférent non plus à l'intention, à la signification légère de cette quantité de particules intraduisibles, mais non pas insaisissables, qui parsèment le dialogue et qui lui donnent avec un air de laisser aller toute sa finesse, son ironie et sa grâce; c'est chez les lyriques, dans les choeurs des tragédies ou dans les odes de Pindare, deviner et suivre le fil délié d'une pensée sous des métaphores continues les plus imprévues et les plus diverses, sous des figures à dépayser les imaginations les plus hardies, c'est, entre toutes les délicatesses des rhythmes, démêler ceux qui, au premier coup d'oeil, semblent les mêmes et qui pourtant diffèrent, c'est reconnaître, par exemple, à la simple oreille, dans l'hexamètre pastoral de Théocrite autre chose, une autre allure, une autre légèreté que dans l'hexamètre plus grave des poètes épiques . . . Que vous dirais-je encore? savoir le grec, c'est l'apprendre sans cesse et poursuivre une étude qui ne saurait être un hors-d'oeuvre dans la vie, et qui, comme un Ancien l'a dit du métier de la marine, doit être et rester jusqu'à la fin un exercice de tous les jours, de toutes les heures: sans quoi l'on se rouille et l'on ne sait plus bien.[44]

Sainte-Beuve, by his own judgment, failed to accomplish this sort of knowledge of the Greek language, but there were, indeed, few men in the nineteenth century who did attain it.[45]

Notes

1. Clément Falcucci, *L'Humanisme dans l'enseignement secondaire en France au 19ᵉ siècle* (Toulouse: Privat, 1939), p. 99.
2. Louis Liard, *L'Enseignement supérieur en France 1789–1889* (Paris: Armand Colin, 1888), 2 vols., II, 29.
3. Falcucci, p. 11.
4. Badolle, p. 323.
5. Liard, I, 298–99.
6. See: Liard, II, 27–28. "Il ne faut pas enseigner ce que chacun peut apprendre soi-même [i.e., French culture]." And also: Liard, II, 102: " 'D'après ma propre expérience, dit Napoléon, les cours de littérature n'apprennent rien de plus que ce qu'on sait à quatorze ans.' "
7. Badolle, p. 344.
8. Liard, II, 153–54.
9. Liard, II, 86.
10. Gustave Dupont-Férrier, *La Vie quotidienne d'un collège parisien pendant plus de trois cent cinquante ans. Du collége de Clermond au Louis-le-Grand (1563–1920)* (Paris: E. de Boccard, 1921–25), 3 vols., p. 220. See also: p. 223.
11. *Volupté*, p. 9.
12. *N.L.* XIII, 39–40.
13. *C.g.* I, 34, n. 1.
14. M-L Pailleron, *François Buloz et ses amis* (Paris: Calmann-Lévy, 1919), pp. 177–80. See also M-L Pailleron, "Les Petits

Carnets de Sainte-Beuve," *Revue Hébdomadaire* n.s. 31 (29 juillet 1916), pp. 620–29; and also *Sainte-Beuve à 16 ans* (Paris: Le Divan, 1927) by the same author.
15. *Notes inédites de Sainte-Beuve,* ed. Charly Guyot (Neufchatel: Secrétariat de l'Université, 1931). Henceforth this volume will be referred to as Guyot.
16. *C.g.* I, 43.
17. *C.g.* I, 26.
18. Canat, I, 193.
19. Pierre, Moreau, "Sainte-Beuve latiniste," *Revue d'Histoire littéraire de France* 44 (1937), pp. 45–64. Also, by the same author, "Sainte-Beuve poéte latin," *Annales littéraires de la Franche-Comté* LV (1949), pp. 55–63.
20. Antoine Guillois, "Notes inédites de Sainte-Beuve sur un exemplaire de la première édition des Oeuvres d'André Chénier," *Bulletin du Bibliophile* (1902), pp. 212–24. This article was also reprinted (Paris: Leclerc, 1902). The page numbers refer to the latter printing. I am inclined to doubt M. Guillois's terminal date of 1838, since Sainte-Beuve continued to read Chénier after that date. He also continued, very probably, to read the poet in the same edition he had been accustomed to use.
21. The idea for such an edition was not new even in 1839, for in 1835 Sainte-Beuve had written to Alexandre Bixio, whom he had met when he wrote for the *National,* asking him for Brizeux's corrections because Renduel wanted to reprint Chénier's *Oeuvres.* He added in the same letter that if Renduel were the sole proprietor of the work "il ferait faire une édition annotée avec l'indication des imitations grecques et latines au bas des pages, telle que nous en avons souvent causé avec Brizeux" (*C.g.* I, 510).
22. Manuscript D. 571, Collection Spoelberch de Lovenjoul, p. 45.
23. *Bibliog.* III (seconde partie), 472. Entry 77 shows that Sainte-Beuve took the *Anthologia graeca cum versione Hugo Groti de Bosch* (t. 1–2) from the Bibliothèque Nationale on November 3, 1838.

24. Ms. D. 571, Collection Spoelberch de Lovenjoul, p. 75.
25. Gabriel Faure, *Sainte-Beuve, Voyage en Italie, Notes inédites* (Paris: Variétés littéraires, 1922), p. vi.
26. Faure, p. 14.
27. Canat, III, 7. See also Canat, II, 263–64.
28. *C.g.* III, 356.
29. *C.g.* IV, 155.
30. *C.g.* V, 595.
31. Jules Troubat, *La Salle à manger de Sainte-Beuve* (Paris: Mercure de France, 1910), p. 104.
32. Felix Duquesnil, *Souvenirs littéraires* (Paris: Plon, 1922), p. 210.
33. Jules Troubat, *Souvenirs et Indiscrétions* (Paris: Michel Lévy Frères, 1872), p. 15 n. 1.
34. Troubat, *Salle à manger* . . . , p. 106.
35. *Bibliog.*, III, 481–84.
36. This new edition showed evidence of Sainte-Beuve's readings in ancient literature by the numerous quotations added from ancient authors. See: Gustave Michaut, *Quibus rationibus Sainte-Beuve opus suum de XVIe seculo iterum atque iterum retractaverit cui dissertationi adjectus est ejusdem operis apparatus criticus* (Paris: Fontemoing, 1903).
37. *C.g.* V, 340. See also Charly Guyot, "Sainte-Beuve et Jacques Adert," *Journal de Genève* (14, 16, 17 août, 1933). Adert introduced Victor Cherbuliez to Sainte-Beuve and also, much later, provided the critic with the biographical material for Dübner's funeral oration.
38. Ms. D. 573, Collection Spoelberch de Lovenjoul, p. 9.
39. *C.g.* VI, 341–42.
40. *Mes Poisons*, pp. 10–11, *C.g.*, VII, 34–35. In 1847 he wrote: "et moi, j'ai tenté, en lisant Théocrite, de *réveiller mon âme pastorale*, cette âme de l'âge d'or que tant de couches d'airain et de plomb recouvrent et qui est enfouie au fond de notre passé." The italics are Sainte-Beuve's.
41. Ms. D. 573, Collection Spoelberch de Lovenjoul, pp. 60 and 71.

42. *C.L.*, II, 44.
43. *Cahier de notes grecques*, ed. Ruth Mulhauser (Chapel Hill: University of North Carolina Press, 1955), p. 15.
44. *N.L.*, VI, 93–94.
45. *C.L.*, VI, 333. Sainte-Beuve himself restricted this number to five or six in Europe.

Chapter 3
The Activist

When Paul Dubois invited Sainte-Beuve to write for *Le Globe*, he was offering the lad entrance into one of the most active intellectual groups in Paris. Dubois himself had been relieved of his teaching post because of his liberal political views, and when he and his friend Pierre Leroux founded *Le Globe* in 1824, their basic tenet was freedom and active curiosity in all forms of literary and intellectual thinking.[1] Dubois gathered around him from the beginning a very capable group of men who were not confined to a single editorial policy, but in general held to middle-of-the-road, liberal ideas in both politics and literature. In politics this meant, among other things, a philhellenic attitude, and in literature, sharp criticism of the pallid contemporary neoclassicism. This criticism was nevertheless coupled with an explicit admiration for seventeenth-century French Classicism as well as with a cautious tolerance toward the Romantic innovators. These attitudes combined to produce a particularly happy receptivity toward the new concept of antiquity that was beginning to take concrete form in French intellectual life.

The new points of contact with both ancient and modern Greece are reflected in the *Globe* articles from the very first issue, which carried verses composed in modern Greek on the death of Byron. Jouffroy wrote seven major articles in the following months analyzing the Greek revolution, and Lieutenant Colonel Maxime Raybaud's *Fragment de Mémoires sur la Grèce* appeared in serial form, as did translations of some of the Greek folk songs collected by Claude Fauriel. Count Giuseppi Pecchio reported on Greece in a dozen articles in the spring of 1825. There were even announcements for benefit collections, concerts, exhibits, and sales for Greek relief. In December 1826 two articles appeared on the "real" causes of the Greek revolution. The next year, beginning in July 1827, there was a series on the University of Corfu, which had been founded with the sympathetic help of Lord Guilford and Cambridge University. Two years later the *Globe* published a series of five letters on the "Greek Affair" and the new Greek state. The political philhellenism of the *Globe* is impressively attested to by the constancy of its reporting on the war, but in addition to this significant political philhellenism the *Globe* also gave ample coverage to the new renaissance of interest in the culture of ancient Greece.

Jouffroy reviewed the third volume of Cousin's new translation of Plato's complete works in the pages of the *Globe*. Villemain's famous lecture on the superficiality of Racine's conception of Greece was reported with special praise for Villemain, who made his own translation of Euripides' *Iphigenia*. Patin's course on Greek tragedy was also reported with the comment, "Monsieur Patin refuse de s'appeler classique ou romantique; il veut le point de vue grec."[2] Creuzer's book on ancient religions was discussed in Guigniaut's translation.[3] The archaeological expedition of the younger Champollion, which led to deciphering the Rosetta Stone, was reported in fourteen articles from 1825 to 1829. In 1825 the *Globe* reported on a temple discovered in Corfu by John Wright; B. G. Niebuhr's *Römische Geschichte* inspired three articles in favor of reforming critical historical writing in France; Charles Magnin, writing about Eichoff's *Etudes grecques sur Virgile,* contrasted French erudition and criticism with the work from across the Rhine and concluded that a happy union was the new ideal. Wolf's death was reported, and a tribute article at the death of Voss discussed Voss and Wolf as successors to Heyne. In 1827 Raoul-Rochette was severely criticized for not revising the translations or taking German scholarship into account in his reediting of Brunoy's *Théatre des grecs.* It would be uselessly repetitive to continue to catalog the *Globe* articles as evidence of the intellectual atmosphere in which Sainte-Beuve lived and worked from 1824 to 1830.

When Sainte-Beuve entered this group he was twenty years old, hardly capable of providing the same type of articles as his more mature colleagues. What Dubois asked of him was a series of historico-geographic articles on the places whose names were then prominent in the Greek War.[4] The series ran from October 1824 to January 1825. The five articles are youthful journalism, and were never considered worthy of republication by the mature critic, but the series served a definite purpose in his formation by associating his schoolboy knowledge of antiquity with a live issue of the day. The general pattern of the articles is as direct as the moral: each place should be worthy of illustrious ancestors or compensate for the lack of ancient luster by modern heroism. In keeping with the *Globe* outlook, the articles are characterized by intellectual restraint at a time when many other journalists were indulging in lyric prose on the same general subjects. The critic's restraint made him critical of exaggerated partisanism, even in favor of the Greeks; he berated Madame Belloc for seeing in the Greek War a sort of holy crusade. The sturdy minds of the Greeks were sufficient without the hand of God.[5] In general, Sainte-Beuve's political philhellenism was not so much an emotional enthusiasm as an intellectual political sympathy for a popular cause supported by his liberal colleagues and by a people whose heroic history he knew. Enthusiasm he had, but there was no desire to go to Greece and no poetic expression of his sentiments. Forty years later, in his article "La Grèce en 1863," Sainte-Beuve recalled the atmosphere of these philhellenic years of his youth with deep feeling, and mentioned his own articles in an almost offhand manner which would seem to indicate, even at that distance, an active psychological adherence to the cause.[6]

More important to the formation of the young critic was the exposure to progressive scholarship and criticism, and the personal contact with leaders like Villemain, Patin, and his lifelong friend, Nicolas Piccolos. Abel Villemain, twelve years Sainte-Beuve's senior, was in the golden years of his teaching career, as Sainte-Beuve later called them. He had already translated Cicero's *Republic,* and had prefaced a collection of Greek stories in 1822. Although Sainte-Beuve wrote to his old school friend Loudierre on December 6, 1828, that he had not yet heard Villemain, he added that his course was very popular. He very probably began attending soon after that date, for Juste Olivier noted that he saw Sainte-Beuve there in 1830.[7] The friendship between the two critics was not destined to endure. The break came around 1839, when Sainte-Beuve wearied of Villemain's constant need for flattery. Although some of the comments about Villemain in *Mes Poisons* are quite emotional, Sainte-Beuve always remembered with deep admiration Villemain's capacity as a professor to fire youthful minds and to create vast literary syntheses which opened new horizons.[8] It was Villemain who encouraged the young writer toward a university post in 1828, and during this period the two men occasionally had pleasant walks together, exchanging ideas on literature.[9]

The reports on Villemain's Sorbonne lectures which appeared in the *Globe* had been written by another friend of Sainte-Beuve, Henri Patin, who was to hold the chair of Latin poetry at the Sorbonne and to write his important *Etudes sur les Tragiques grecs* (1841–43). Like Villemain, he was somewhat older than Sainte-Beuve (eleven years), and farther along in his career. In 1838 Sainte-Beuve wrote from Lausanne to Charles Labitte regretting his enforced absence from Patin's course on Virgil's *Georgics*. On at least one occasion, in 1847, Patin, after reading Sainte-Beuve's article on "François Ier Poète" for the editors of the *Journal des Savants*, suggested to the author two more analogies with Latin authors.[10] A third friend of the same generation as Patin and Villemain, Charles Magnin, a specialist in the theater, deserves special mention here because it was Magnin who served as a replacement for Fauriel in 1834–35, and who lectured on the origins of the modern theater. In this course he discussed Greek drama, especially Sophocles.[11] An older friend of this period, not writing for the *Globe*, was the Hellenist Viguier, about whom Sainte-Beuve spoke warmly in 1867, and who, according to the critic, had heard Wolf on Homeric poetry.[12] Sainte-Beuve also recounted a dinner party at Viguier's house where the guests included Cousin, Loyson, and Patin as well as Sainte-Beuve.[13] Perhaps the most charming recollection was that of meeting Viguier on the Vanves plain, strolling along reading Greek.[14] The recollections themselves are convincing evidence of the impression made on the young man during the period of his intellectual formation.

One young *Globe* writer just about Sainte-Beuve's own age

was Jean-Jacques Ampère, who in 1825 certainly promised a more brilliant future than the career Sainte-Beuve was to record in 1868.[15] Already Ampère had accompanied Madame Récamier and Fauriel to Rome. With Fauriel he studied Sanskrit, and in 1827 he went to Germany. Despite this fine classical background, however, he seemed to prefer the early northern literatures for his courses. These Sainte-Beuve attended quite regularly, despite certain comments on Ampère's painful manner of lecturing.[16] In these early years, however, Ampère's classical culture provided a rich intellectual stimulus for Sainte-Beuve. It was also Ampère who introduced Sainte-Beuve to the salon at the Abbaye-aux-Bois in 1834, and in an 1842 article for the *Revue des Deux Mondes* he rejoiced over Sainte-Beuve's decision to reread Greek literature.[17]

The *Globe* group would not be complete without some mention of Nicolas Piccolos, a native speaker of Greek, who was trained as a doctor of medicine at Montpellier, and who was a friend of the Greek patriot and philologist Adamantios Coray. Piccolos's friendship with Sainte-Beuve deepened with the years as each helped the other interpret a literature foreign to his own nation.

After the first Greek series, Sainte-Beuve's articles in the *Globe* were short reviews of a miscellaneous nature—books handed over by Dubois, probably as not meriting a major article by one of the mature writers, but for that very reason providing a challenge to the young journalist. In these early years Dubois kept a tight rein on the young man, and the articles echo the *Globe* attitude: criticism of the academic neo-classicists for their overuse of mythology or of insignificant erudite classical allusions; even philhellenism was regarded as no excuse for bad verse. There were two articles which reviewed new translations of Anacreon and Tacitus. The problem of translation, raised at this beginning of his career, continued to interest Sainte-Beuve throughout his life as he readjusted his judgment on the possible degree of success in such an undertaking. Two other points, of some concern to the critic later, were also hinted at in this first article, in his remarks on the scarcity of historic facts about Greek authors, and in his own typical treatment of these authors by analogy with French counterparts. Anacreon's genius resembled French genius, and Marot's poetry was compared to that of Anacreon. Neither of these articles required any profound knowledge of antiquity, but for a young man oriented to classical culture they brought to mind one of the major problems with which Sainte-Beuve continued to grapple as his convictions matured: the unbroken line of the French cultural heritage from Greece through Rome.

In addition to his discussion of the translation of the ancients, Sainte-Beuve was already practising a stylistic device characteristic of his mature prose, that of associating a modern with his classical "counterpart." Boileau did not have Horace's sense of nature; Corneille's style must inevitably please those who appreciate Demosthenes, Pascal, and Caesar; Mathurin Régnier's religious and philosophic emotion is such as Lucretius and Buffon could have had. At times the references are purely stylistic ornament: "Et d'abord, à commencer par Dieu, *ab Jove principium*," Madame Hausset seemed made for the role of Suetonius, etc. On first sight these references seem hardly more than a youthful display of knowledge, but further analysis shows that what was perhaps display in this early period, these quick references, were characteristic of Sainte-Beuve's style throughout his life. They have the evocative value of the poetic image, and like the image are particularly significant when they carry an element of surprise in their aptness. The result is, of course, that references to antiquity were rarely absent from Sainte-Beuve's early articles.

As the philhellenist enthusiasm quieted down in Paris, and the young critic learned his journalist's trade, he continued to write for the *Globe* but he also turned his attention to other forms of writing and made new friendships. His meeting in January 1827 with Victor Hugo, and their subsequent intimacy, have tended to encompass and dominate the interpretation of this creative literary period of production, insufficient regard being paid to the fact that it was an enrichment of rather than a substitution for his previous life. In August 1826 Sainte-Beuve learned that the subject for the French Academy competition for 1827 was the history of the language and literature of the sixteenth century, and it was Daunou who advised him to compete, promising to aid him in his research.[18] The tone of the *Tableau de la Poésie française* may well reflect a new intellectual climate, but the decision to study the Pléiade was quite independent of the Hugo group.

During the decade 1830–40, Sainte-Beuve published only five articles treating ancient literature directly, and two of these articles were never republished in his collected works. His attack in 1830 on Pongerville's translation of Lucretius sprang from literary politics rather than from a desire to bully a mediocre translator.[19] The result was that, although the brief article *does* show Sainte-Beuve's easy familiarity with Lucretius's poetry, it neither indicates a preoccupation of the moment nor a critical interpretation of the Latin philosopher-poet. The article on Théry's *De l'esprit de la critique chez les peuples anciens et modernes* (1832) can hardly be called an article; it is an announcement, no more, of a compendious anthology of critical thought. The 1830 note on Quinet, which was no longer than the Théry announcement, became only a footnote to the final form of the 1836 article on Quinet. This note, however, does give clear evidence of Sainte-Beuve's enthusiasm for Quinet's scholarship, which was the fruit of contact with Germany and of a trip to Greece itself. The critic was somewhat less enthusiastic in 1836 over Quinet's attempt at epic poetry; he devoted the major portion of the article to the thesis that popular epic of the Homeric variety was no longer possible in literate times, that the Napoleonic legend confirmed scholars' theories on the evolutionary quality of medieval and Homeric epic poetry, but that it could not evolve to create a popular epic again as Quinet had suggested in the preface to his poem on Napoleon. At the end of the article Sainte-Beuve defined his position clearly if obliquely on the subject of such popular epic poetry. After pointing out sections of Quinet's work which, as a critic, he believed gave evidence of real poetic talent, he concluded: "Toutefois, Français de la tradition grecque et latine rajeunie, mais non brisée, ami surtout de la culture polie, studieuse, élaborée et perfectionné, de la poésie des siècles d'Auguste et, á leur defaut, des époques de la Renaissance," he, Sainte-Beuve, "le lendemain qui suit le jour de cette lecture," would pick up, "(tombant dans l'excès contraire sans doute) une ode latine en vers saphiques de Gray à son ami West . . . et aussi je me mets à goûter à loisir . . . le plus cristallin des sonnets de Pétrarque."[20] Certainly, the critic's attitude is open on the point of fine poetry, but his position is also equally clear and negative on modern primitivism.

The fourth of these five articles treated the critic Nisard and was written after many requests by the latter. It was occasioned by the *Histoire des poètes latins de la décadence*, despite a two-year interval between the publication of the book and the article.[21] Since Nisard had simply used the late Latin poets as a means of attacking the Romantic poets, the article has a tone of acerbity which is usually attributed to Sainte-Beuve's defense against personal attack.[22] The critic did, nevertheless, make at least two very constructive, objective points. He stated that "forgotten" authors, especially those of antiquity, must be treated with sympathy in order to create a desire to read them, for critical consideration of such authors serves almost inevitably as an invitation and an introduction for the reader. Sainte-Beuve also made a second point that allegoric criticism like Nisard's does justice neither to the literal nor to the allegoric line of interpretation, and thus falsifies both. Nisard accepted, not without grace, Sainte-Beuve's unmasking of his allegory,[23] but though their paths continued to cross throughout their lives, their interests and minds were too different for any fruitful exchange.

The same article on Nisard was revised three years after the original publication in 1836, and the second version contained a long note on Statius in which the critic, with knowledge and taste, responded to Nisard's negative judgment of the poet with a limited but definite, positive, and sympathetic appreciation of Statius's qualities. In the unusually long note, Sainte-Beuve quoted four different passages from Statius and concluded by translating into his own French verse a whole poem from the *Sylves* entitled "Somnus."[24] By this long addition the critic extended and reaffirmed his point on the necessity for a sympathetic consideration of ancient authors less frequently read by the modern public. He himself would exemplify this belief a few years later by a series of articles. Both the note and the later articles, therefore, validate his criticism of Nisard's work as something beyond the obvious personal contribution to the quarrel over Romanticism.

The final article in this group appeared in 1839 and treated Victor Leclerc's *Des Journaux chez les Romains*. Bonnerot has suggested that the immediate inspiration for this article probably came from Sainte-Beuve's reading of Labitte's review which immediately followed his own "Notes et Sonnets" in the *Revue de Paris* for January 6, 1839.[25] Such circumstances might aid in explaining the orientation of the article, but do not invalidate the critic's major theme in his essay, namely that modern erudition, with its complexities and dynamic qualities, was an important facet of contemporary literary life in nineteenth-century France. Since this theme was a constant preoccupation of the critic in his mature writings, it will be considered more fully elsewhere, but it is important to note here its appearance as a major theme in 1839. Each of the five articles, then, was written for some circumstantial reason, but each one implies an awareness of changing ideas, standards, and problems in the study of classical antiquity.

The next years were concentrated on his masterpiece, *Port-Royal*, in Lausanne, but 1837 also brought the article on Chénier in February that suggested a special Greek source edition, and the article on Leclerc in November that discussed the subject of classical scholarship. Less than a year after his return to Paris and the Leclerc article, Sainte-Beuve published the controversial "Dix ans après en littérature," which was literally a sequel to the essay immediately preceding it, entitled "De la littérature industrielle." The generation that had promised so much in literature at the end of the Restoration had almost spent itself in nonliterary activities. Some sort of program or doctrine was necessary to give form and character to the now-mature generation. The very loose tenets suggested by Sainte-Beuve—tolerance and freedom—would principally combat the immediate enemies, industrialism, cupidity, and pride; for, as he added, what he envisaged was sympathetic collaboration rather than a strict program. He further made a specific appeal to the men who had grouped themselves around the *Globe* to return to literary and intellectual studies. This appeal to his friends to fulfill the promise of their youth was equally the enunciation of a personal program on Sainte-Beuve's part. He did not envisage either a literature of "art for art's sake" or a return to worn-out neoclassicism.[26] His general concept remained much the same, but very much clearer: Romantic freedom in invention under the discipline of an "Attic" genius. He himself set about to strengthen and insure his own grasp on Greek culture, the source of the purest Attic taste.[27]

Sainte-Beuve's active study of Greek with Pantasidès soon led to a series of articles on the ancients, beginning with an important double article on Homer and continuing until his departure for Liège. During this same period the critic was also active in other ways for the knowledge and study of antiquity. One of the most important monuments to Sainte-Beuve's active interest in classical scholarship was the royal decree of September 17, 1846, creating the Ecole Française d'Athènes, of which Sainte-Beuve was "le père spirituel" according to Radet.[28] The idea was not completely new in 1846, and Radet traces it back to various memoirs, notably those of Legrand between 1802 and 1807.[29] Radet also describes the political maneuvers of England, Russia, and France in Greece after the Treaty of Adrianople. Additional pressure from the Académie de France in Rome, in a memoir dated February 1845, for similar facilities in Athens furthered the cause as it was presented by Salvandy a few months later.[30] Sainte-Beuve, on the other hand, recorded that as early as 1841 he had talked with Eynard and Piscatori of his own concept, formed in conjunction with Pantasidès for a school in Athens for advanced research in Hellenic studies of all sorts.[31] At that point Victor Cousin had suggested to them, however, that the idea be withheld until his own return to power as prime minister; he was not called to form a new ministry, though, and as a result the idea lay dormant. In late April or early May 1845, Sainte-Beuve was again speaking of this interest with Madame Piscatori during a reception at the home of Madame d'Arbouville when Salvandy, then minister of Public Instruction, joined the group, listened with interest, smiled, said nothing, but "Quelques jours après, l'idée était couvée et éclose. *Il ne m'en a jamais parlé depuis.*"[32] In March 1846, M. Alexandre was commissioned to go to Greece to investigate the possibilities of a French Academy. Obviously Sainte-Beuve was piqued by Salvandy's ungenerous attitude in the affair, but in justice it should be added that Sainte-Beuve had no egotistic vanity in the matter, for he fully recognized that such a plan could not be the inspiration of, much less be implemented by, any single person. All of these disparate interests came together chronologically, nevertheless, to exert the pressure on the government that resulted in the royal decree of foundation the next September.

Sainte-Beuve did, however, make one further positive gesture of no small importance with his unsigned article on August 25, 1846.[33] This article, published just as Piscatori arrived back in Paris on leave from his ambassadorial post in Athens, provided a lucid and concrete plan for such a school, harmonizing political, cultural, educational, and artistic interests, and recorded it in a discreet fashion which permitted its publication in a newspaper, even before the project was acted upon and became approved by royal decree in September of the same year. Such publication brought the project to the attention of a much wider public, and Bonnerot has implied that the proximity of dates between the article and the royal decree is not fortuitous.[34] In addition to Sainte-Beuve's activities on a semipolitical level, it is important to note that the 1845 article is quite clearly oriented in the direction of the critic's own interest in Greek culture: to study the language and literature in the country itself, to revivify the French university outlook by a transfusion from Greece. It is not too difficult, especially after the Homer articles of 1843, to read between the lines Sainte-Beuve's impatience with the dominance of German philological scholarship, and to infer that he had dreamt of a French Academy in Athens as the French response. The Academy, though founded in 1846, was only reorganized as a "centre de recherches et de hautes études,"[35] according to the pattern of Sainte-Beuve's original suggestion, in 1850. Of the four Academies presently active in Athens, the French School of Classical Studies is the oldest, for the German School was not founded until almost thirty years later, in 1874, followed by the American School in 1881 and the British School in 1883.[36] It would be an exaggeration to credit Sainte-Beuve with all the illustrious work of the four schools, but certainly his original vision has greatly vivified Hellenic studies in occidental Europe and America in the past century.

Even while Sainte-Beuve was actively engaged with the French Academy in Athens, he was reading Greek with Pantasidès; he noted what he termed a "bonne journée" in 1846, for he had read Homer in the morning and seen Madame d'O[rtigues] in the afternoon.[37] He was also reading in preparation for two articles on another of his particularly favorite Greek poets, Theocritus. In September (1846) he noted that he had translated the fourth idyll.[38] Just about ten days later he wrote a long letter to Boissonade on the nature of Greek poetry as part of an exchange of letters between the two men on Sainte-Beuve's translations from Apollonius Rhodius, and a month later, in a letter of Nicolas Martin, he defended his previous judgment on the importance of Anacreon.[39]

His year in Liège also permitted, even required, him to create a synthesis and thus gain a perspective on the literature of his own century and its traditions. He said in his opening lecture, "1802 marqua une ère nouvelle, il y eut renaissance, retour à l'antique esprit ou du moins à de nobles formes de la tradition. . . . "⁴⁰ His overall estimate of Chateaubriand as "l'Homère de notre siècle" likewise signals his point of comparison for the great Romantic descriptive artists. In general Sainte-Beuve saw *Le Génie du Christianisme* as the source of the nineteenth-century enthusiasm for the Middle Ages and found the style like that of the late Latin writers. He analyzed the nature imagery in *Atala* in other terms, however, clarifying Chateaubriand's technique in his vast paintings of nature by the vivid contrast between his procedure and that of the early Greeks. The discussion of *Les Martyrs* provided Sainte-Beuve the opportunity for a penetrating analysis of the types of epic poetry, beginning, of course, with Homer. These discussions were not the fruit of quick study or of schoolboy memories; they attain their richness and concreteness because Sainte-Beuve was thoroughly familiar with the Greek epic in Greek as well as in French. In the *Itinéraire*, Sainte-Beuve found some of Chateaubriand's finest pages, those in which René forgets his systematic Christian pose and "il est Grec et païen malgré lui."⁴¹ For all the severity, even harshness at times, of his judgments on Chateaubriand as a man and as an author, Sainte-Beuve did, all the same, attribute to him a high place in literature when he said, "Tel nous a paru, au vrai, dans les principaux traits de sa physionomie, celui que notre siècle, jeune encore, salua et eut raison de saluer comme son Homère."⁴² Such was Sainte-Beuve's interpretation of Chateaubriand-Homer, a prose-poet who would not be ill at ease with Sainte-Beuve's other Romantic ancestor, Chénier. Sainte-Beuve's return from Liège in August 1849 preceded by only two months the inaugural article of the great double series which continued to the critic's death. It is hardly fortuitous that before the end of 1849 Sainte-Beuve had treated three contemporary critics in his articles and that in each case, he expressly considered the critic's attitude toward antiquity.⁴³

Sainte-Beuve's library borrowings for 1850 show nothing in Greek; the borrowings tend to parallel his articles with no evidence of any new serious personal study. He continued to quote Horace and Virgil in his correspondence, and even at one point Lucian in Greek, but these quotations are probably spontaneous recollections and not evidence of reading. The next three years quickened the rhythm of library borrowings, but when Sainte-Beuve borrowed a Greek text, he took also a French translation. Rossignol and Egger also continued to furnish the critic with any specialized information he needed. In September 1852 Sainte-Beuve refused the succession to Villemain at the Sorbonne, excusing himself by pleading his lack of the required academic degrees.[44] In 1854, however, he actively solicited Boissonade's help in obtaining the chair of Latin poetry at the Collège de France, to which he was appointed in December 1854.[45]

In the four and one half years between his return from Liège and his appointment to the Collège de France, there were but two articles directly on ancient authors. Two other lines of thought related to his Greek studies become apparent. One resulted in two articles in October 1850: "Qu'est-ce qu'un classique" and "Madame Caylus et ce qu'on appelle *l'Urbanité*." The other had to do with French poets, translators and commentators of ancient literature: Fénelon, Florian, Pasquier, Amyot, Le Brun-Pindare, Perrault, Walkenaer, Rollin, Courrier, Barthélemy, Madame Dacier. Gibbon may well be classed with this latter group though he could hardly be termed French.

Of the two articles on antique subjects, one dealt with the poet Firdousi, and, except for underlining the limits of Greco-Roman-Christian civilization in the mind of the critic, lies somewhat outside our province. The second article is on Pliny the Elder. This was occasioned by Littré's new translation, published in two volumes, the second of which had appeared only on March 9, 1850, less than six weeks before Sainte-Beuve's article. Ten years later Sainte-Beuve would write three long articles on Littré, and on the subject of translation, one perennially interesting to him, but neither of these possibilities was developed in the 1850 article, which is truly about Pliny. The introductory paragraphs are particularly revealing in the perspective of the apparent decline of interest in antiquity by the critic.

Sainte-Beuve begins by saying that he would like to write about antiquity, if only for variety, and that he does not lack serious books worthy of his study, such as Emile Egger's *Histoire de la Critique chez les Grecs*. "Mais, pour aborder convenablement les anciens, il faut des préparations singulières. . . . Et puis, ce n'est pas tout de les approcher; si l'on veut encore les présenter et les faire agréer aux autres. . . . "[46] The general public is interested solely in what is immediately related to itself. The study of antiquity has a part only in "retirement plans" and "projects never carried out for lack of time." Later in the same essay Sainte-Beuve, discussing the *Letters* of Pliny the Younger, described the conditions for pleasant reading:

> Les après-midi d'été à la campagne, si vous voulez vous redonner un *léger goût, une saveur d'antiquité*, si vous n'êtes trop tourmenté ni par les passions, ni par les souvenirs, ni par la verve (car je vous suppose un peu auteur vous-même, tout le monde l'est aujourd'hui) prenez Pline, ouvrez au hasard et lisez.

The expressions "léger goût, une saveur d'antiquité" evoke linguistically the critic's statement in 1847 of what he sought in reading ancient literature. Similarly, the introduction to the Pliny article states the other side of the coin for the same evolution; namely, that Sainte-Beuve was very well aware that he was not a professional Hellenist, and that perhaps he suffered unduly from the tension created by his desire for meticulous accuracy and helpful corrections on the part of specialists who read his articles. This single article on Greco-Roman antiquity during the period 1848–54 transmitted to his sympathetic public an explanation for discontinuing the series started during the decade 1840–50. Further, it made clear to this same public his rather characteristic and personal distinction between specialist and amateur. He was soon to accept the challenge to lecture in public on Latin poetry, and although the subsequent events were disastrous, the experience did result in the publication of the critic's only book-length study of an ancient author.

Sainte-Beuve's appointment to the chair of Latin poetry at the Collège de France seemed to mark the climax of his career. He was already distinguished as a man of letters and critic, well embarked on the great series of *lundis*, and almost at the end of his master work *Port-Royal*. The new appointment seemed to recognize the one facet of his work which had hitherto been recognized only outside his own country. The vote in the election to the post had been unanimous in the first ballot on the part of the constituted body of professors.[47] The critic had wanted and had actively sought the post; his colleagues were enthusiastic. Rigault announced the appointment in the *Journal des Débats* of January 11, 1855 in appreciative terms, as the last step in the education of a true critic, one that would change Sainte-Beuve from "un des causeurs les plus agréables, un des chroniqueurs littéraires les plus spirituels, un des grands amuseurs publics . . . " into "un critique véritable, et l'un des meilleurs maîtres de son temps."[48] In addition to affording him a highly honorable position and added economic security, the post also permitted Sainte-Beuve to come into contact with a more sophisticated audience on subject matter which had always been close to his heart. His decision to request the chair takes on additional significance in the light of his refusal of Villemain's chair at the Faculty of Letters when it was offered by Fortoul in 1852. He had told the minister that he was neither academic nor traditional enough for the Sorbonne position, but in the Collège de France he probably felt freer and more adequate. This third venture into the academic world was, nevertheless, nothing short of scandalous in its brevity, for reasons only indirectly connected with the conditions of his appointment and with the volume which resulted from his brief experience.

Before the first course ever began one apparently unimportant change was made which, in retrospect, might conceivably have influenced the series of events that took place. The critic had first chosen to study and lecture on Ovid, but as he prepared, his enthusiasm for Ovid cooled, and he chose rather to begin with the "greatest monument," the *Aeneid* of Virgil, the official poet of the emperor Augustus.[49] It is almost impossible not to speculate on whether certain analogies drawn between Virgil-Augustus and Sainte-Beuve-Napoleon III would have been avoided had the subject been Ovid. At any rate, Sainte-Beuve gave his first public lecture on Friday, March 9, 1855 in the smaller of the two amphitheaters in the Collège de France. His first lecture, and particularly the appropriate opening remarks of gratitude to the Minister and government for his appointment and his praise of his predecessors in the chair of Latin poetry, were interrupted by politically liberal students. After the police ejected these latter, the critic continued his lecture in relative peace. On March 14, however, the demonstration was larger and better organized. The room was packed. The critic was unnerved by the booing students; he unfortunately answered some of their remarks. Again the police found it necessary to interrupt in order to restore order before the critic could complete his lecture. Naturally the newspapers immediately laid hands on the story, each one giving the color of its own political bias to the account.[50] In a long letter to Fortoul, dated March 20, 1855, Sainte-Beuve made his own analysis and concluded that two types of enmity had joined forces: enmity against the literary critic and enmity against the man apppointed by the government. He concluded his letter with an official resignation. This resignation was not accepted, and the affair dragged on for some time, but Sainte-Beuve did not, after the end of the school year, accept his salary or make any further official appearance at the Collège de France. Until his death his chair was filled by replacement professors. The incident had quite deeply wounded Sainte-Beuve, but at least the course he was to have given did appear as the *Etude sur Virgile*.

At its serial publication in the *Moniteur* the *Etude* was excellently received and inspired a certain number of enthusiastic letters to the author.[51] It is not, however, usually considered a major work like *Port-Royal* or *Chateaubriand et son groupe littéraire sous l'empire*, the fruits of his first two teaching experiences. In his special study of the work, Professor Boissier undertook to set the *Etude* into the context of nineteenth-century classical studies and the liberal tradition of the Collège de France. He noted in particular Sainte-Beuve's methodology as partaking of both the traditional French point of view and that of the new schools. Even in teaching matters, continued Boissier, the critic lent an ear to what came out of Germany, for he was not hostile by prejudice to the reforms desired by the German scholars. Boissier further added that criticism would not succeed unless it added to the German philological method, the delicacy of trained taste. "Il me semble que c'est là ce que l'enseignement de Sainte-Beuve aurait mis en pleine lumière."⁵² If the *Etude sur Virgile* had done no more than make eminently clear the fundamental point of methodology, it is particularly regrettable that the critic was not allowed to give his course peacefully to the end. Sainte-Beuve's interpretation of Virgil, with its insistence on the poet's originality, was equally important, as we shall see later, for a large cultivated audience of the nineteenth century. For the present, however, it is more important to point out that all the translations in the *Etude* were new ones done by Sainte-Beuve.

Unpleasant as the experience at the Collège de France undoubtedly was for Sainte-Beuve, it was not his last venture into academic teaching. With the reform of the Ecole Normale in October 1857, which retired Michelle as director and appointed Désiré Nisard in his place, a new group of professors was also named. Among these new appointees was Sainte-Beuve as professor of French language and literature. The entire new group was installed on November 3, 1857, but Sainte-Beuve did not actually begin to teach until April 12, 1858. This fourth and final incursion into university life was the most stable and, judging from the critic's own comment to Adèle Couriard, it was pleasanter and less demanding than his earlier experiences, since it called for less public lecturing and more true classroom teaching.⁵³ The sojourn at the Ecole Normale permitted the critic to enunciate his philosophy in his first lecture, later published as the essay "De la Tradition," and he continued to elucidate this central idea in the years that followed. Before, Sainte-Beuve had always used a complete written text when he lectured, but no precise text for these classes is known, perhaps because of the more informal nature of his teaching. There are, nevertheless, at least two, probably three, articles which are reworked forms of studies begun for the Ecole Normale.⁵⁴ Since we shall consider separately the concept of tradition, it is only important to underline here that Sainte-Beuve was actively occupied with the question of literary tradition from 1857 to 1861 at the Ecole Normale with an elite public, trained in both Latin and Greek and preparing to teach.

Sainte-Beuve's teaching at the rue d'Ulm also brought him into close personal contact with specialists. Some, like M. Viguier, "l'helléniste délicat de l'Ecole Normale,"[55] under whom Sainte-Beuve had sat some forty years earlier, were old friends; others, like the young Hellenist Gandar, were new friends of another generation. Gandar's thesis on Ronsard and Homer had interested the critic very much, and, ironically, his premature death permitted Sainte-Beuve to write the eulogistic article of 1868. Sainte-Beuve also came to know A. Chassang, whose charming New Year greetings in Greek verse must have touched and pleased the critic very much since he laid them away carefully.

Sainte-Beuve did not put aside his active sympathy and interest in the Ecole Française d'Athènes during this period at the Ecole Normale or during his brief career at the Collège de France. He continued to note, either in passing or in articles, significant findings or reevaluations resulting from work done at the Ecole. At the end of his commemorative article in 1863 on the Hellenist Boissonade, there is a veritable charge to the young Greek scholars to bring distinction to France in this area.[56] It can hardly be an exaggerated interpretation of the paragraph and its context to think that Sainte-Beuve had in mind the scholars trained at the Ecole d'Athènes. Renan, Rigault, Gandar, About, Boissier are but a few of these young scholars who found sympathetic attention from the official critic. This new erudition seldom resulted in full-scale articles, but the allusion to Renan in 1854 as "un jeune savant qui a déjà fait ses preuves en haute matière"[57] was not only encouraging to the young man, but also brought his work to the attention of a broad public. Even cursory reading kept the critic oriented to new trends in classical erudition during an important period of change in France. Such benevolent awareness of young scholars brought in turn their sympathetic treatment of the critic.

This mutual sympathy was not universal, however, and during the last decade of his life Sainte-Beuve was rather sharply attacked by young critics on the point of his knowledge and views of antiquity. Without too much lack of charity, one is inclined to see these attacks as attempts to gain notoriety by engaging the dean of critics in journalistic combat. In such cases Sainte-Beuve was too shrewd to give this kind of victory to his opponent. H. Babou, in the *Revue française* of 1859, charged Sainte-Beuve with merely changing taste with the times.[58] Two years later, Bernard Jullien attacked Sainte-Beuve's "idolatry of antiquity," using as a basis for this charge the article on Meleager published almost twenty years earlier.[59] In both these cases the specific issue seems almost ludicrous in light of the facts, but the evidence remains that Sainte-Beuve's position on such matters was clear enough to inspire opposition and independent enough not to be merely the opinions accepted.

On the whole this teaching period of the critic's life was marked only by the publication of the *Etude sur Virgile*, with the accompanying studies on Horace and Quintus of Smyrna. In 1862, however, after he left the Ecole Normale, he began to write on ancient subjects again with the article on "Le Roman dans l'antiquité et Apulée," to which he later added a second essay on Courrier's translation of *Daphnis et Chloé*. These two articles were followed in 1863 by the double article on Terence and the evocative article on "La Grèce en 1863." The following years brought, at the steady, if reduced, pace of one a year, articles on the *Greek Anthology*, on Grote's

History of Greece, which provoked the critic's last word on the Homeric Question, on Benoist's edition of Virgil, and on Pongerville's translation of Lucretius. Neo-Latin poetry also inspired him to write two articles; one, on Jean Santeul, the other, on Sénécé.[60] The critic very probably read much of this poetry during the long years of study on Port-Royal and by this period felt equal to the task of treating it in articles. He could also thereby fill very real gaps in the usual knowledge of the culture of modern France. The articles on *Salammbô,* moreover, are oriented completely to the question of Flaubert's use of his historical source material, and it is clear that Sainte-Beuve wrote his articles with his Polybius before him on the desk. To this list should be added the commemorative articles on Magnin, Boissonade, Viguier, Dübner, Gandar, and Ampère, whose contributions to the field of Hellenic studies were signaled so concretely in each case by the critic. One other article belongs with this group, although it is not primarily on a Greek subject: the article on Becq de Fouquière's edition of Chénier, for this was the edition Labitte had started at Sainte-Beuve's suggestion. Boissonade had collaborated in the reading for sources, and finally, in 1862, Sainte-Beuve had the pleasure of reviewing the edition he had wanted for almost thirty years, but which he could not do personally. Each of these articles stands out as a kind of summation of Sainte-Beuve's thought on a work or an author read many times since the critic's youth. Terence alone is a relatively new name, but in all probability Sainte-Beuve had read Terence before this period in his life. In 1850 Sainte-Beuve had begun his article on Pliny with the words, "Il y a déjà longtemps que j'ai envie, ne fut-ce que par variété, de parler une fois d'un ancien et je n'ose. Mais pour aborder convenablement les anciens, il faut des préparations singulières."[61] Two years later he had also written to his friend Lerminier his hesitations about reviewing the latter's book on the legislative and constitutional history of Greece: "Tout sujet qui concerne l'antiquité est une rude affaire, même quand on vient après vous et sous les auspices de votre talent."[62] The rich harvest of articles from 1862 until his death reflects both of these earlier remarks. The conscientious, severe, and often tedious preparation was compensated for only at times by the critic's own deep inner satisfaction at meeting an intellectual challenge with integrity.

Sainte-Beuve's personal standards of accuracy in detail did not lessen in these last years of his life. In 1862 he took the poet Pontmartin to task for misquoting Horace in Latin—to the amusement of his less disciplined colleagues in criticism.[63] He was equally severe on Honoré Bonhomme, editor of the *Correspondance de Collé*, for his versions of Ovid and Horace.[64] For his own studies his specialist "collaborators," supplying scholarly verification and detail, continued to be, in the main, Egger, Rossignol, Patin, and even Leclerc, who verified Cicero for him.[65] Occasionally another friend would supply a bit of information, either on request, as when Sainte-Beuve asked Dezeimeris about the profession of Paul the Silentiary,[66] or gratuitously, as when, after reading the critic's articles on the *Greek Anthology*, Professor Egger sent him a note to correct two minor errors.[67] At least once, moreover, Sainte-Beuve dared to disagree with an editor about a textual reading. In his review of Benoist's edition of Virgil, Sainte-Beuve rejected a new reading for a passage in the third Eclogue which was suggested by Benoist and corroborated by his own friend Dübner as well. The critic preferred the more traditional reading and punctuation, nevertheless, until such a time as a new reading would give a more satisfactory meaning to the passage. Incidentally the German classical scholar Peerlkampf, in a letter to the critic, agreed with Sainte-Beuve about this reading. Such incursions into textual criticism were relatively rare, however, and only with certain

Latin authors with whom Sainte-Beuve was completely familiar, having studied them in detail and even translated for publication portions of their works. In the main his own standards of meticulousness led him to recognize his limitations in the field of textual criticism.

In direct contrast to the detailed erudition required for textual scholarship, one more facet of Sainte-Beuve's active interest in Greek culture might be mentioned. During the last decade of his life the bond of common interest in Greek culture and literature seems to have brought individual friends and groups to the critic's home on Montparnasse. Troubat has described in *Souvenirs et Indiscrétions* the gay, hellenizing social circle which met at Sainte-Beuve's house. Pantasidès read and commented on Homer, Aristophanes, or the *Anthology* in such a fashion that: "les dames elles-mêmes y prenaient goût, tant il y apportait de passion, de conviction, de chaleur et d'enthousiasme."[68] Another frequent visitor in the group was M. Garsonnet, who had replaced Sainte-Beuve at the Ecole Normale, "sémillant d'esprit, la gaieté même, en grec, en latin, en français." Frederick Dübner, to whom is owed a great debt for the nineteenth-century Didot Greek editions, was a close personal friend of the critic. He frequently stopped at 11 rue du Montparnasse, occasionally bringing excellent pears from his garden as well as his profound, scrupulous, but unpedantic knowledge of Greek. According to Professor Regard, even Sainte-Beuve's cat was graced with the name of Polémon in honor of the third-century Greek archaeologist and historian.[69] On at least one occasion, in 1866, the famous Magny dinners generated a good deal of passion over Homer, when Jules Goncourt announced his preference for Hugo and the critic Saint-Victor became violently angry in his defense of Homer. The Goncourts were extremely caustic about Saint-Victor's defense, and it took Sainte-Beuve's intervention to calm the turmoil: "Sainte-Beuve, fort ému de la querelle, me [Goncourt] fait venir auprès de lui, essaye de me calmer, en me promenant les mains sur les bras, et tâche de tout raccomoder en proposant de fonder un club des *Homérides*."[70] No such formal group seems to have been organized, but there can be little doubt about the fact that a bond existed among the sympathizers.

Troubat also reported that Pantasidès was among the faithful friends who joined the vigil at the bedside of the dying critic.[71] Quite apart from the personal friendship, it was very appropriate to have Hellenic culture represented at the final moments of Sainte-Beuve's life, for it was never really absent from his mature intellectual life. In some measure, at least, it had replaced a lost faith in religion and a human happiness which had not been his lot. He himself had written:

> Esprits immortels de Rome et surtout de la Grèce. Génies heureux qui avez prélevé comme en une première moisson toute fleur humaine, toute grâce simple et toute naturelle grandeur, vous en qui la pensée fatiguée par la civilisation moderne et par notre vie compliquée retrouve jeunesse et force, santé et fraîcheur, et tous les trésors non falsifiés de maturité virile et d'héroïque adolescence.
>
> Grands hommes pareils pour nous à des Dieux et que si peu abordent de près et contemplent, ne dédaignez pas ce cabinet où je vous reçois à mes heures de fête; d'autres sans doute vous possèdent mieux et vous interprètent plus dignement; vous êtes ailleurs mieux connus, mais vous ne serez nulle part plus aimés.[72]

His tie was not, however, sheer sentiment and faith. We have seen by now that the critic actively pursued a continuing program of reading and study of Greek literature within the confines of the Greek language itself.

Notes

1. G. Michaut, *Sainte-Beuve avant les lundis* (Paris: Fontemoing, 1903), p. 52 ff. It is a pleasure to be able to acknowledge a general indebtedness to Michaut's perspicacious and full discussion here. Canat seems to me overenthusiastic when he wrote that the program of the *Globe* "est celui du romantisme le plus avancé" (Canat, I, 307).
2. *Globe*, 19 février 1825.
3. *Globe*, 11 décembre 1824, 13 août 1825, 24 décembre 1825, etc.
4. Adolphe Lair, "Un Maître de Sainte-Beuve," *Le Correspondant*, 23 avril 1900, pp. 318–19. See also: A. G. Lehmann, *Sainte-Beuve: A Portrait of the Critic 1804–1842* (Oxford: Clarendon Press, 1962), p. 28. Profesor Lehmann describes the tight rein held by Dubois on the young journalist in these articles and wonders what importance to give the articles as the expression of Sainte-Beuve's thought. This is indeed a delicate question. Personally I tend to take them on faith. These articles are now all easily available in the Pléiade edition of Sainte-Beuve's *Oeuvres*.
5. *Oeuvres*, I, 170–74.
6. *N.L.*, V, 308–17.
7. Juste Olivier, *Paris en 1830 Journal de Juste Olivier*, ed. André Delattre and Mark Denkinger (Chapel Hill: University of North Carolina Press, 1951), p. 114. See also: *C.g.*, I, 506.
8. *Mes Poisons*, pp. 62–64. See also: *C.g.*, III, 142.
9. *P.C.*, II, 393. See also: *C.g.*, I, 534 and V, 245–48; Lehmann, *Sainte-Beuve*, pp. 290, 292 and 310.

10. *Bibliog.*, I, 336–37.
11. Canat, II, 300.
12. *N.L.*, XI, 423.
13. *N.L.*, II, 229.
14. *N.L.*, XI, 422.
15. *N.L.*, XIII, 183–265.
16. *N.L.*, XIII, 226 and 229–30.
17. "Vous, critique si délicatement inspiré, vous qui pénétrez d'un jet si rapide et si lumineux toutes les conceptions de l'esprit, tous les arcanes de la sensibilité, tous les détours de l'imagination et du coeur, je vous ai vu vous éprendre toujours plus de la beauté grecque, remonter à Homère de Ronsard et d'André Chénier, qui après tout étaient de la famille. Continuez mon aimable ami. Cette antiquité que souvent des interprétations si fausses ont si lourdement travestie, livrera à vos mains ingénieuses et légères ses richesses les plus cachées, ses perles les plus exquises. L'antiquité peut se rajeunir, rapprochée de ce qui a été conçu hors d'elle, mais dans un esprit semblable au sien. Vous l'avez bien montré naguère en retrouvant si finement dans Electre la soeur aînée de Colomba." J-J. Ampère, "Une Course dans l'Asie-Mineure: Lettre à M. Sainte-Beuve," *Revue des Deux Mondes* 29, 4ᵉ série (1842), p. 174.
18. *C.g.*, I, 69, n. 1.
19. *N.L.*, XII, 445.
20. *P.C.*, II, 325–26.
21. *P.C.*, III, 328–57.
22. See: Michaut, *Sainte-Beuve*, pp. 340–41.
23. See: *Bibliog.*, I, 159–67.
24. *P.C.*, III, 340, n. 1.
25. *Bibliog.*, II, 163.
26. For Sainte-Beuve and "l'art pour l'art," see the detailed studies of W. M. Frohock, "The Critic and the Cult of Art: Sainte-Beuve and the Esthetic Movement," *Romanic Review*, XXXII (1941), pp. 379–88; Edna C. Frederick, "The Critic and the Cult of Art: Further Observations," *Romanic Review*, XXXIII (1942), pp. 385–87.

27. Sainte-Beuve returned to the same subject in 1843 with "Quelques vérités sur la situation en littérature" (P.C. III), 415–42. See also: Claude Pichois, *Philarète Chasles et la vie littéraire au temps du Romantisme* (Paris: Corti, 1965), 2 vols. Chapter 4 (I, 422–56) is particularly interesting to compare with these two essays of Sainte-Beuve, for it deals with Chasles's characterization of Romanticism at about the same period.
28. Georges Radet, *L'Histoire et l'oeuvre de l'Ecole française d'Athènes* (Paris: Fontemoing, 1901), p. 422.
29. Radet, p. 5. Note, however, that the Legrand memoir was not published until 1896 and that while oral circulation of the idea must not be entirely discounted, it could not have had the force necessary for imposing direct action.
30. Henry Lapauze, *Histoire de l'Académie de France à Rome* (Paris: Plon, 1924), 2 vols., II, 274–76.
31. Charles Pierrot, *Table générale et analytique des Causeries du lundi, Portraits de femmes et Portraits littéraires* (Paris: Garnier, 1881), p. 41.
32. Pierrot, p. 41. The underlining is Sainte-Beuve's.
33. *P.L.*, III, 478–84.
34. *Bibliog.*, I, 386.
35. Gabriel Vauthier, "Une lettre de Thouvenel sur l'Ecole française d'Athènes en 1848," *L'Acropole, revue du Monde hellénique*, II (1927), p. 255.
36. John Edwin Sandys, *A History of Classical Scholarship* (Cambridge: University Press, 1903–8), 3 vols., III, 222, 469, 413.
37. *P.C.*, V, 467.
38. *C.g.*, VI, 500.
39. *C.g.*, VI, 507–8.
40. *Chat.*, I, 25.
41. *Chat.*, II, 70.
42. *Chat.*, II, 91.
43. Saint-Marc Girardin, Villemain, Feletz.
44. *C.g.*, IX, 178–79.
45. *C.g.*, IX, 512.
46. *C.L.*, II, 36.

47. *Le Livre d'or de Sainte-Beuve* (Paris: Fontemoing, 1904), p. 208.
48. Hippolyte Rigault, *Oeuvres complètes*, précédées d'une notice biographique et littéraire par M. S-Marc Girardin (Paris: Hachette, 1859), 4 vols., III, 396.
49. *C.g.*, X, 197.
50. See: Abel Lefranc, "Sainte-Beuve au Collège de France," in *Le Livre d'or*, pp. 203–20. Harold Nicolson, in his biography of the critic (*Sainte-Beuve* [London: Constable, 1957]), gave a somewhat less sympathetic version of this incident, which may be used to compare with the measured, sympathetic version of Abel Lefranc.
51. *C.g.*, X, 239–52.
52. Gaston Boissier, "L'Etude sur Virgile de Sainte-Beuve," in *Le Livre d'or*, p. 9.
53. *C.g.*, X, 510.
54. "De la Tradition" (*C.L.*, XV, 356–82); "Des Origines de la langue . . ." (*Pr. L.*, III, 72–133); and possibly the article "De la lecture des poètes latins sous Louis XIV," published by Jean Bonnerot (*Mercure de France*, No. 1152, août, 1959), pp. 588–613.
55. *N.L.*, II, 229.
56. *N.L.*, VI, 112.
57. *C.L.*, IX, 474. Rigault was an exception to this rule, for Sainte-Beuve wrote two full-scale articles about his thesis on the *Querelle des Anciens et des Modernes* (*C.L.*, XIII, 132–71).
58. H. Babou, "Des Amitiés littéraires," *Revue française* XVI (20 février 1859), pp. 177–84.
59. Bernard Jullien, *Thèses supplémentaires de métrique et de musique ancienne, de grammaire et de littérature,* (Paris: Hachette, 1861), pp. 433–39.
60. *C.L.*, XII, 20 and *C.L.*, XII, 280. Profesor Hutton seems unduly severe in his implication when he writes about this article, "Sainte-Beuve's remarks on the history of the epigram in his *causerie* on Sénécé owe much to Sénécé's sketch, though the reader might not be aware of it." (James Hutton, *The*

Greek Anthology in France and in the Latin Writers of the Netherlands to the year 1800 [Ithaca, New York: Cornell University Press, 1946], p. 510, n. 13.) It seems incredible that either the critic or his readers could be unaware that he was using information from the book he was reviewing.
61. *C.L.*, II, 36.
62. *C.g.*, IX, 85.
63. *N.L.*, II, 13.
64. *N.L.*, VII, 359-60.
65. *N.L.*, IX, 8, n. 1
66. *C.g.*, XIII, 404.
67. *C.g.*, XIII, 390-91.
68. Troubat, *Souvenirs*, p. 143.
69. Maurice Regard, *Sainte-Beuve* (Paris: Hatier, 1959), p. 168.
70. Edmond Goncourt et Jules Goncourt, *Journal; mémoires de la vie littéraire*, éd. R. Ricatte (Monaco: Imprimerie nationale, 1956-) 22 vols., II, 213-15.
71. Troubat, *Souvenirs*, p. 15, n. 1.
72. *P.C.*, V, 467-68 (Pensée XXXVIII).

Chapter 4
Library and General View

One significant body of evidence has been purposely omitted from all consideration up to this point, namely, Sainte-Beuve's fine personal library. This procedure has been chosen because, in spite of the careful and entirely credible reasoning of scholars who have published marginal notes from the critic's books, there is yet great uncertainty about the chronology of these notes. The evidence advanced thus far from notes, books, articles, and correspondence has led repeatedly to the conclusion that Sainte-Beuve never definitely terminated any study to put it completely out of his mind. Simple logic would make this strong personal characteristic of his written works even more true of his reading, and especially of his reading in books he had chosen to own. In short, his personal library contained one kind of synthesis of his intellectual life, chronologically valid only at his death.

Of the 1,009 books listed in the sale catalog, 246 or roughly about 24 per cent deal with Greco-Roman antiquity in some fashion.[1] Many of these books were naturally books of erudition, criticism and translations published during the critic's lifetime and sent to him by the hopeful authors. Sainte-Beuve's notes of thanks for such books indicate that even when he did not review a book he did not put it aside without at least a cursory reading, with the result that the critic easily obtained a kind of overview of specialized knowledge not common among the writers of his own generation. It also meant that he was aware of trends in research and of new interpretations by classical scholars.

Texts, including translations, comprised a sizeable portion of the Greco-Roman collection. Relatively few of the classical texts belong to the category of pure bibliophilic interest. Rather, it is particularly noteworthy that multiple editions of the same work most frequently range from traditional or popular texts, easily available in any bookstore, to scholarly critical editions. One concrete example will help a great deal to elucidate this point. The texts of the Homeric poems, to which should be added the books of criticism and commentary on the poems, formed one of the largest single groups of books. They also represent a subject which particularly interested the critic, and one on which he wrote professionally. In addition to the Boissonade edition of Homer, which Sainte-Beuve used constantly and which is now famous for his marginal notes,[2] there figured in the sale catalog of Sainte-Beuve's library at the time of his death the scholarly editions of Barnes (1711), Clark-Ernesti (1814), and Wolf (1804–7). Three more editions of the *Iliad* were also listed: Villoison (1788), Heyne (1802), the incomplete edition annotated from notes of ancient commentators by the Greek patriot Adamantios Coray (1820), and that of Dugas-Montbel (1833), about which Sainte-Beuve had written. Among the translations of Homer, Sainte-Beuve owned that of Madame Dacier, about which he had written,[3] and Leconte de Lisle's translation, of which, for good reason, he never took public note.[4] He also owned a copy of Hugues Salel's incomplete translation of the *Iliad* (1574), obviously a bibliophilic item of great interest to the critic.[5] In addition to these Greek and French editions, the critic owned several *scholia* editions. He possessed both the 1825 Bekker edition of the *Scholia in Homeri Iliadem*, containing only the commentary, and the 1858 *Carmina Homerica graeca*, which contained the Greek text and the emendations. Of the *Odyssey* he had Dindorf's *Scholia Graeca in Homeri Odysseam* (1855). The *Commentarii* of Eustathius was also in the critic's personal library, as was Theil's *Dictionnaire complète d'Homère et des Homérides*. Sainte-Beuve's copy of this dictionary was from the 1841 Paris edition, a presentation copy from the author with twelve lines of Latin verse inscribed to the critic. Ruhnkenius's edition of the *Homeri Hymnus in Cererem* (1808) also belongs with this group. One rather curious fact is the presence of only one book of Homer criticism in French, *Les Hommes d'Homère* (1861) by Delorme. One can almost suppose that it figured because of the author's name rather than for any intrinsic value to the critic or any selective criterion touching the subject matter of the study.

There can be little doubt that with such a collection Sainte-Beuve was interested in the best texts he could have from modern scholarship. It is also apparent he was interested in the commentary of ancient authors on the texts, but that he evidently did not keep modern studies on Homer as they came into his hands. In this connection it should be noted that Bareste's translation of the *Iliad*, which partially occasioned the two articles on Homer in 1843, does not figure in the sale catalog of his library. It is hardly surprising to find that his library was more selective than that of many people, for he was absolutely forced to cull from the tremendous numbers of books sent to him by publishers and authors; hence, his collection represented the books he actively chose to possess and, in the case of Homer, it seems to have been textual scholarship and the tools for reading the text accurately that Sainte-Beuve wanted at hand. By almost any standard it was an outstanding Homer collection for his time and certainly indicates the critic's long-lasting and serious interest in the poet.

The same preoccupation in reading that eventually resulted in Becq de Fouquière's edition of Chénier is apparent in the critic's copies of other French authors, with their numerous marginal notes. His Montaigne contains precise comparisons of Montaigne's thoughts with those of Latin authors unnoted by the essayist.[6] In addition to such notes, his La Bruyère shows evidence of disagreement with the author's opinions. Sainte-Beuve did not agree, for instance, with La Bruyère on the qualities of Greek style.[7] His copy of *Les Oeuvres d'Alain Chartier* is "bourré d'exemples empruntés à l'antiquité et d'allusions que la mémoire de Sainte-Beuve identifie aussitôt."[8] This characteristic form of reading was, moreover, not limited to original literary works, for Sainte-Beuve's copy of Eugène Gandar's thesis *Ronsard imitateur d'Homère* also contains notes with precise citations and allusions as well as commentaries on Gandar's findings.

The critic's library of Greco-Roman authors was no less annotated. The exhibit organized by the Bibliothèque Nationale to celebrate the one hundred and fiftieth anniversary of the critic's birth contained copies of Horace, Anacreon, Aeschylus, and Sophocles' *Oedipus Rex*, all annotated by the critic.[9] His copy of the Boissonade Homer, with its abundant annotations, so temptingly described in the sale catalog, made a brief appearance in a Paris book sale in 1955, but disappeared from sight again.[10] Each time a book is recovered and the notes deciphered, additional evidence of Sainte-Beuve's meticulous and precise reading is provided. The fact of his reading

Greek as well as Latin authors, and the method of his reading, are by now quite clear, however, and although the lack of chronology is regrettable the varieties of pen and handwriting in many of these books seem to point in the direction of reading over the years rather than at definite dateable periods. In any event, the critic's library bears out the evidence of his correspondence, notes, and public writings on his knowledge and constant reading of Greco-Roman authors.

A similar body of evidence is also undated, but is sizeable enough to deserve mention with the personal library. This is the collection of manuscript notes on "feuilles volantes" gathered together in the Collection Lovenjoul under subject-matter headings.[11] On a variety of papers, in handwriting of different periods of the critic's life, are notes dealing with authors like Hesiod, Terence, Theocritus, Horace, Homer, and with the collection of the *Greek Anthology*. Since he had written publicly about five of these six subjects, it is not surprising to find these reading notes. In the case of Hesiod the notes were undoubtedly preparatory to the somewhat developed discussion of Hesiod's concept of nature found in the article "Le Poème des champs."[12]

Some of the notes are purely bibliographic, such as the ones on the first page of the Hesiod group: "—Ampère article sur la Grèce Revue des 2 Mondes; —Léopardi dissertation [?]; —Daunou chronologie; Petite Anthologie tome I page 237 épigramme D'Alcée." The notes on the next leaf are more revelatory about the working of the critic's mind: "Confuscius meurt à 72 ans, l'an 479 avant Jésus Christ, et neuf ans avant la naissance de Socrate—ainsi Hésiode précède—Salomon en Judée et l'Ecclésiastique. C'est un peu comme si Franklin avait mis ses préceptes du bon homme Richard en vers." Other notes on the same page are briefer, but still in a comparative, categorizing vein: "Autant l'Odyssée est aimable autant Hésiode est chagrin. On s'est trop accoutumé à livrer les Grecs à une pure jeunesse, déjà expérimentée, triste à sa manière quoique sans le repli chrétien. Réfuter les dernières pages de Reinius sur l'amer du Minmerme, du Simonide, de l'Euripide." In the margin, next to this last comment is written "de [sic] Hésiode à Crabbe." The final page of notes on Hesiod is literally covered with writing at all angles and in all directions. The central part is very clearly a translation, though probably not from Hesiod. In the side margins are comments on imagery or on different versions of the translation. At the top of the page is a note "Pour épigraphe mettre ce mot de La Fontaine dans Philomène et Baucis." Such notes and translations are by no means rare; one finds them scattered throughout the Sainte-Beuve manuscripts, usually grouped under the heading of an article or study that the critic was making. We can be sure in this fashion of his close reading and study of Apuleius, Longus, Meleager, Quintus of Smyrna, Pindar, Ovid, Terence, Theocritus, and the *Greek Anthology*. There are also notes for his course on Latin poetry, and there is a whole packet of notes to consult at the reprinting of the Homer articles.[13] All of these little slips of paper bear mute testimony to Sainte-Beuve's precise method of reading and preparing his published articles as well as to his wide-ranging intellectual interests.

The evidence which we have attempted thus far to present in an orderly, concrete fashion in order to trace the course of the critic's intellectual life has, at times, seemed perhaps to suggest mountains of minutiae, implying, perhaps, a depth of study apparently incompatible with the critic's demanding professional preoccupations. Such a study has been necessary, however, in order to reach some clear factual conception of the basis for certain opinions Sainte-Beuve held, and to attempt to distinguish in his thought between prejudices and consciously acquired beliefs, between sentimental attachment and selection by experience. The chronology and identification have needed to be established quite precisely in the light of the nineteenth century's evolving views of Greco-Roman antiquity and "the classical tradition." It is apparent at this point, however, that Sainte-Beuve read Greek most of his adult life, that at all periods he was in close touch with philhellenes and scholarly specialists, with thinkers, and that all of this voluntarily sought-out contact had an impact, not only on his personal taste and mode of thinking, but on his literary criticism as well.

Before proceeding to the consideration of the specific relationships between the critic's massive reading of ancient authors and his own critical production it seems desirable, at the risk of oversimplification, to attempt to draw a synthetic picture of his view of antiquity. Here, again, the emphasis will be laid on Greece, since Sainte-Beuve's attitude toward Rome and Latin culture was not different from that of any other cultured Frenchman—namely, that French culture is a direct descendent of Latin. There was perhaps one incidental point of difference in that Sainte-Beuve interpreted Rome always, not as a culture in itself, but rather as a splendid mediary between Greece and France, renewing and re-creating her predecessor.

There can be little doubt that the first forty years of the nineteenth century brought a rapid and notable increase of interest in Greece. Sainte-Beuve himself wrote, in 1841, that Greece had become the style.[14] It was not a simple, unified view of Greece, moreover, which emerged; rather, as René Canat has pointed out, the various kinds and degrees of Romanticism could be categorized according to their attitudes toward Greece. There is a poetic Romanticism closed or hostile to the Greeks, a doctrinaire Romanticism favorable to Greece, a Romanticism of the critics, the historians, the philosophers, a Catholic, conservative Romanticism which looks defiantly at Hellenism, and a liberal Romanticism which rallies to it.[15] The neoclassicists had equally diverse views, with the result that the tremendous variety of points of view and the persistence of the discussion tended to confuse the issue completely, rendering any view inevitably eclectic and without clear outline. What distinguishes Sainte-Beuve from all these is his defense of Romantic poetry and its revolt against tradition together with his active study of the Greek tradition and his political philhellenism. In this combination Sainte-Beuve formed an individual, independent conception of Greek civilization and its value for modern French culture.

The first and a very important characteristic of the critic's interest in Greece was that after the Greek War of Independence, Sainte-Beuve's interest was almost wholly concentrated on *ancient* Greece.[16] Modern Greece existed for him generally only insofar as it contained monuments and vestiges of the ancient civilization, or as its modern citizens could clarify, consciously or unconsciously, the great culture of the past. It is also completely apparent that one aspect of Sainte-Beuve's view was a personal and lyric one, which found its expression typically in the 1846 "jamais vous ne serez plus aimé,"[17] and in his directions on how to approach the study of the ancients, which remind one of certain religious purification rites.[18] Sainte-Beuve also regretted very much the loss of the legends about Greece through the new scientific studies. Using the example of Hippocrates, Sainte-Beuve in 1863 listed the few bits of certain information about the founder of Greek medicine, as opposed to the more developed picture of him, the product of legend and apocryphal writings, that was deemed inadmissible by modern critics on guard against the siren voice of "tout ce que cette Grèce aimable et mensongère a imaginé." But, added the critic, if we destroy the legend, we should attempt to replace it in another fashion so that human memory and the pantheon of the past may not be impoverished of a great image.[19] The very next year, in a review of Viollet-le-Duc's *Entretiens sur l'architecture*, Sainte-Beuve reported with noticeable pleasure that Viollet-le-Duc, reputedly a foe of Greece, appreciated Greek talent and differentiated well between Greek and Roman architectural genius. The critic also observed that, as Henri Estienne had realized, "il y ait dans notre génie, dans notre tour naturel d'esprit et de langage . . . quelque chose qui nous rapproche d'avantage des Grecs," that the Roman filiation is rather "par réflexion, par habitude et routine."[20] One immediately recognizes the reiteration of the cultural myth—the wishful thinking—that inspired the Renaissance writers to make Trojan genealogies for the French nation. These various expressions of sentiment in both religious and mythological language do not, however, contain any sort of nostalgia for a lost Golden Age; they express, rather, the critic's admiration on a nonintellectual level, a vital reenforcement of feeling. Through the eyes of his love, Sainte-Beuve saw the ancient Greeks as "la race d'élite et privilégiée entre toutes."[21]

A related aspect of the Greek civilization that held particular meaning for Sainte-Beuve was the Greek ethical view of life. He once said that Chateaubriand was always in a dilemma of choice between Christianity and Greece, and later in his own life he wrote that the concept of transcendental perfection found in Christianity was not to be found in the writings of any ancient moralist.[22] He had developed and explained the same conflict in a letter to Adèle Couriard in 1858 when he pointed out that the greatest opposition to Christianity is "Pan-Nature." The reader is reminded immediately of the critic's earlier verses:

> Paganisme immortel, es-tu mort? On le dit;
> Mais Pan tout bas s'en moque et la Sirène en rit.[23]

Sainte-Beuve continued to explain his point in the same letter to Adèle Couriard, writing that "derrière mon scepticisme poli" he was a naturalist.[24] Lest these remarks seem to be of only relative importance, it is appropriate to recall here that Sainte-Beuve turned to the study of Greek culture in the same period when he began *Port-Royal,* and that the letter to Adèle Couriard was roughly contemporary with the famous epilogue to *Port-Royal* rejecting the Jansenist Christian ascetic view of life. In short, Sainte-Beuve felt more spiritual affinity with the Greek than with the Christian concept of life. Though this sense of philosophic affinity was frequently expressed in almost religious terms, it would be wrong to construe it as a sentimental nostalgia for a lost utopia capable of being recovered in the nineteenth century. Sainte-Beuve was too much of a Lucretian realist, philosophically, to lose himself in such idle dreams. Writing about the Atticism of the period of Louis XIV, he compared it to that of Greece, but added that it was also nice to live in the nineteenth century, "sous notre Code civil et notre régime d'égalité, même lorsqu'on est gentilhomme comme lorsqu'on ne l'est pas."[25]

Sainte-Beuve's view of antiquity, and of Greek culture in particular, has often been characterized as dilettante. "C'était un alexandrin qui devait finir bibliothécaire . . . philologue à la Boissonade," wrote Bertrand, adding that his Alexandrianism and epicureanism were bourgeois in character, like those of Chénier.[26] Anatole France too doubted the Greek taste of Sainte-Beuve.[27] Even Réne Canat has posed the question: "Le prudent Sainte-Beuve n'a-t-il pas fait une antiquité trop charmante? . . ." although his answer is somewhat weakened by its negatives and generality.[28] Desonay implied the same general attitude when he commented specifically on Sainte-Beuve's translations from the *Greek Anthology,* saying that they reminded him of the "versifications mignards du dix-huitième siècle, pastoral, embaumé et fleuri de roses."[29] Each of these statements has a great deal of truth in it, but is seen to be inaccurate when set in the wider context of a more developed, synthetic view. The critic's serious preoccupation with the late writers of the Alexandrian, and even of the Greco-Roman, periods of literature is evident to any consistent reader of Sainte-Beuve. At least two causes for this that are not strictly literary present themselves immediately, and should be borne in mind: a historical approach, and scholarly curiosity.

Like his contemporaries Sainte-Beuve was penetrated by the organic concept of historic process which, following the ideas of Vico, regarded general progress as going through cycles of birth, flowering, and decay. This concept, applied to French cultural history, viewed the Middle Ages and the Rennaissance as the birth, the reign of Louis XIV as the apex, and the eighteenth and nineteenth centuries as a decadence, containing perhaps the seeds of a new genesis. From the beginning of his career, Sainte-Beuve tended to view his own age as postclassical, analogous to post-fifth century Greece.[30] He turned, then, to Alexandria to find brothers, artists whose problems were similar, whose historic circumstances were analogous, to those of the nineteenth century. Another facet of this same attraction to the writers of the Alexandrian period was that, as anthologists and catalogers, these writers were the nearest contemporary source for much of our modern knowledge about Greek culture.[31] Less original and inspired in their own work, they could provide much information about earlier authors, and even real insight into their works, for they had revised the texts and written the first serious commentaries on them. In an 1844 letter to Juste Olivier, containing his *Paris Chronicle*, Sainte-Beuve noted a new tendency in French literature and criticism, what he called the erudite and scientific method of studying the language, vocabulary, and text of the seventeenth-century authors. He continued that, on a smaller scale and with more ease, it recalled the work of the Alexandrian critics and grammarians on their language. "Les classiques français du dix-septième siècle sont déjà devenus des Anciens. La critique française entre décidément dans son époque alexandrine."[32]

Alexandrian and Greco-Roman authors attracted the critic for yet another, more purely literary, reason: they belonged to a time of fusion (and differentiation) of the two great expressions of ancient culture. Just as, in individual studies, Sainte-Beuve looked particularly closely at the moment of budding and then at the first sign of decay, so, with the Greco-Roman culture, it was natural that a period of change should attract his attention as one that could make clear the essential qualities of its genius. In 1845, at the end of the article on Meleager, he questioned and defended the validity of his appreciative essays on less well-known ancient authors. Neither scholarly nor philological, but "à la vieille manière française légèrement rajeunie," these essays might interest and instruct a cultivated, though not erudite, audience that customarily judged antiquity by a few great names on everyone's lips. Sainte-Beuve continued, moreover, with a more personal and perceptive answer, saying that one knows a country well only when one has crossed it not only on the broad, well-traveled highways but also on its pathways, and even, perchance, among its brambles. The *Anthology* and its poets are like the pathways of ancient, interior Greece; Sainte-Beuve can only indicate the way. If anyone questions "ce souci perpétuel du nouveau," he will answer in the words of Ulysses in Alcinous's palace.[33]

It is also important to recall, in this connection, that Sainte-Beuve did not write of the "victory" of Rome over Greece or of the opposition between the two cultures. Rather, it was the sense of continuity, the natural succession or evolution of a single culture, which he emphasized. In one of his fruitful digressions from a discussion of Duveyrier's lecture on "Civilization," Sainte-Beuve pointed out that the word itself might be of modern invention, current only since Turgot, but that Greece, and Rome after Greece, had had the concept, and indeed, the fact. Civilization in such terms had been less expansive with the Romans perhaps, more defensive, and he added that "les modernes se remettent en marche et entreprennent désormais l'oeuvre progressive de la civilisation proprement dite; la différence des proportions et des mesures méritait en effet un mot tout nouveau."[34] Here again Greece and Rome are portrayed as the source and the microcosm of modern thought. Earlier, in the essay "Qu'est-ce qu'un classique?" Sainte-Beuve had said explicitly, "Il ne s'agit pas ici de distinguer entre les Grecs et les Latins; leur héritage pour nous et leurs bienfaits se confondent."[35] He recognized differences between the two nations, nevertheless, but was less interested in an analytical definition of the separate entity of each than in the cultural fusion which was the heritage of the whole Latin world.

The ever-changing concept of this heritage, in the process of its transmission to the nineteenth century, evolved in the critic's maturity as a concrete example of one of his fundamental historic and literary concepts. The brief essay prompted by Maurice de Guérin's poem *Le Centaure* mentioned the poem only quite incidentally; the real body of the essay established four periods in French Hellenistic culture, from the Greek colony at Massilia to the nineteenth century. According to Sainte-Beuve, it was only the modern (i.e., nineteenth-century) school which put aside a somewhat mannered, overrefined Greece to express "le sentiment grec grandiose, primitif, retrouvé et un peu refait à distance par une sorte de réflexion poétique et philosophique."[36] In his doctoral research Professor Scheel concerns himself specifically with this question of Sainte-Beuve's interest in the survival of the Greco-Roman tradition throughout French literature. Dr. Scheel finds that although Sainte-Beuve did not set about in a systematic, scholarly fashion to make such a study he was, nevertheless, constantly preoccupied with the question and treated it in the majority of his separate essays.[37]

Greece was, then, a complex, multifaceted civilization, interpreted by each succeeding generation to suit its own needs. It had its own organic development (rise, classicism, decadence); it was, in effect, a microcosm of occidental civilization. This complex microcosm, however, had, according to the critic, certain characteristic traits which he emphasized repeatedly. Greece, for Sainte-Beuve, was a full-blooded, heroic nation, vibrant and alive, not the cold, insipid ideal of pure white plaster which had for so long frozen French poets.[38] Simplicity and naturalness, a certain graceful naïveté, deeply rooted in human nature and true in its physical images, characterize Greek literature in all its periods from Homer to the followers of Theocritus. Certain Latin poets, such as Horace and Virgil, were very sensitive to this simplicity without being able to express it completely, for their poetry was born of artistic sophistication. The Greek spirit ("spiritus graiae tenuis camoenae") "est une fraîcheur qui tient à la source; il est des images vives et légères qui tiennent aux impressions du berceau, et dont la trace se perpétue à travers les âges."[39] Natural simplicity was, furthermore, not solely a literary characteristic, a kind of expression; it contained also a philosophic view of life. For Sainte-Beuve, Greece, not Palestine, was the nation of the Elect.

The diversity of Sainte-Beuve's reading in Greco-Roman authors, which has become increasingly evident during the first part of this study, is quite as impressive as the sheer quantity of his critical production. Were these characteristics the only conclusions to be drawn, however, they would be somewhat meaningless and empty. From this very broad panorama must still be disengaged those particular authors who might naturally affect, or who did indeed affect, the critic's concept of literature and criticism in some tangible way. In disengaging one aspect for examination there is always, however, the risk of putting the total view out of focus. In the particular context of his study, it nevertheless seems wiser to risk such a distortion than to try to encompass the critic's total estimate of the ancient writers who attracted his attention from diverse points of view. By way of introduction to the group of works commonly recognized for their relationship to the critic's literary and intellectual orientation, there is certainly some value in considering at least one group of ancient prose writers for whom Sainte-Beuve might reasonably have felt some affinity, in an effort to clarify his apparent preference for the poets in both the Greek and the Roman literatures. The choice for this first attempt has been the historians. This group has been chosen because it is prominently represented in Sainte-Beuve's own reading, and while the critic reviewed many books of history, including books on ancient history, he never wrote an essay on an ancient historian as a mature critic. Such a consideration can at best be only partial, therefore, and oblique. It can, however, help to uncover in a positive way the critic's attitudes both toward antiquity and toward his own contemporaries. Other authors are more easily distinguishable, even to the casual reader, since in every case they prompted specific essays by the critic. Sainte-Beuve's predilection for Homer, Virgil, and the *Greek Anthology* has been noted many times by students of Sainte-Beuve, although the implications of these preferences for his criticism have not been studied in detail. Theocritus and the elegiac poets have received less critical attention, but, upon closer inspection, his study of these poets seems to have direct bearing on Sainte-Beuve's own poetic creation and his personal poetic theory. The *Greek Anthology* provided the critic with much of the material for one of his favorite pastimes, translation. These translations and the numerous reviews he did of both verse and prose versions of foreign works give very concrete evidence concerning his theory of translation, his views on its efficacy, and the manner of performing the task. Finally, Sainte-Beuve's general concept of tradition and the place of Greco-Roman antiquity in the life of a modern cultured person is a subject which emerged frequently from the critic's pen. It was an essential *prise de position,* and will serve here also to synthesize the more fragmented views of the other chapters.

The question of the language of his reading will not be of paramount importance in these studies, since our argument on this point has, hopefully, made apparent that Sainte-Beuve read both Latin and Greek frequently, although it has also shown that time did not always permit him this luxury. In the chapters that follow, therefore, it has been assumed that Sainte-Beuve was familiar with his texts in the original, that he very probably had help from specialists for bibliography, points of scholarship, or even in reading the original in the case of the Greek authors. Whenever he wrote a complete article he had already worked with, and probably had before him, the original text, but allusions and references, particularly for Greek authors, were frequently based on reading in translation. One further point that needs to be made here is that Sainte-Beuve obviously learned a great deal about antiquity from secondary sources in the contemporary scholarly books he reviewed. It would therefore be practically impossible to distinguish precisely the provenance of his information.

Such precision has seemed less important than the establishment of a correct overall view and an understanding of the role which this information played in his own critical attitudes. Finally, whatever the source of his knowledge, whatever the outside help, one point is clear: namely, in the published articles, it was Sainte-Beuve who initiated the line of thinking and chose to take the position to which his study led him.

Notes

1. *Catalogue des livres composant la bibliothèque de M. Sainte-Beuve dont la vente aura lieu le lundi 21 mars 1870 et les cinq jours suivants à sept heures du soir* (Paris: L. Potier, 1870), 2 vols. Henceforth this work will be referred to as: *Cat.*
2. Troubat, *Souvenirs,* p. 139, n. 1. "L'Homère de M. Sainte-Beuve, celui dont il se servait dans ses lectures avec M. Pantasidès (édition Boissonade, texte grec, 4 vol., 1824), est tout chargé de notes, de commentaires, de remarques, de rapprochements littéraires: c'est la critique même en formation, à l'état d'ébauche, d'éléments, telle qu'il l'applique ensuite et la développe dans ses travaux destinés au public; on la surprend là sur le vif, on la voit saillir et jaillir de son esprit: vous retrouverez ce premier mouvement dans n'importe laquelle de ses études."
3. *C.L.,* IX, 473–514. *Cat.* (deuxième partie) No. 142: "*L'Iliade et l'Odyssée d'Homére* trad. en français avec des remarques par Mme Dacier (Paris, 1741), 8 vols. in-12 fig. v. m. Aux armes du duc de Chevreuse."
4. A letter from Frederic Dübner, the eminent Hellenist, to Sainte-Beuve, refusing the latter's invitation to do an article on Leconte de Lisle's Homer makes very clear Dübner's opinion of the work. It also confirms an opinion that Sainte-Beuve saw the problems in a review and felt that only a professional Greek scholar could speak with the proper authority. The letter says in part:

"Je suis content de n'avoir pas eu occasion de demander un exemplaire à l'éditeur et d'être resté sans engagement; car quelque édifiant que soit pour moi cette preuve d'un vigoureux amour pour le prince de l'antiquité et ce signe d'un public français ayant conservé quelque piété pour le père de la poésie, je déplore cette publication et je suis convaincu qu'elle fera beaucoup de mal à Homère dans le public contemporain, si elle doit se répandre. Tous ceux qui n'ont pas lu le grec ou l'ont lu sous des maîtres incapables ou absurdes, croiront à une reproduction rigoureuse, à un calque sévère, à une photographie du texte, et mettront toute cette raideur, toute cette monotonie, toute cette affreuse pauvreté de mouvement (si on peut joindre ces mots) *sur le compte d'Homère,* qui est dans sa simplicité naturelle, le plus souple, le plus délié des poètes, qui a une liberté de mouvement, avec laquelle Virgile a voulu quelquefois lutter, sans succès, comme lui-même le sentait sans doute mieux que personne. Je déplore les Veilles d'un homme zélé si mal employées, mais je ne crois pas qu'on calomnie M. Leconte en disant qu'il a fait d'Homère une momie." (Ms. D. 601, Collection Spoelberch de Lovenjoul, p. 74.)

5. *Cat.* No. 183: "L'Iliade d'Homère, traduict de grec en vers françois, par Hugues Salel; l'augmentation outre les precédentes impressions, l'Umbre dudict Salel, par Olivier de Magny, avec le premier et le second de l'Odyssée d'Homère, par Jacques Peletier du Mans. Autres poésies par P de Ronsard, et par autres poëtes du ce temps, à l'imitation dudit Homère. Paris, Claude Gautier, 1574. . . . La continuation de l'Iliade d'Homère (livres douze à seize inclusivement), par Amadis Jamyn. Paris, Lucas Breyer, 1574. . . . En 1 vol. in-8, v. f. fil. tr. dor. (Simier) Bel exemplaire."

6. See: Emile Faguet, "Montaigne annoté par Sainte-Beuve," *La Revue Latine,* 5 (25 août 1906), pp. 449–76.

7. Gustave Michaut, "Le 'La Bruyère' de Sainte-Beuve," *Revue d'Histoire littéraire de France,* 13 (1906), pp. 505–44 and 714–26.

8. Jean Seznec, "L'Alain Chartier de Sainte-Beuve," *Romanic Review*, XXXV (October, 1944), pp. 203–19.
9. *Sainte-Beuve* Exposition organisée pour le cent cinquantième anniversaire de sa naissance (Paris: Imprimerie de la Bibliothèque Nationale, 1955), pp. 60–61.
10. *Cat.*, p. viii. I am grateful to MM. Paul Jammes and Frédéric Lolié for providing me with this information on the sale of the book. I should also like to thank Professor Guy Tosi, Director of the French Institute in Florence (Italy) for his efforts to obtain information about the present whereabouts of this book.
11. Manuscript D. 572 contains the "feuilles volantes" of D. 571. D. 569 is labeled "Notes historiques et littéraires prises par Sainte-Beuve." Collection Spoelberch de Lovenjoul.
12. *N.L.*, II, 272–78, and Ms. D. 552 fols. 351–55. Collection Spoelberch de Lovenjoul.
13. Notes on all these authors are found in the manuscripts of Sainte-Beuve in the Collection Spoelberch de Lovenjoul.
14. *P.C.*, III, 186.
15. Canat, I, 31.
16. Sainte-Beuve did, of course, write on *La Grèce en 1863* by Grenier. See: *N.L.*, V, 308–9.
17. *P.C.*, V, 468. See also: *C.g.*, VI, 341–42. Sainte-Beuve wrote to Félix Ravaisson on January 17, 1846: "Je n'ai pas eu le temps de l'apprendre [l'antiquité] ni d'y pénétrer assez avant en ces années qu'on ne retrouve plus, mais je l'adore et je me prends à ceux qui en savent les avis."
18. *C. L.*, II, 44–45; and more especially *C.L.*, XI, 288.
19. *N.L.*, V, 219–20. The context here is important for the critic's thought and his perception that where legend is destroyed, man creates new legends.
20. *N.L.*, VII, 164.
21. *N.L.*, XIII, 50.
22. *N.L.*, III, 253.
23. *Poésies complètes* I, 330.
24. *C.g.*, XI, 97. See also Canat III, 119–20. Canat quotes

Gautier: "le Christ n'est pas venu pour moi," and Jules Janin: "l'étrange querelle qui oppose le monde religieux aux humanistes."
25. *P.C.*, V, 118.
26. Bertrand, pp. 395–96.
27. *Poésies complètes*, I, xxv.
28. Canat, III, 180. Canat's answer is: "Sainte-Beuve dans l'ensemble ne l'a pas déparée et le charme des anciens a passé dans sa manière."
29. Fernand Desonay, *Le Rêve hellénique chez les poètes parmassiens* (Louvain: Librairie universitaire, 1928), p. 36.
30. See for example: *C.g.*, V, 448.
31. *P.C.*, V, 443–44.
32. *C.g.*, V, 448.
33. *P.C.*, V, 444.
34. *N.L.*, X, 243–46. Incidentally, on the comparison of Greece and the Middle Ages, fashionable among enthusiastic medievalists of the nineteenth century, Sainte-Beuve reacted in a strongly negative fashion. See: *N.L.*, III, 395–97.
35. *C.L.*, XV, 362.
36. *Pr. L.*, III, 387.
37. Hans Ludwig Scheel, *Die Ürteile Sainte-Beuves über das Verhaltnis der französischen Literatur zur Antike (1500–1800)* (Kiel: University Press, 1950), p. 145–50. I should like here to express a special gratitude to Dr. Scheel's work, which parallels so closely parts of my own, although each of us worked quite independently. We have often corroborated each other's findings.
38. *N.L.*, V, 417. See also: *P.C.*, V, 413.
39. *P.C.*, V, 417. But see also the slightly different version of this idea in 1852: "L'idée qu'on faisait de la Grèce, de cette littérature et de cette contrée célèbre n'a pas toujours été la même en France, et elle a passé depuis trois siècles par bien des variations et des vicissitudes. Si l'on nous faisait autrefois de l'ancienne Grèce une image trop amollie et trop riante, ne nous le fait-on pas trop dure et trop sauvage aujourd'hui?" (*C.L.*, VII, 216.)

PART II
Implications for Criticism

Il ne s'agit pas ici de distinguer entre les Grècs et les Latins; leur héritage pour nous et leurs bienfaits se confondent.

Causèries du lundi XV, 362

Chapter 1
Historians and Historiography

In 1862 Sainte-Beuve wrote that his epoch lived on retrospection, that it flattered itself particularly, if not for having invented history, at least for having found its true key—even though this key was both used and abused.¹ Everything was subject to new evidence and/or a new interpretation. Certainly no single characterization of the nineteenth century could be much more telling. The critic himself had taken pleasure in reading history ever since his childhood experiences with Rollin's *Histoire ancienne* and the Abbé Barthélemy's *Voyage du jeune Anacharsis*²; he had even written a monumental work of historic analysis on Port-Royal. Still, as his work differed from that of many of his contemporaries, so did his views on historiography. His commentary on Greco-Roman historians may perhaps enrich the background of his independent position, and will at least make clear his opinion on some of the functions of historical writing by providing his reasons for the continued study of the ancient historians.

During his years of apprenticeship at the *Globe*, Sainte-Beuve had the opportunity of reading, if not the books themselves, at least the *Globe* reviews of several important historical works published in that period. In 1825, Jouffroy wrote for the *Globe* "Comment les dogmes finissent," and we have already seen that Sainte-Beuve was acquainted with Michelet, who translated Vico, and with Quinet, who translated Herder. He frequented the Sorbonne lectures of Cousin, who spoke of his own views on historiography; he also heard Guizot's lectures on the history of civilization. His friend and mentor Daunou gave a course at the *Collège de France* in 1829–30, entitled *Systèmes de philosophie applicables à l'histoire*. A letter from Sainte-Beuve to Michelet in 1831, thanking the historian for the copy of *Histoire romaine* sent to Sainte-Beuve, perhaps in hope of a review, provides evidence of an early enthusiasm (which did not last) for Michelet's kind of history. It also gives some concrete evidence of the critic's general background in Roman history. It says in part:

> J'achève toute à l'heure de lire, Monsieur, votre *Histoire Romaine* que vous avez été assez bon pour m'envoyer. Vous dire tout ce que j'ai appris, combien j'ai été heureux d'y retrouver sous le jour d'une critique moderne et originale, ces récits et ces hommes avec lesquels on nous a fait vivre si jeunes, mais que tant de préjugés ont enveloppés à nos yeux d'un voile romanesque, c'est ce que je ne puis assez faire, Monsieur. Depuis longtemps je vous avoue que je n'osais jamais parler d'histoire romaine ni même m'en appuyer dans mes séries de pensées intérieures. Des origines j'avais lu deux volumes de Niebuhr, et je savais que rien n'est bien certain que la négation de la fable convenue; des derniers siècles de la République, je me disais que l'histoire n'en était pas faite et que tous les jugemens [sic] classiques sur les hommes et l'esprit des événemens étaient à réviser. . . . Je n'ai abordé la lecture de vos volumes qu'avec des connaissances générales, des souvenirs vagues de mes his-

toriens, de Tite-Live, de Plutarque, et sur les choses comme sur les personnages, il ne m'a pas été difficile d'être de votre avis et de m'abandonner, dans l'ensemble comme dans les détails, au développement continu de votre pensée.

The same year also witnessed Sainte-Beuve's brief flirtation with Saint-Simonism, with its systematic and doctrinaire interpretation of the present and future events. Sainte-Beuve was not long, however, in returning to his broader and less restrictive views, no longer susceptible to any systematic philosophy of history. Thirty years later, he wrote "on ne donnera jamais des coups de canifs assez profonds dans toute philosophie de l'histoire."[3] Even his enthusiasm for Michelet's increasingly rhetorical and imaginative re-creation of history waned to the point that in 1864 he declared that Michelet's particular gift escaped him entirely.[4]

Although there are no more than fleeting allusions to Vico, Sainte-Beuve found the Viquian concept of an organic succession of critical ages sufficiently sympathetic to utilize it against Boileau in 1829 and, as we have seen, to create a parallel between the Alexandrian period of Greece and his own age.[5] Such a general intellectual sympathy does not constitute a contradiction of his strong statement against systematic philosophers of history, however, nor did it lead the critic on to accept totally, like Madame de Staël, an absolute faith in continual progress. Shortly after the Revolution of 1848 Sainte-Beuve, commenting on the recent events, remarked that "la civilsation, la *vie* est une chose apprise et inventée," and that after a period of peace men forget this truth too easily, and come to believe that culture is innate and synonymous with nature. Savagery is always near at hand, continued the critic, and as soon as the defenses are relaxed it takes over. Professor Guyot, in quoting this view, has recognized that it does indeed express a philosophy of history, but one based on the observation of events rather than on the grandiose dreams of 1830.⁶

Sainte-Beuve was no less opposed to another form of interpretative history, popular among the Romantics, that of the "man of destiny," who by his greatness was released from any moral judgment of his acts. Even among intellectuals and poets "l'idée obsédante du grand homme a substitué presque généralement la *force* à l'idée morale."⁷ At precisely the same period, Sainte-Beuve expressed the same ideas in another fashion in *Volupté* in the character of Monsieur de Couaën, who talks at some length with Amaury about the number of great men who do not succeed.⁸ Professor Guyot has followed the evolution of the critic's thought to its final crystallization in the La Rochefoucauld article, where Sainte-Beuve wrote: "Le philosophe systématique et le moraliste sont volontiers mal ensemble. Le moraliste souriant importune l'autre; il sait la ficelle secrète et gêne les grands airs du conquérant."⁹ Sainte-Beuve thus "escaped from the ubiquitous temptations of Romantic history with the conjoined lines of transcendental schematism and hero worship."¹⁰ Thinking independently in a manner that did not always please his contemporaries, Sainte-Beuve, in the end, brought more true sophistication to history and historiography than the work of some of his contemporaries. He expressed his concept and method best in 1864, when he wrote:

> Le sage et le critique qui a d'avance purgé son esprit de toutes les idoles et de tous les fantômes continue, chaque jour et à chaque instant, de servir à sa manière l'avancement de l'espèce, d'étudier, de chercher le vrai, le vrai seul, de s'y tenir sans le forcer, sans l'exagérer, sans y ajouter, et en laissant subsister, à côté des points acquis, tous les vides et toutes les lacunes qu'il n'a pu combler.¹¹

Against this background, it is of some interest to look briefly at Sainte-Beuve's manner of reading ancient historians and the various judgments he made of their works. It is hardly surprising to find that the critic read the Roman historians in his youth, and read thoroughly the Greek historians only later. At one point, however, the critic approved M. Troplong in his judgment that no Roman historian had the perception of Aristotle on the Spartan republic or of Xenophon on that of Athens. Roman historians, wrote Sainte-Beuve, explained by very general causes or simple ethical decisions very complicated and diverse results. Even Tacitus, who was normally perceptive about the human heart, lacked the talent for analyzing the underlying motives of great historic events.[12] In the same article, Sainte-Beuve considered the applicability, to the contemporary scene, of the history of the transition from the Roman Republic to the Augustan Empire, only to point out that it is less frequently the case that ancient history clarifies a modern situation than that modern experience gives new meaning and clarity to the picture transmitted by an ancient historian. Valid as his conclusion is, the critic nevertheless habitually utilized allusion to ancient historians as a means of clarifying by comparison the work of a modern writer. Since the allusions were intended to facilitate the understanding of a cultivated but not erudite reader, they rarely went beyond obvious characteristics known to every educated adult.

We find few surprises, then, in the critic's specific comments on the Greek historians. Sainte-Beuve appreciated Polybius's historic method in its precision and clarity,[13] but found this historian's work less interesting, as well as less fecund for his own studies perhaps, than that of other historians. He seems to have read Polybius only for the long article on *Salammbô*.[14] Herodotus, the antithesis of a scientific historian, was read by Sainte-Beuve, on the other hand, at every period of his life. The anecdotal chronicle was not without its own special value for Sainte-Beuve. The critic particularly enjoyed the life of Homer falsely attributed to Herodotus because he appreciated the story for its mythic value. Herodotus was a source for Greek cultural tradition, then, not historically accurate, of course, but with a particular value for a cultural historian. Once, in discussing the late fourteenth-century work *Le Combat de trente Bretons contre trente Anglais* as an antidote to the *Roman de Renart*, Sainte-Beuve wrote that he was moved to hunt in antiquity among the memorable contests for a combat comparable to that of the Thirty Bretons. He found his comparable battle in Herodotus, and though he ended his discussion by a literary comparison between Simonides and the trouvère, his narrative source was indeed Herodotus.[15] Somewhat earlier, in the article on Volney who, as he pointed out in passing, did not have the "religion of Antiquity," Sainte-Beuve explained quite clearly his reasons for cherishing and reading Herodotus by saying that the life of Homer falsely attributed to him, "si fabuleuse qu'elle soit, exprime très bien le fond des légendes populaires qui circulaient sur le poète."[16] The mythic value of popular legend is important to our understanding of literary works and artists as well as the more positivistic information of the modern erudite discipline, according to Sainte-Beuve.

Of all the Greek historians it was in fact the one who was not truly a historian at all, but a biographer, that Sainte-Beuve frequented the most. For the critic, as well as for his compatriots since the sixteenth century, the Amyot translation of the *Parallel Lives* played no small role in Plutarch's popularity. The importance of this translation, in the opinion of Sainte-Beuve, was that it provided a natural entry into the Greek work and a kind of marriage of two artists to the extent that it is difficult to distinguish the two in the critic's mind. The article which he wrote on Amyot, however, was not used as a pretext to discuss the Greek writer. Quite apart from the Amyot translation, Sainte-Beuve had other reasons for his appreciation of Plutarch. Biography is the best introduction to history, wrote Sainte-Beuve many times, and Plutarch is an excellent introduction to the indispensable knowledge of Greek history.[17] Even Shakespeare, the least classic of great authors in French eyes, had read Montaigne and Plutarch.[18] Beyond providing easy access to Greek civilization, Plutarch was also "une mine féconde pour ce genre d'indication dans l'Antiquité."[19] In fact, Sainte-Beuve's first refusal of the Wolfian hypotheses on Homer arose in large measure because they contradicted Plutarch's evidence on the Homeric poems, and particularly on the Pisistratean recension.[20]

The *Parallel Lives* had also served generations of less erudite Frenchmen as a model of moral elevation,[21] just as they continued to be read by the Greeks themselves in 1863. But, added Sainte-Beuve, quoting Guizot, Coletti alone is a Greek statesman worthy to take his place among Plutarch's men.[22] It is hardly surprising either to find a parallel frequently drawn by subsequent critics between the Greek biographer-moralist and Sainte-Beuve. Jules Troubat once asserted that Sainte-Beuve "restera le Plutarque du XIXe siècle."[23] It would be easy to exaggerate the aptness of this parallel, and perhaps its real value should be seen in the same light as the critic's own parallels between authors, that is, as a quick, apt, provocative, but hardly profound juxtaposition of two similar talents. The most comparable traits in the two talents are those of the social observer and the *moraliste*, along with a certain command of dramatic narrative style able to create a vivid scene in masterly fashion. Plutarch had been well known in France for so long that Sainte-Beuve tended as a rule to use him for clarifying comparisons rather than to interpret him to the nineteenth-century public, despite the similarity between the two authors.

It was to the style of Xenophon that Sainte-Beuve returned most easily. In the discussion of Napoleon I as a historical writer, the critic chose Xenophon to provide the rich contrast in style and manner which could facilitate the analysis and comprehension of Napoleon. Xenophon was the leader of all the Attic writers of every language and country, of "tous ceux qui sentent le prix d'une persuasion aisée, d'une simplicité exquise et d'une douce négligence mêlée d'ornement."[24] Professor Emile Egger of the Collège de France, one of the critic's faithful readers, wrote to him about this appraisal of Xenophon's style, underlining the military simplicity which is not entirely covered over by the elegant Atticism. Sainte-Beuve replied by clarifying that he completely agreed on Egger's point, and even went further than simplicity and familiarity to "au besoin même, la crudité d'expression," but this did not negate the Attic quality which is found "dans une certaine façon à la fois négligente, aisée et choisie."[25] It is curious to note that Sainte-Beuve says nothing about Xenophon's method or theory of history; in fact, he referred in a meaningful manner only to the "Retreat of the Ten Thousand."

Sainte-Beuve's admiration for Xenophon's style is surpassed by his more comprehensive esteem for Thucydides. This Greek historian embodied, in the critic's opinion, the several qualities he admired separately in the other Greek historians. We have already noted that Thucydides' style was the real test of one's knowledge of Greek, according to Sainte-Beuve. This historian used to the full the inherent possibilities of his language which give delicacy, nuance, precision to his prose.[26] Beyond that measure, Thucydides' veracity and dependability are sufficient in the eyes of the critic to be convincing even in silence. He discounted a legend about Hippocrates, "dont Thucydide ne dit mot."[27] Most importantly, however, Sainte-Beuve turned to Thucydides for the words to define the great books of history. In considering Lamartine as a historian, the critic wrote "Oh! ce n'est pas ainsi qu'on écrit la grande et sérieuse histoire, celle qui est, comme dit Thucydide, une oeuvre éternelle et à toujours."[28]

Of the great Latin historians, Sainte-Beuve only rarely turned to Suetonius, and once merely to comment that Suetonius might have told a certain story which he deemed too vulgar for the *Moniteur*. Sallust commanded slightly more attention. Though the critic termed him "ce Romain dissolu," he admired the firmness and concision of his style[29] and recognized him as a historian of conscious moral principles.[30] Two Roman historians, however, come to the fore very frequently in Sainte-Beuve's work: Livy and Tacitus. Both were authors with whom the critic was completely familiar. He had received a copy of Livy as prize for Latin verse in 1820, and Tacitus had long been a part of every cultured Frenchman's education. Livy, according to Sainte-Beuve, was a historian "dans sa belle et large manière qui est la vraie voie romaine dans l'histoire."[31]

Livy also had a timely value in the nineteenth century, for the German philologist Berthold Niebuhr, working in the tradition of Vico, had recently seemed to destroy the historic validity of Livy's work. He constructed a whole new theory of interpretation, based in large measure on the loss of the *Annales pontificales* by fire during Numa's reign, to the effect that parts of Livy's history dealing with early Rome had only mythic value. He saw Livy as a poet rather than as a historian, and criticized him severely on points of historic fact which he himself frequently deduced or reconstructed on fragmentary evidence, so that, though his theories were often brilliant, they were shortly proved no more dependable than Livy's own evidence.³² In 1839 Sainte-Beuve reviewed Victor Leclerc's book *Des Journaux chez les Romains* and after an unusually long introduction on the difficulty of judging erudition, the criteria for such judgment, and the internecine quarrels among learned men, the critic discussed in detail the first essay in Leclerc's volume.³³

This essay treats the *Annales Pontificales,* intending to restore to them the authenticity which Niebuhr and his disciples had so seriously called into question by attributing them to popular imagination. When Niebuhr had questioned the validity of Livy and other historians before the reign of Vespasian in their accounts of early Rome, the key phrase which inspired his questioning and his new interpretations of Livy's source material had been a phrase (*pleraque interiere*) found in Livy's own history. Professor Leclerc, by close scrutiny of texts of Livy as well as those of Polybius, Dionysius of Halicarnassus, Cato, Cicero, and Varro reestablished the existence of at least some of the *Annales* after the fire in Numa's reign. He thereby discredited Niebuhr's position by answering the questions and doubts he had raised. With his usual undue modesty ("à ne juger qu'en ignorant et en simple amateur"), Sainte-Beuve gave evidence of his sound judgment in these matters by pointing out the inadequacy of the interpretation that Livy's phrase *pleraque interiere* was the facile excuse *"d'un rhéteur ingénieux* qui voulait se soustraire au long travail de l'historien."³⁴ Philosophically and conceptually, Niebuhr's method and work, while hardly definitive, remained important because it did at least upset the much more limited traditional view à la Rollin and resulted in Professor Leclerc's meticulous evaluation of the extant evidence. Sainte-Beuve also perceived the speciousness of certain Leclerc arguments by analogy between prehistoric and historic centuries of ancient

Rome. Similarly, he rejected Leclerc's opinion on the "candor" of the narrative in the *Annales* with the jest that only the tablets were *in albo*. The critic also indicated to Leclerc that, while he had reestablished the validity of the *Annales*, he had not, and perhaps could not, detail the exact points of their veracity. Finally, though Sainte-Beuve judged that after Leclerc's work the discussion of the authenticity of the *Annales* should be closed, he himself raised several cogent questions on the transferral from tablets to books, the identity of the "editor" of the project, and the fidelity of the revision. Leclerc had not had evidence enough to conjecture answers to these questions, which show therefore the weak link in his argument, a potential point of departure for new discussions.

Almost twenty years later, in 1857, Sainte-Beuve returned to the same subject, quite naturally, in his article on Taine, for the younger critic's *Essai sur Tite-Live* had been awarded the prize by the French Academy in 1855. But if Niebuhr had erred in seeing Livy as a poet, Sainte-Beuve judged that Taine was also in error to make of him solely a historian "qui a un génie d'orateur." Although the objection arose from a fundamental disagreement with Taine's rigidly unilateral method, resulting from a systematic approach, Sainte-Beuve limited his discussion to showing the artificiality and the conjectural weaknesses of Taine's approach with reference to Livy. He accomplished this, in part at least, by drawing in quick, telling strokes his own portrait of Livy and his life, and by calling attention to the fragmentary state of his history. Sainte-Beuve then took up again Taine's phrase, "historien orateur," which had a certain literary exactness, he said, in the sense of Cicero's *opus hoc oratorium maxime*. But, the critic continued, Cicero in the *Laws* distinguished history from oratory. History has the special qualities of "l'horreur du mensonge, la vérité des faits pour base, la description fidèle des événements, des lieux, l'exposé intelligent des entreprises, et un courant de récit plus égal, plus doux, répandu, naturel, exempt des violences et des secousses de l'action oratoire."[35] This historian was not an orator; he was, rather, an eloquent historian. And, according to Sainte-Beuve, it was Livy who became this Roman historian thirty or forty years after Cicero's definition. By an apt comparison of Livy and Thiers the critic explained that a historian differs from a biographer, that the historian presents people by means of their public and memorable acts, leaving aside the anecdotes which are important to a biographer. Livy had taken Thucydides for a model just as Virgil had taken Homer, Sainte-Beuve continued, but Livy had also similarly expressed his own special kind of genius, his clarity, emotion and feeling. Livy, Sainte-Beuve wrote, was an orator, but he was also a painter, a dramatic writer, a moralist, and probably could have been a political analyst if necessary.

Sainte-Beuve's criticism of Taine's rigid system refined and clarified the portrait of Livy; it also juxtaposed Livy and two nineteenth-century historians, at least, in such a fashion as to allow us to perceive the critic's preference and also some of the underlying reasons for his lack of enthusiasm for Michelet. One other Roman historian provided a similar kind of historic perspective, namely, Tacitus. Since the Renaissance Tacitus had been the Roman historian most admired and studied in France, and though Sainte-Beuve noted that Tacitus was perhaps less in favor in 1849 than he had been in the eighteenth century, when he was so universally admired and even imitated, Sainte-Beuve nevertheless continued to use Tacitus as a point of orientation in his discussions of historiography. Two characteristics of Tacitus's talent recur in such discussions: his style and his concept of history.

Sainte-Beuve characterized Tacitus's style repeatedly as

"serious and majestic" in tone, marked by an *imperatoria brevitas* which occasionally created difficulties for the reader. Tacitus was also one of the greatest portrayers of antiquity, and some people even gave him first rank in this area.[36] Thus far Sainte-Beuve was merely repeating time-honored judgments of Tacitus's style and quality as a writer. His commentary became more distinctive, however, when in the face of this esteem he explicitly criticized the tendency of French historians to imitate Tacitus. In 1849 Sainte-Beuve wrote that he would certainly not advise anyone to imitate Tacitus, but added that a little Tacitus, "une réflexion forte" now and then, would not hurt any historic narrative.[37] This note of strength or interpretative judgment would nevertheless be quite different from the studied imitation, to the point of pastiche, that was done by Madame Roland in prison. Success in imitating Tacitus is possible for a few pages, yet in the end such an imitative style is tiring. Daunou had tried to do this in his *Histoire de la Convention*, but he gave up the venture after the first chapter. "Laissons Tacite avec sa manière à lui et son gènie," added the critic. Mankind is too variable to be poured into a single mold and "l'histoire ne saurait trop ressembler à un grand fleuve. Moins de talent, moins d'art et plus de largeur et d'impersonnalité: c'est là aussi une belle manière de talent."[38]

In this final point, with its positive definition of historical style and its implicit plea for freedom for the writer's individuality, as well as for a multiplicity of acceptable styles, Sainte-Beuve was echoing the defense of Thiers's historic style he had written several years earlier. Among the critics of Thiers's style, M. Lanfrey had specifically reproached the historian, in that he lacked "un certain cachet à la Tacite." Certainly that is true, Sainte-Beuve agreed, but went on to ask if Tacitus's manner is, then, the sole, or even the best, style

110 • *Implications for Criticism*

for history? Even Tacitus's contemporary and friend, Pliny the Younger, was not so absolute. Tacitus had great and admirable parts, wrote Sainte-Beuve, but ordinarily he is difficult and dense; the facts are often encumbered by his thought. Certainly this is not the only way to narrate, or even the sole manner of observing and judging well.[39]

To understand fully the import of this type of commentary on Tacitus it is necessary to set it back into the context of the nineteenth century, with its various schools of the philosophy of history. We have observed earlier in this chapter that Sainte-Beuve opposed historians who saw their material only in the light of a preconceived system. When, for example, he cited Tacitus's *De Oratore* as an example of objective analytic criticism, "où toutes les opinions, même celles des romantiques du temps sont représentés; aucun système n'est sacrifié dans cet excellent dialogue, et chaque côté de la question est défendu tour à tour avec les meilleures raisons et les plus valables,"[40] he is explicitly contrasting Tacitus's analysis and critical evaluation with the one-sided bourgeois criticism of his own contemporary, Saint-Marc Girardin. Likewise, his defense of Thiers should be seen as a protest against an overly rigid theoretical approach and style rather than as an implied denigration of Tacitus. His note that Thiers could best be compared with Polybius further underlined Lanfrey's ineptness, or his limited knowledge of ancient historians, rather than expressing judgment upon either Tacitus or Thiers. We have already seen that, much as Sainte-Beuve admired Polybius, his own taste led him rather to Tacitus's historic concept.

In the second article on Froissart (1853), Sainte-Beuve differentiated first between the simple chronicler with a mobile, curious mind, gifted for narrative, and the historian who adds to these qualities a deeper reflection, a search for causes and understanding without, however, letting this last quality stifle the former. He then stated quite flatly, "Il n'y a pas, notez-le bien, de formes d'esprit plus opposées que celle de l'historien proprement dit, narrateur et chroniqueur, et celle du philosophe et de l'homme de doctrine." After quoting Royer-Collard's joking remark about the insignificance of a fact, and repeating the fundamental opposition in type of mind between the philosopher and the historian, he added, "L'historien et le philosophe, du moins le philosophe moraliste, se rejoignent dans Tacite et c'est sa gloire."[41] In short, Tacitus could hardly be a model for a meticulous, erudite nineteenth-century historian, but the historian could learn a very important lesson from his Roman predecessor. This lesson was one of balance between naïve, straightforward chronicle and overly rigid, preconceived principles of interpretation. For Sainte-Beuve history always remained an art, a many-faceted art, even, in which the practitioners, forced to choose among methods and points of view, made choices in order to give an honest, sympathetic, artistic interpretation of the material at hand.[42]

What conclusions, if any, may be drawn from this brief consideration of the critic's attitudes toward the historians of Greece and Rome? One point which will be reenforced as we progress in our study of various groups of writers is already evident to some extent: Sainte-Beuve certainly did not look to the ancient historians as models. Completely committed to and aware of modern scientific methodology in history, he did not frequently discuss the ancient historians from this point of view. There can be little doubt that Sainte-Beuve, as a critic, esteemed Greek historiography over that of Rome, but he discussed Roman historians more frequently and fully in his articles. This custom was not merely due to his own greater familiarity with the Roman writers; it resulted at least equally from the fact that his public generally had a better knowledge of the works of the Roman historians. Since Sainte-Beuve so frequently used the ancient historians as a "sounding board" or basis of discussion for the works of contemporary writers, he could make his distinctions more clearly and economically through Roman historians. Sainte-Beuve was by no means unique among his contemporaries in this type of orientation, but by his technique Sainte-Beuve accomplished more than merely the clear comprehension of his public.[43] He was reminding his readers of the direct descent of French literary tradition from those of Rome and Greece; he was at the same time using literary tradition, not as a straitjacket, but as a corrective to exaggerations of contemporary scientific theories.

A second point of importance is that Sainte-Beuve read and judged the Greek and Roman historians as literary men. It is true that he read them with interest for the information and light they give about their own civilizations. As the rare, or, even more frequently, the sole witnesses of their times, their information was particularly precious to a critic who wanted to place any literary monument in the larger context of its epoch or civilization. Sainte-Beuve tended, on the whole, to believe whatever the ancient historians told him, unless modern scholarship effectively proved otherwise, but his personal preferences among them are quite independent of considerations of historic validity. The critic preferred the historians who were interested in individual people and in biography. He also admired an elevated, simple, and even elegant style. His quotations and allusions are most frequent apropos of this last point. Whether their contributions were stylistic or conceptual, the Greek and Roman historians helped Sainte-Beuve to define the new history in relation to the known tradition.

Notes

1. *N.L.*, I, 362.
2. *C.g.*, I, 247–48.
3. *N.L.*, VIII, 98.
4. *N.L.*, IX, 9.
5. See: Part I, Chapter 4 for the discussion of this parallel. See also: A. G. Lehmann, "Sainte-Beuve and the Historic Mind," in: *The French Mind: Studies in honor of Gustave Rudler*, Will Moore, Rhoda Sutherland, and Enid Starkie, eds. (Oxford: Clarendon Press, 1952), pp. 256–73. Professor Lehmann speaks of Ballanche as the importer of Viquian ideas. Sainte-Beuve wrote a long article on Ballanche in 1834 but only quite incidentally mentioned Vico. The casual mention does demonstrate, however, his understanding of Vico's work: "les vieilles expressions latines, les étymologies essentielles de Vico ont passé intégralement dans leur langage." (*P.C.*, II, 40.)
6. Charly Guyot, "Sainte-Beuve et les philosophes de l'histoire," *Revue de Suisse* (octobre 1952), pp. 75–76.
7. *P.C.*, III, 279. Sainte-Beuve says this about Napoleon I in the same place (p. 277): "Je n'ai pas la prétention de juger ici en quelques mots un personnage comme Bonaparte, qui offre tant d'aspects, et dont la venue a introduit dans le monde de si innombrables conséquences; mais pour rester au point de vue qui m'occupe, j'oserai dire qu'il est l'homme qui a le plus *démoralisé* d'hommes de ce temps, qui a le plus contribué à subordonner pour eux le droit au fait, le devoir au

114 • *Implications for Criticism*

bien-être, la conviction à l'utilité, la conscience aux dehors d'une fausse gloire." The underlining is Sainte-Beuve's.
8. *Volupté*, pp. 76–77.
9. Guyot, "Sainte-Beuve et les philosophes de l'histoire," pp. 77–78. (*P.F.*, p. 319-Pensée XXXIX.)
10. Lehmann, "Sainte-Beuve and the Historic Mind," pp. 270–71.
11. *N.L.*, IX, 105.
12. *P.L.*, III, 46–49.
13. *C.L.*, I, 154.
14. *N.L.*, IV, 31–95. See also *C.L.*, II, 193, where Professor Egger pointed out to Sainte-Beuve a similarity between Frederick II and Polybius.
15. *C.L.*, VIII, 323.
16. *P.C.*, V, 309.
17. *C.L.*, I, 289–91.
18. *C.L.*, XIV, 366.
19. *N.L.*, XI, 193.
20. *P.C.*, V, 338, 341.
21. *C.L.*, XIII, 119, 300, 313–14.
22. *P.C.*, V, 328.
23. Troubat, *Salle à manger*, p. 213.
24. *C.L.*, III, 52.
25. *C.g.*, VIII, 70–71.
26. *N.L.*, VI, 93.
27. *N.L.*, V, 219.
28. *C.L.*, XI, 462.
29. *C.L.*, VII, 64–65.
30. *N.L.*, XI, 170.
31. *C.L.*, VII, 382.
32. See: Hippolyte A. Taine, *Essai sur Tite-Live* (10e édition [Paris: Hachette, n.d.]), pp. 106–23 for an authoritative nineteenth-century discussion of Niebuhr's theories.
33. *P.C.*, III, 442–69.
34. *P.C.*, III, 448. The underlining is Sainte-Beuve's. He is quoting Victor Leclerc (p. 70), even though he does not identify him, preferring the general "*on.*"

35. *C.L.*, XIII, 274.
36. *C.L.*, XV, 280.
37. *C.L.*, I, 153.
38. *N.L.*, VIII, 230.
39. *C.L.*, XV, 280–81.
40. *C.L.*, I, 14.
41. *C.L.*, IX, 98–99.
42. *P.C.*, V, 239. See also: *N.L.*, VIII, 44–47, where, in the field of literary history, Sainte-Beuve gives high praise to Professor Egger for being able to combine rigorous, scientific historical method with humanistic admiration and warmth.
43. See: *C.g.*, XII, 70–72, where the critic refused to review Etienne Dubois Guéhan's book on Tacitus and his century because it pleaded a case for a transitional empire. According to Sainte-Beuve, this argument was outmoded in France in 1861, and particularly inappropriate for the *Moniteur*. It is also worthy of note that Sainte-Beuve reedited Sénac de Meilhan's edition of Tacitus's *Annales* in 1868.

Chapter 2

Homer and Erudition

Of all the authors Sainte-Beuve studied and admired, Homer held a unique place, not only intellectually as a writer and as the central example of an aesthetic theory, but also on a less formal basis, as a guide, guardian, a god, even, for the man who had divested himself of transcendent religious beliefs. In the introduction to his article on Gresset, Sainte-Beuve affirmed "qu'il y a telle chose que la religion et même que la dévotion littéraire."[1] Some years later he called Eugène Gandar an "adorateur d'Homère," immediately defining the epithet: "et j'appelle adorateurs ceux qui le sont par un voeu tout spécial et par une pratique fidèle."[2] The critic himself belonged to this particular religion and cult. Scherer reported that the copy of Homer used constantly by the critic is "tout couvert d'une écriture fine," and another copy of the *Odyssey* carries the note "achevé de lire l'Odyssée pour la troisième fois, le 30 juillet 1856."[3] The critic looked forward to retirement and the opportunity to read the *Iliad* again. Pantasidès, in reporting this fact, also remarked that though he himself understood the literal sense of the *Iliad* better than the critic, "avec son sentiment de poète, il me faisait comprendre la pensée littéraire du texte."[4] In 1846, Sainte-Beuve reported a good day as one during which he read Homer and saw Madame d'O——. Few men have thus equated Homer and the woman they loved![5] When he enlarged the "Temple de goût" he brought in many great writers, but first of all "Homère, comme toujours et partout, y serait le premier, le plus semblable à un dieu."[6] Indeed, Homer is never really absent from much of the critic's writing; even the *Etude sur Virgile* is an attempt to bring Virgil up to Homer's greatness. Any article on epic writing tacitly or explicitly presupposes Homer's unique position. Writers have occasionally approached him from one certain point of view, but as a totality Homer stands alone, apart, "semblable à un dieu," whose text Sainte-Beuve read, commented upon, and analyzed with the devotion and reverence of an initiate.

Though we can only describe and accept Sainte-Beuve's cult of Homer, it is possible to synthesize his analysis of the poet's genius, his intellectual judgments on the poet, the theology of his cult, so to speak. One point, however, needs to be clarified at the outset. Quite contrary to his normal procedure, Sainte-Beuve almost never wrote of Homer the man. He said at one point that he regretted the utter lack of information about the author, but that this very lack set the poems apart.[7] The name Homer, then, although never completely depersonalized, is frequently just a synthetic signal for the *Iliad* and/or the *Odyssey*.

Two adjectives recur most frequently in Sainte-Beuve's writings to characterize the Homeric poems: *primitif* and *naturel*. These reflect concepts which do not noticeably change during the critic's life and hence require precise definition. Sainte-Beuve's use of the word *primitif* is complex and subtle. His friendship with Fauriel, Ampère, and Quinet, and his knowledge of German scholarship, made him well aware of the technical usage for this word in Romantic scholarship. In areas with which he was not particularly concerned (i.e., Middle Ages, folk songs, non-Greco-Latin literature), he used the word as his friends did to mean roughly "pre-self-conscious art."[8] A closer examination of Sainte-Beuve's examples of primitive artists reveals a more specialized meaning closer to the Latin etymon *primus*. *Primitif* here carries the idea, etymologically, of "early," "first," before a high point in a given civilization. Sainte-Beuve sets the high points, what we might call the classic cultures, as those of fifth-century Greece, Rome in the Augustan Age, and the court of Louis XIV. In 1829 primitive geniuses are "fondateurs originaux sans mélange, nés d'eux-mêmes et fils de leurs oeuvres, Homère, Pindare, Eschyle, Dante et Shakespeare." The same passage states further an unequivocal judgment upon the self-conscious artist (Horace, Virgil, Tasso) as of "cette famille secondaire, réputée, *et avec raison, inférieure à son aînée*, mais d'ordinaire mieux comprise de tous, plus accessible et plus chérie."[9]

Professor Carl Viggiani has made a careful and perceptive study of the whole cluster of words used in conjunction with the word *primitif* by Sainte-Beuve.[10] He pointed out that at the end of the eighteenth century the concept of "original genius" was widespread in England, through Young's *Conjectures on Original Composition*, as well as in Germany, where Herder produced the notion of *Natur-Genius*, but that in France only Diderot had really come near Young's concept when he opposed taste to genius. Schiller added to the discussion another adjective, *naïve*, which also belongs to this same cluster for Sainte-Beuve. It is more probable, however, that Sainte-Beuve's use of the word is less dependent on Schiller's exposition than on that of Chénier in his "Essai sur les causes et les effets de la perfection et de la décadence des Lettres

Homer and Erudition · 119

et des Arts," considering Sainte-Beuve's intimate knowledge of the French poet's work. Professor Viggiani therefore sees the 1829 statement quoted above as "a variation of the late eighteenth-century concept of original genius" to which Sainte-Beuve tied the Romantic-Neoclassic quarrel.[11] Professor Viggiani completes the cluster of adjectives with: *fécond, franc (franchise), simple (simplicité), instinctif (instinct), facile, fort, vraie, naïve, genuine, abondant*. To these adjectives must also be added the phrase "dont le caractère est l'universalité, l'humanité éternelle intimement mêlée à la peinture des moeurs ou des passions d'une époque."[12] Most of these adjectives are drawn from the 1835 article on Molière where, according to Professor Viggiani, Sainte-Beuve chose his exemplary authors more freely because the meaning of *primitif* was now clear for him. For our study it is important to note that the critic had drastically reduced the number of ancient representatives. Homer is now specifically the sole Greek author to be termed "un génie primitif." Here as elsewhere the etymological sense of "first" seems apparent in the critic's definition. With these adjectives is also associated the adjective *sublime* which for Sainte-Beuve is not the same as for Longinus: *sublime* is contrasted with *beau; sublime* is innate, not learned. In short, says Professor Viggiani, "these are the principal traits of the ideal artistic imagination as seen by Sainte-Beuve and his contemporaries. . . . In addition to its force, fecundity, and facility, this imagination is innate, its genius is instinctive. Sainte-Beuve employs as many different terms as he can find to communicate and stress his idea."

For Sainte-Beuve, Homer is the epitome of this kind of creative genius, and his peculiar position of primacy is a unique guarantee of his creative power.[13] Sainte-Beuve was accustomed to describe the Homeric poetic style in terms such as "la force, l'abondance, la veine pleine,"[14] or "l'abondance impétueuse et le plein courant d'Homère," or "qualités vives, brillantes, harmonieuses, musicales."[15] *Force* is qualified as "chaste et sérène,"[16] in contradistinction to Balzac's unbridled kind of creative power. Apart from the serene force of Homer's true genius, which is only speciously and not truly paradoxical, the recurrent qualifiers are all active, dynamic, and even musical. Sainte-Beuve insisted in one place on the sophistication of the Homeric prosody.

The adjective *naturel* is very closely but not reversibly allied to *primitif* in the vocabulary and thinking of Sainte-Beuve. A particularly clear explanation both of the nuance of meaning for *naturel* and its relationship to *primitif* may be found in the introduction to the 1835 article on Alfred de Vigny, where in quick intense brush strokes the critic paints a picture of an evolution from popular tribal poetry of spontaneous character through the emergence of the individual poet who is increasingly limited by highly organized society and an inclement atmosphere.[17] Sainte-Beuve uses two images to clarify his thought: the contrast between wild fruit, with its variable quality from bitter to very sweet, and the magnificent, tasty, carefully ripened products which are no longer fruit: "ce sont des produits rares, précieux peut-être mais non pas nourrissants." The pearl and incense are two further examples of artificial "irritations" of great beauty. If such deviations from nature be art or poetry, adds Sainte-Beuve, they are not the art, the poetry of Homer, Sophocles, Dante, Shakespeare, Molière, or Racine, for the poetry of these authors remains "le riche et heureux couronnement de la nature, *ramis felicibus arbos*." Natural poetry, then, is frequently, but not necessarily, spontaneous or folkloric. It is nevertheless a positive product, the synthesis of the poet's mind and heart.[18]

Sainte-Beuve's choice of concrete examples of the *naturel* matches, with one exception, his list of "les grands génies primitifs." The inclusion of Racine, one of his favorite examples of the self-conscious poet (*poète studieux*), marks the difference in meaning between *primitif* and *naturel*: the former adjective is one used of form, technique, sources of external inspiration; *naturel* defines the poet's own internal inspiration and emotional climate with its resultant expression. In his discussion of Vigny, Sainte-Beuve further pointed out that one poet (Vigny, in this case) may write both kinds of poetry.

Homer, nevertheless, is constantly the greatest of the *naturel* poets. In his study on *Chateaubriand et son groupe* Sainte-Beuve made Homer the exemplary of "le poète naturel," both for his imagery and his epic structure. Homer's images are distinguished from those of Virgil and Chateaubriand by a vast amplitude, in which an essential point of contact makes the image relationship clear, but beyond which the images flow free and "comme s'oubliant," resembling "en realité à la nature, qui a des harmonies et non des symétries, et qui ne sait ce que c'est que de calquer."[19] Homer is never premeditated; when an image or detail is strikingly different, "c'est que le trait sort de soi et que l'auteur n'y a pas songé," for the poetry of Homer lies, not in elegance and precision, but in the lively, brilliant, harmonious, and musical qualities of a growing language. "Souffle, véhémence, torrent, abondance, grandeur, feu et richesse, voilà les caractères contenus de l'*Iliade*."[20] In analyzing the structure of the epic, Sainte-Beuve makes a tripartite division: popular (Homer), cultivated (Virgil), and systematic (Chateaubriand). Even though he describes the Homeric poems as popular epic poetry, he does not admit the multiple authorship of the Wolfian school. Similarly, he is not led by his classification to apply the adjective *naturel* to the formal aspects of the poem.[21] The *naturel* may result in a certain form, but it is not form in itself, even when closely related as with popular epic form.

Sainte-Beuve also used the adjective *naturel* in reference to the external landscape. The ancients began by observing and depicting directly pure nature which, in the Greek climate and setting, was beautiful, accessible, and even elegant, in contrast to the impenetrability of the Gaulish natural setting which, left to grow wild after the barbarian invasions, became ugly, forbidding, and repulsive. As a result French descriptions of nature might be charming, witty, literary, but they were seldom *naturel* until Bernardin de Sainte-Pierre really looked at nature in Mozambique.[22] Two points are involved here: first, the differentiation which we have already noted between natural poets and latter-day writers seems to remain constant in their view of external nature, but on a geographical rather than chronological basis; secondly, natural emotion is in contrast to compensatory parallels. Direct observation of nature and the consequent description are in sharp contrast to the literary creation of nature. French poetry does not have a long tradition of this kind of natural poetry; it is much more frequently of a literary nature, with a beauty quite its own. The *naturel* is not only simple and straightforward, both in feeling and expression, but contains also an easy elegance.

The idea of elegance is not without importance, for Sainte-Beuve differentiates carefully between realism and its exaggeration. When Ponsard wrote that Chénier recoiled before Homer's "brutalité," Sainte-Beuve replied, with some feeling, that Homer is *naturel* and not at all vulgar, like the critic who used the word.[23] Sainte-Beuve was quite aware of the ridiculousness of the dispute over Homeric language as it was carried on in the Quarrel of the Ancients and Moderns, but as nineteenth-century naturalism emerged in literature the critic drew an even sharper distinction between truth to nature, with appropriate linguistic expression, and vulgarity, lack of taste. The blind Homer was natural, without vulgarity but also without overrefinement, and the truth and accuracy of the Homeric observations, both of human nature and of the external world, were further enhanced for Sainte-Beuve by the manner of their expression. In a period when Greece was being idealized by Cousin and his disciples Sainte-Beuve saw in Homer the great realist.[24] Again a contrast with Virgil is made, for Virgil was a poet who did not want "la réalité pure."[25] Such realism can only spring from profound truth to human values; Sainte-Beuve spoke of the natural tears of the Homeric heroes.[26]

The critic's cult of Homer was far from blind, however, and the polarity established in his criticism as early as 1829 between primitive and cultivated poets was not at all exclusive. It is, rather, an analytic polarity to aid in clarifying the nature of genius. As a result, Homer almost automatically called up the name of Virgil, not at all pejoratively, but as a poet different from Homer. The most developed consideration of the Homeric poems is to be found in the *Etude sur Virgile,* where Sainte-Beuve explicitly analyzed Virgil's dependence on Homer for inspiration and material, which he took freely for his own independent artistic use. The *Etude sur Virgile* has generally been examined for its new views or interpretations of Virgil, and hence judged mediocre.[27] The idea of studying Virgil's debt to Homer was by no means new with Sainte-Beuve.[28] Why, then, did he choose this particular focus for his course at the Collège de France? The critic explained his reasons for considering this approach almost as a duty, which he as a serious critic was performing for the literature of his own epoch. He believed that nineteenth-century literary men needed the Virgilian pattern of care, taste, restraint, and awareness of tradition brought before their eyes again.[29] For his own part, however, he added that anyone could easily guess that his admiration for Homer was "très-supérieure" to his very real admiration for Virgil, but that since the qualities of the Homeric epic were more naturally appreciated in 1855 than those of Virgil, he believed, as a responsible critic, that contemporary literary men needed the lessons which Virgil could teach. He reiterated the same lesson ten years later in his review of Benoist's edition of Virgil.

The last chapter of the *Etude sur Virgile* is a study of the relative reputation and popularity in France of the two poets. The critic pointed out that Homer needs, in a fashion that Virgil does not, a special devotee priest in France to put him into context, to bridge the centuries and the distance between the civilizations. Although Homer's Greek is simple, only intellectuals learn Greek, and even Voltaire had only skimmed Homer in French: a fact which explains his lack of perception in his remarks on the poet.[30] Translation, then, must serve. Each translation loses some quality of the poems, but, except for travesties such as that of Lamotte, who did not read Greek and undertook to "imitate" Homer, each sincere translator brings his sympathetic understanding of the poet to his contemporaries. Madame Dacier's translation might shock the ear of her contemporaries by its style, which had not been polished by Boileau and Racine, but it had a "certaine naïveté et *magniloquence* qui se retrouve dans sa langue naturelle plus qu'élégante." By dint of her great knowledge and good faith, she attained in general a certain Homeric effect which she brought to her readers as no previous translator had done.[31]

To name Madame Dacier is to evoke a second important facet in Sainte-Beuve's consideration of Homer, namely, the Homeric Question, which stemmed from Wolf's hypothesis of popular authorship in his *Prolegomena*, published in 1795.

Homer and Erudition • 125

The critic's interest in Homeric scholarship was more than an interest in the single question of the poet's existence, although, as we have seen, the cultlike quality of his admiration shows to a great extent the characteristics of a belief in a single, quasi-divine Homer. Furthermore, Sainte-Beuve's ambivalent attitude toward modern erudition was not restricted to classical erudition, but this does provide a compact example, giving a limited but fair picture, of his attitude toward one of the major literary problems of his century.

We have already noted that Sainte-Beuve read ancient historians with pleasure for the commentary they provided on literary men and their works; hence, it is natural to find that he read ancient commentaries on Homer, and that he particularly liked the ἐνάργεια of Aristotle as a critic.[32] Among contemporary critics and scholars the picture was more complex, and Sainte-Beuve remarked nostalgically in 1867 that Virgilian critics "ne s'entremangent pas comme ceux d'Homère."[33] He, himself, had a distinct preference for certain positions rather than others. Even a private reading of La Bruyère's statement, "L'on n'a guère vu jusques à présent un chef d'oeuvre d'esprit qui soit l'ouvrage de plusieurs," evokes a note in the margin, "Koechli et Wolf ne sont pas de cet avis pour l'*Iliade*."[34] This kind of petulant note does not, however, truly reflect the critic's serious concern for the poems themselves and for erudition and criticism in general.

It is not uncommon, even in twentieth-century histories of classical scholarship, to find the France at the end of the eighteenth century is discounted as dormant, stagnant, or lost in neoclassic digressions. There can be little question of the general truth of this picture, but its incompleteness should be equally not surprising. The source of French strength in classical scholarship lay in the very literary quality which impeded its growth in the period when British, and, later,

German scholars were turning to topographical, archaeological, and scientific linguistic considerations. It should be noted, moreover, that it was Anse de Villoison's discovery of the Venice scholia which touched off Wolf's pyrotechnics in 1795.[35] In 1863, when the fireworks were pretty well over, Sainte-Beuve reproached Boissonade that he had not written about the controversy in 1809. Sainte-Beuve pointed out that Boissonade had been trained under the Leyden school of classical scholarship, and that a young German scholar, Bast, "le mit au courant de l'érudition allemande."[36]

We have already seen that the *Globe* milieu was the center for progressive thinking on Greek subjects, cultural as well as political, in the years 1824–30. It was also Charles Magnin, Sainte-Beuve's close friend, who wrote a series of articles for the *Globe* in 1830 on the Homeric Question. We further found that Sainte-Beuve was well acquainted with Claude Fauriel, the leading French exponent of Wolfian theory. A cryptic note in Sainte-Beuve's notebook (1825–29) says: "Il y a des gens qui doutent que l'Iliade soit l'oeuvre d'Homère,"[37] and in 1830 Juste Olivier noted in his journal a conversation with Sainte-Beuve which is clearer, for Sainte-Beuve replied to the statement of Olivier that he had a Hellenist specialist friend who believed that Homer had not existed as a single author of the *Iliad* and the *Odyssey*, "Oh cela me paraît évident, tout le prouve, l'analogie, etc."[38] The comment points up clearly the young critic's position. He was already willing to accept the two poems as of different authors, but his reasoning is literary, i.e., analogy or the lack of it, rather than linguistic. In short, there is no lack of evidence to conclude that Sainte-Beuve was well-acquainted with contempoary scholarship and theories on the Homeric poems. At least two articles on poets begin with introductions on primitive or popular poetry.[39] In the article on Jasmin, the blade is two-edged, for if Sainte-Beuve used the vogue for popular poetry to give status to Jasmin, a hairdresser in Agen, as the critic explicitly informed his readers, he also used Jasmin to make the point that even popular poetry has, in the final analysis, an author. The Vigny article has the same stricture, somewhat less clearly stated: "La poésie ... a été une faculté humaine, générale, populaire, aussi peu individuelle *que possible*, une oeuvre sentie par tous, changée par tous, *inventée par quelques uns sans doute*, mais inspirée d'abord et bien vite possédée et remaniée par la masse de la tribu, de la nation."[40] The progress of civilization, he continued, is the progressive individualization of the poet to the point that he is divorced from his society, like Vigny. In short, even in 1837 Sainte-Beuve did not accept strictly the idea of folklore poetry created by a people; he judged that such poetry must have a single poet at some point.

This same attitude is very evident in his two articles in 1843 on the Homeric poems. These articles were occasioned by the publication of two new books: Bareste's translation of the *Iliad* and Dugas-Montbel's *Histoire des poèmes homériques*. A cursory reading of the January article could quite easily result in the conviction that Sainte-Beuve was simply an ultraconservative, a left-over disciple from the schools of La Harpe and Madame Dacier. But closer examination reveals that his argument centers on two major points: first, that, with all regard for modern scientific erudition, the poem must still be read as an artistic unit; secondly, that the new philological erudition is in fact no more scientific than the older literary criticism, for both schools reason by induction. Despite his praise for the elegance and lucidity of Dugas-Montbel's exposition of the Homeric Question according to Wolf, Sainte-Beuve refused to accept completely his conclusions. The major point of difference lay in the importance given to the Pisistratean recension. According to Wolf, the overall plan of each poem was created at the moment of the recension, but Sainte-Beuve, relying on ancient commentary, maintained that this recension only brought together again dispersed pieces of the poems. The critic's major objection to the Wolfian position, however, concerned its method. He charged that the Wolfians minimized the value of traditional arguments for the unity of the poems as purely inferential, and hence unscientific. At the same time, their own conclusion of multiple authorship was based on inferences from the two newly-found scholia, one of which contained a gross textual error. In the name of legitimate skepticism Sainte-Beuve concluded that he would oppose the systematic conjectures of the Moderns and, if forced to choose an extreme position, he would take that of the Unitarians rather than the Wolfian one, adding quickly that there was no necessity for extremes, since Guigniaut represented "une sorte d'opinion moyenne" which he gladly accepted. The critic nevertheless questioned the basic concept of popular poetry and instinctive genius, for, he asked, do popular poetry and national imagination ever rise above the romance or lyric song? He also called Vico's statement about all Greece being the poet specious, and he rejected the idea of "Homère *par une Société de Gens de Lettres*."[41] The focal point of the article, therefore, is less the critic's actual position on the Homeric Question, though this is not without interest, but rather the carefully nuanced attack on contemporary erudition for arrogating to itself all claims to "scientific reasoning" and, perhaps even more importantly, for ignoring the literary-artistic values of the poems. A certain national prejudice, which declares itself most clearly in the critic's contrast between French and German criticism, also appears as a constant factor in this discussion.

The second article developed Sainte-Beuve's reasoning for

the existence of one Homer, whom he placed between two different groups or generations of Rhapsodes before the Pisistratean recension. Aristarchus did not cover the poet with a golden veil, as Athena did Odysseus, but he did wash the spots. Sainte-Beuve then attacked the scholars for beating a dead horse. No one, he said, believes in neoclassic rules any longer, but there is equally no reason to question all unity. The *Iliad* has unity of subject in Achilles, who dominates the poem even when not actually present. Sainte-Beuve also quoted Choiseul-Gouffier's geographic study of the *Iliad* (*Voyage en Troade*) and Napoleon on the precision of the battles. Between Homer and Virgil, said Sainte-Beuve, the one who "did not exist" is the more concrete. Furthermore, the poetic imagery is consistent throughout the poem—although inconsistencies in themselves would not necessarily prove multiple authorship, he continued, citing one such inconsistency from the *Aeneid*. He concluded the defense with a discussion of the Homeric tones of moral grandeur and human dignity apparent in the poems today, and of the place of antiquity in modern civilization. Sainte-Beuve, like many contemporary scholars, was conservative about accepting completely Wolf's radical hypotheses but at the same time he was neither unaware of German philological work nor inimical to its principles.[42]

Although Sainte-Beuve did not write again specifically on the subject until 1865, allusions to a single authorship were not infrequent in the period 1843–61.[43] In 1847, he read "with attention and interest" Egger's *Conclusions homériques*.[44] The rather flat statement would seem to imply some lack of enthusiasm for Professor Egger's position that the new Homer of the scholars was even more attractive than Aristotle's Homer, and that if a single Homer was a miracle of nature, a concept difficult to give up, he, Egger, still chose progress and the new knowledge.[45] This conclusion was in fact very near to the one finally accepted by the critic some fifteen years later. By 1850 in the essay "Qu'est-ce qu'un classique?" Sainte-Beuve was ready to announce publicly that Homer was not one person, that the unifying pattern came later, and yet only a few pages later in the same essay he wrote, "Homère est là comme un dieu." The *Cahier de notes grecques* also indicates that the critic read, or at least wanted to read, Wood's *Essay on the Original Genius of Homer* (1769) some time after 1855 as well as other Homeric criticism.

Textual scholarship became the subject of central importance in Sainte-Beuve's article on the new edition of Madame de Sévigné's letters in 1861. Sainte-Beuve discussed at some length the importance of an accurate complete text for an author. He pointed out that in the case of Madame de Sévigné the new accurate text did not eliminate any of the famous fine passages, nor did it add any really fine new ones. The new text was corrected in detail, rounding out the picture better and more fully. Since Sainte-Beuve had been trying to convince a nostalgic friend, Sacy, who did not want his Madame de Sévigné to change, Sainte-Beuve tactfully turned his discussion to a personal confession. He applied the same criticism of lethargy toward a new text to himself in connection with Homer, saying that he too found himself from time to time regretting that nothing is definitive in the literary world. "Pourquoi retourne sans cesse, avec les érudits allemands, le texte d'Homère?" Is it not sufficiently fixed after Pisistrates, Aristotle, Aristarchus, and the Alexandrians? "Qu'avons-nous à faire de mieux que d'en jouir et d'en repasser à souhait les immortelles beautés?"[46] The very nostalgia of the passage, however, only gives evidence for the critic's conviction, for his gradual acceptance of the modern position. Two years later he indicated this same position from another point of view.

In considering Boissonade he no longer used a tone of nostalgia for the good old ways, but rather a sharp critical tone on this very point, different from that of the rest of the article, which is generally eulogistic and sympathetic. Boissonade, he wrote, acted in regard to Homer as if everything had been said, as if Wolf had not existed. "On est tenté de s'écrier de l'impatience en le lisant: *Sparge, morite nuces . . .* Homme aimable, vous vous amusez à la bagatelle, et les grandes batailles de la science se livrent sans vous." Sainte-Beuve's final remark was even more trenchant: "Il s'en tire par une plaisanterie, une défaite."[47]

The next year, in his discussion of Emile Deschanel's *Essai de Critique naturelle*, Sainte-Beuve took up the point in literary criticism which even today evokes passionate partisans on both sides; namely, the importance of a knowledge and understanding of the author, the period, the literary scene, in short, the social and literary context of a work read. The critic used a first series of examples, like *Paul et Virginie* and *Manon Lescaut*, to argue that one appreciates them, not necessarily more but with better understanding, with a knowledge of the context. As for the greatest works of the past, those of a Homer, Dante, or Shakespeare, Sainte-Beuve became categorical to an unusual degree: "Je nie absolument qu'on les puisse bien comprendre, et par conséquent bien goûter, sans des études fort longues et où la méthode a sa grande part." Using Homer as his example, Sainte-Beuve sketched the amount of falsification or misunderstanding that had occurred in proportion to the distance in time from the poet. A regular structure to the poems, invented beauties, subtle expressions which were the bases of prescriptive laws, were read into Homer's works. The universally touching scenes, like Hector's farewell to Andromache, continued, of course, to be understood by the heart, but whatever depended on the cultural context: qualities of savagery or naïveté, crudity of passions and language, either eluded the reader or were disfigured by the admiration of critics like Eustathius and Madame Dacier.⁴⁸

Only a few months after this statement Sainte-Beuve returned to the Homeric Question in his articles on the French translation of Grote's *History of Greece*. As the critic explained in his introduction, both Mérimée and Léo Joubert had reviewed the English version of the book much earlier.⁴⁹ A comparison of the three reviews points up Sainte-Beuve's practice of limiting his articles to one aspect or part of a work rather than giving an overall view, as did Joubert, or even of doing the kind of general critical review common among the journalists of the twentieth century. Such a comparison also underlines Sainte-Beuve's preoccupation with the Homeric Question, for it is the focal point of his articles on Grote's work, but certainly is not central to the twelve-volume *History of Greece*.

A careful comparison of the 1843 articles on Homer with this one in 1865 can leave little doubt that Sainte-Beuve was completely aware of the evolution in his own attitude, for it was less a change of position midway between the two extremes than an evolution toward a sympathetic, even if cautious, acceptance of what had come to seem to him "scientific truth." His characterization of Wolf carries an echo of the 1843 article, for he wrote in 1865 that whatever one's final opinion of Wolf's work might be, he was endowed with German critical genius, creating a science, instituting a new form of study, and "il renouvela d'emblée, en y entrant, toute l'étude d'Homère."⁵⁰ Sainte-Beuve was, on the other hand, less than kind to Villoison, and he repeated his criticism of Boissonade, despite the fact that Goethe had shared Boissonade's opinion. Grote, however, had found a means of conciliating the positions. His point of view was, briefly, that the question of writing was not an important issue since feats of oral memory are not uncommon even in modern times among actors. He further pointed out that the rather loose thematic unity of the *Odyssey* facilitated oral transmission of the entire poem, and hence that the crystallization of our poem, except for some details, probably dates from legendary times. The *Iliad*, however, presented many more difficulties which Grote recognized. His explanation accepted a certain aggregate poem well known to Greek audiences before Pisistratus, but which was losing its identity in the individual versions of various rhapsodes. The Pisistratean recension, then, was not the "construction" of the *Iliad* but "simplement de réunir 'les membres en lambeaux d'un Homère sacré.'" Such an explanation still left many problems to be resolved in detail, and Sainte-Beuve outlined Grote's reasoning on separate points, but the basic attraction to Grote's explanation was the reasonable moderation of his position between the extremes of a single poet and a society of literary men. While not accepting literally the idea of one poet, Grote did recognize poetic genius and individual hands. And Sainte-Beuve reacted to this conclusion by saying:

> Le génie d'Homère n'est donc pas si morcelé et épars qu'on l'a dit? C'est un esprit poétique, vaste et exubérant sans doute, mais propre aussi à organiser, et conservant encore, à ce second moment, cette fraîcheur d'observation et cette vivacité de détail qui constitue le charme de la *ballade*, de la *saga*, de l'*épos* primitif . . . et c'est à bon droit que le nom d'Homère reste attaché en propre à ce premier grand travail de composition épique.[51]

For Sainte-Beuve, science and literary intuition had been reconciled in a new, enriched, and solid knowledge without renouncing completely the accumulated interpretations of centuries.

At the beginning of the present discussion it was asserted that Sainte-Beuve had perhaps a personal reason for feeling so strongly on the Homeric Question in 1843. It seems apparent that Sainte-Beuve's return to the study of Greek and his reading in ancient authors formed a part of the resolution of his depressed mental state of 1839–40. He had discovered that religion, politics, and love held no absolute answers for him. He turned to the study which was to result in his magistral *Port-Royal* but which ended on a note of rejection in the famous epilogue.[52] At the same time he also turned to antiquity, only to find his gods being attacked. He said this clearly only in this 1865 article, after he had found a position compatible with modern scholarship and with his own sensitive reading.[53]

The last word had not yet been written by Sainte-Beuve on the Homeric Question. His article inspired "des lettres furieuses ou plaintives," according to a letter to Professor Egger, who had announced to Sainte-Beuve that a young scholar, Campaux, was going to translate Wolf's *Prolegomena*. Egger termed this project, in his letter to Sainte-Beuve, "le succès même d'un de vos conseils."[54] Ironically enough, the discussion of Homeric authorship continues to our own day in similar if not identical terms. What Sainte-Beuve's literary critical intuition opposed to nascent philological study seems now to be a tenable position based on scientific evidence. Sainte-Beuve's regretful acceptance of "truth" in 1865 is therefore only the more poignantly ironic with one hundred years' perspective.[55]

The specific subject of the Homeric Question leads quite naturally to some brief commentary on Sainte-Beuve's general attitude toward nineteenth-century erudition, particularly on the aspect of the almost chauvinistic rivalry between the traditional French *explication* approach and the new German philological studies. The critic's position has been variously evaluated, both during his own lifetime and since his death. Gaston Boissier saw the central core of the course not given at the Collège de France as the happy marriage of German erudition and French taste.[56] Professor Regard, however, made a somewhat different estimate when he wrote that Sainte-Beuve taught a preference for sensitive appreciation of the text over the heavy erudition which masks the text.[57] Professor Scheel concluded "that he [Sainte-Beuve] so seldom carried out accurate confrontation of sources and imitation."[58] René Canat perceived a change of position, or at least an evolution in Sainte-Beuve's opinion of French philology: "Sainte-Beuve, au temps de ses ferveurs germaniques, ne la ménage pas; il est vraie que plus tard, il attenuera et même rectifiera.[59] A young contemporary, William Reymond, wrote in 1854 that Sainte-Beuve represented the Germanic School, "mais avant tout il est l'homme de la fusion des deux principes ou de l'éclectisme littéraire."[60] All of these judgments meet on the ground of positive and sympathetic knowledge of German erudition on the part of the critic. They all equally note some reservations. Boissier and Reymond further perceived a positive attempt at compromise. The restricted field of classical scholarship provides the opportunity to look at the critic's attitudes quite concretely, and to draw some conclusions at least for that one important area of nineteenth-century erudition.

Sainte-Beuve repeatedly contrasted French and German erudition. Generally such statements are not at all to the disadvantage of his compatriots, although diffident professors occasionally interpreted them so.[61] One of his clearest definitions of the difference is to be found in his study of Chateaubriand, where he pointed out that French literary criticism was different from that of Germany and her other neighbors. Some people would say that French criticism was superficial, but Sainte-Beuve simply did not believe that. Rather, he said, it was "plus vive, moins chargée d'érudition, moins théorique et systématique, plus confiante au sentiment du goût." The French are not "synthétiques" like the Germans: the very word is not French. As French criticism became more erudite, Sainte-Beuve felt a regret for the old freer form. The Greeks, he concluded, were a happy people, for they did not have such a long literary history behind them to be learned.[62] This distinction between scientific erudition and urbane taste is a constant which may be found in all periods of Sainte-Beuve criticism. Late in life he praised Benoist and Zeller for their capacity to combine the two kinds of criticism. In short, Sainte-Beuve admired the scientific methodology and meticulous detail work of German scholars, which produced excellent texts and frequently filled lacunae in knowledge. His admiration was not complete acceptance, nevertheless, as we have seen in the case of Wolf's theories on Homer. His desire to found a French school of classical studies in Athens was also part of the desire to evolve a distinguished French classical erudition, using all the German techniques but keeping and further refining French taste and judgment.

The critic's explicit attitude toward French erudition appears at times to be ambivalent, if not downright paradoxical, but this impression results more from a natural tendency to confuse several separate issues than from true paradox. The first issue, the acceptance of German philological methodology, prompted constant needling from the critic, who found French scholars much too slow in accepting not so much the results as the methodology for philological text criticism. The Didot Greek texts, published in Paris, were not generally edited by

French scholars. It was Sainte-Beuve's close friend, the German Frederick Dübner, who was really responsible for the admirable series and who was so little appreciated by the French university.[63] When Sainte-Beuve wanted to write his articles on Terence, he asked Professor Rossignol for the most recent scholarship on Terence, adding, "Les Allemands, ont-ils parlé?"[64] On the point of critical texts, then, there can be no doubt about Sainte-Beuve's appreciation and admiration for German methodology. In his opinion, however, this was merely the first step to an appreciation of the text, and he reproached Benoist for not going further after having taken the first step so admirably. Benoist's answer, that there are two separate forms of criticism and one person can not do both adequately, did not entirely satisfy Sainte-Beuve, who continued to envisage and write in favor of a high amalgam, a criticism that would incorporate the good qualities of both nations.[65] It should also be pointed out that even among progressive French scholars like Fauriel, whom the critic never tired of praising for his original ideas and theories, Sainte-Beuve made a sharp distinction between method and conclusion. He admired Fauriel's work, but felt his conclusions were too radical, that Fauriel had lost the line between folklore and literature as an art.[66]

The second issue with regard to French scholars is more relevant to the case of students of modern French literature, particularly medievalists, than to that of classical scholars. The issue was what Sainte-Beuve so aptly termed "le culte des vieux papiers."[67] Some people would prefer Thucydides' notes to his history; Sainte-Beuve, although eager for the truth, would not sacrifice the work of art thereby.[68] The numerous rediscovered fragments of antiquity, together with the consequent nineteenth-century commentaries, published without much judgment or selection, could only overwhelm the reading public and either turn it away from literature or dull its critical acumen on the accepted great works. "Le pire qui nous puisse arriver, c'est que nous serons tous plus ou moins immortels, et bien loin que quelques-uns d'un peu intéressants se perdent tout entiers, dignes et moins dignes nous vivrons tous avec part au soleil et presque *ex aequo*. Etes-vous contents?"[69] he wrote at the end of his article on Euphorion. Like the first issue, that of philological criticism, the mad hunt for the unpublished posed a very real threat to the French tradition of the cultivated reader by creating a mediocre mass of material, selected only by the specialists and read only by them.

A third issue with regard to scholars, generally and in all nations, was that of style or manner of expression. In thanking Taine for his *Essais de Critique et d'Histoire*, Sainte-Beuve complimented the younger critic, then added, "Seulement maintenons toujours que le savant doit être artiste."[70] He also praised the scholarly Zeller because "il a de bonne heure uni les deux esprits, celui de la recherche approfondie et de la science, celui de l'exposition nette, claire, et précise."[71] The issue of style was not just a manner of writing, however, since it resulted in a complete divorce between town and gown, between university and lettered public. In spite of all the progress in scholarship since the eighteenth century, Rollin still had one unquestioned merit, namely, his ability to open a window between the university and the world.[72] In 1852 Sainte-Beuve would not promise to review Lerminier's book on Greek legislative and constitutional history because every classical subject was a difficult affair, even under such fine auspices.

The introduction to Sainte-Beuve's article on Joseph-Victor Leclerc's *Des Journaux chez les Romains* is a sharp and serious indictment of what might be termed the "scholarly ethos," for it describes the society of scholars as a closed group characterized by rivalries, even "entre-mangeries," as well as mutual protection. Their writings, esteemed for exactness and rigor, have become specialized as a chemical formula: "il arrive ainsi que des documents, peut-être utiles, s'amassent sans être compromis par les idées de personne." The savants live apart in their own little world, protected even from insolent journalists. There are some men, however, with original ideas, taste, and wit like Létronne and Fauriel. Finally Sainte-Beuve turned his irony to the Franco-German scholarship with the sharp remark: "En France, d'ailleurs, on aime assez que les idées comme les vins, nous reviennent de l'étranger. Un petit voyage d'outre-mer ou d'outre Rhin ne fait pas mal pour mettre en vogue."[73]

Sainte-Beuve was not just a carping critic; he also enunciated a positive program. At the end of his very appreciative articles on Boissonade, an erudite of taste from another era, he made a direct plea to the young Hellenists of France to treat antiquity precisely, but also broadly, and as much as possible in relation to modern times. He sketched a kind of history-of-ideas approach, the history and progress of the human mind and civilization.[74] Criticism itself is a different kind of writing from erudition, and only rarely are the two disciplines found together,[75] but criticism cannot function when it is based only on sentiment and rhetoric like that of Villemain. These two qualities are important but insufficient: erudition is the solid base on which criticism must build. By the same token, erudition must not render the critic's function impossible by the sheer weight of unselected material, written only for specialists by a small "inner circle." The cult of Homer, though frequently expressed in completely fideistic terms, was also highly intellectual, as might be expected with Sainte-Beuve. His passion for truth led him to follow the progress of Homeric scholarship, not only in France, but in Germany and England as well. His acceptance of Grote's position as a tenable compromise between his critical intuition and modern erudition may seem something less than a brilliant critical perception today. Nevertheless, it does give evidence of Sainte-Beuve's continued effort to avoid a complete rupture with the past, and to consider some of the major literary and historic issues of his day. To all of these issues, he brought his extraordinary intelligence and sensitivity: eager curiosity for the new, balanced by a conservative feeling toward the old.

Notes

1. *P.C.*, V, 78.
2. *C.L.*, XII, 77.
3. This edition, noted by Scherer (*Cat.*, p. vii) as "absolument nulle sous le rapport vénal, a été gardé comme souvenir par un des héritiers de Sainte-Beuve."
4. *Cat.*, I, viii.
5. *P.C.*, IV, 467.
6. *C.L.*, III, 51.
7. *N.L.*, III, 15.
8. Note the difference from the twentieth-century anthropological meaning.
9. *P.L.*, I, 69. The underlining is mine.
10. Carl A. Viggiani, "An Introduction to Sainte-Beuve's Critical Vocabulary" (Ann Arbor, Mich. University Microfilms, 1951). 308 p. microfilm. *Primitif* is one of the key words studied by Professor Viggiani, and I am much indebted to him in the present discussion. It would be difficult to set the limit between corroboration and illumination for the present author.
11. Ibid., pp. 57–58. I must, however, disagree with Professor Viggiani's statement (p. 59), "We should note . . . that Sainte-Beuve does not intend the term *primitif* in a strictly time sense," in the light of the statements in the 1835 article on Molière (*P.L.*, II, 1–4, especially p. 3) on the primitive periods. Nor can I agree with his statement that Sainte-Beuve rarely

used the word *primitif* in his criticism. It is a constant epithet for Homer, Shakespeare, and often Molière as well.
12. *P.L.*, II, 1.
13. *P.C.*, IV, 386 and see also *C.L.*, I, 341.
14. *C.L.*, IX, 484.
15. *C.L.*, XIII, 156.
16. *C.L.*, III, 453.
17. *P.C.*, II, 22. Professor Lehmann reads this passages as an evidence of Sainte-Beuve's taking over Nisard's idea of the Romantics as "decadent." (Lehmann, *Sainte-Beuve*, p. 276.)
18. Sainte-Beuve liked Goethe's definition of romanticism and classicism, which he often quoted, but here the implication is that Romantic need not be "sick."
19. *Chat.*, I, 172.
20. *C.L.*, XIII, 154. See also *N.L.*, III, 377–78, where a parallel description of Homeric poetry is used to exemplify and define Sainte-Beuve's concept of beauty.
21. *Chat.*, I, 329.
22. *C.L.*, XI, 46–47.
23. *C.L.*, XI, 522.
24. See Canat, III, Ch. 5, "La Tradition sacrée," in which Canat made his central point this very one of the realism of Homer in Sainte-Beuve's eyes.
25. *N.L.*, V, 122. "Virgile, Racine, des Raphael, de tous ceux qui dans l'art, ne sont pas pour la réalité pure. . . . "
26. *C.L.*, IX, 390.
27. See: Horatio Smith's review of Tommaso Fiore, *Studio su Virgilio Traduzione e Saggio introduttiva sul Sainte-Beuve*, *Romanic Review*, XXXI (1940), pp. 412–14. Professor Smith says, "The truth is the book (*Etude sur Virgile*) is pleasant and not much more—by the standard Sainte-Beuve himself set in his major achievements." Such isolation from the major achievements seems unduly severe.
28. Frédéric G. Eichoff had published such a work in 1825. (Frédéric Gustave Eichoff, *Etudes grecques sur Virgile, ou Recueil de tous les passages des poètes grecs imités dans les*

Bucoliques, les Géorgiques et l'Enéide avec le texte latin et des rapprochements littéraires [Paris: Delalain, 1825], 3 vols.). It is very possible that Sainte-Beuve read this work, although I have been unable to find any concrete evidence of his having seen the text.

29. See: *C.g.*, X, 239, the letter of Henri de Montaiglon congratulating Sainte-Beuve on the serial publication of the *Etude sur Virgile*. See also Virgil, *Oeuvres*, ed. E. Benoist (Paris: Hachette, 1869), 2 vols., II, xx. M. Benoist cites Wagner on the *Etude sur Virgile*, "une oeuvre de polémique contre ceux qui sacrifient Virgile à Homère avec trop d'emportement." And G. Boissier, "Les Théories nouvelles du poème épique," *Revue des Deux Mondes* (2de période), LXVII (15 février 1867), pp. 848-79. M. Boissier also makes a plea for Virgil, saying we need a broad, flexible canon of taste, capable of understanding poets of all times and places "aussi bien ceux des époques civilisées que ceux des époques primitives." He was, in this statement, reiterating Sainte-Beuve's statement of ten years earlier.
30. *C.L.*, VIII, 289.
31. *C.L.*, IX, 491, 496.
32. *N.L.*, VI, 380.
33. *N.L.*, XI, 179.
34. G. Michaut, "Notes sur La Bruyère," *Revue d'Histoire littéraire de France*, XIII (1960), p. 507.
35. Wolf's "pyrotechnics" were, of course, preceded by Vico's theory in 1730, and, as Dugas-Montbel pointed out (Jean-Baptiste Dugas-Montbel, *Histoire des poésies homériques pour servir d'introduction aux observations sur l'Iliade et l'Odyssée* [Paris: Firmin Didot Frères, 1831], p. 126), Scaliger in the sixteenth century saw multiple authorship to the extent of writing "que l'*Iliade et* l'*Odyssée* pouvaient bien n'être qu'une suite de divers épisodes rassemblés par Pisistrate."
36. *N.L.*, VI, 98.
37. Guyot, *Notes inédites*, p. 62.
38. Olivier, p. 228.

39. *P.C.*, II, 52 (Vigny); *P.C.*, III, 64 (Jasmin).
40. *P.C.*, II, 52. The underlining is mine.
41. *P.C.*, V, 336–41. The underlining is Sainte-Beuve's.
42. Neither the British nor Wolf's own compatriots were entirely sympathetic to the new theories. See: Sir John L. Myres, *Homer and His Critics*, ed. Dorothea Gary (London: Routledge and Kegan Paul, 1958). See especially Chapter 5 and pp. 75–93.
43. See e.g.: *Chat.*, I, 329; *C.L.*, VIII, 324; *EsV*, p. 83, etc.
44. *C.g.*, VII, 64.
45. Emile Egger, *Mémoires des littératures anciennes* (Paris: Auguste Durand, 1862), p. 108.
46. *N.L.*, I, 286.
47. *N.L.*, VI, 99.
48. *N.L.*, IX, 83.
49. Prosper Mérimée, *Mélanges littéraires* (Paris: Calmann-Lévy, 1884), pp. 109–219 and Léo Joubert, *Etudes de critique et d'histoire* (Paris: Firmin Didot, 1863), pp. 1–55.
50. *N.L.*, X, 54. See also: *P.C.*, V, 342.
51. *N.L.*, X, p. 67.
52. *Port-Royal*, VI, 244. The epilogue is not long and should be re-read in its entirety. The following sentences leave no doubt in the reader's mind about Sainte-Beuve's beliefs:

> Directeurs redoutés et savants, illustres solitaires, parfaits confesseurs et prêtres, vertueux laïques qui seriez prêtres ailleurs et qui n'osiez prétendre à l'autel, vous tous, hommes de bien et de vérité, quelque respect que je vous aie voué, quelque attention que j'aie mise à suivre et à marquer vos moindres vestiges, je n'ai pu me ranger à être des vôtres. Si vous étiez vivants, si vous reveniez sur la terre, est-ce à vous que je courrais d'abord? J'irais une ou deux fois peut-être pour vous saluer et comme par devoir, et aussi pour vérifier en vous l'exactitude de mes tableaux, mais je ne serais pas votre disciple. J'ai été votre biographe, je n'ose dire votre peintre; hors de là, je ne suis point à vous.

53. *N.L.*, X, 58 and 67–68.
54. *C.g.*, XIV, 197.
55. A 1963 review in the London *Times Literary Supplement* of Wace and Stubbings, *A Companion to Homer*, said on the subject:

> Professor Davison had the hardest task, that of ssumming up the whole history of the Homeric controversies and he has done it fully and fairly. His verdict is, summarily, this: a unitary plan of the Homeric poems can now be firmly based on the evidence for design which both poems provide; the inconsistencies in language, narrative, and other matters are tolerable in public, oral, and traditional poetry; the *Iliad* and the *Odyssey* were hardly written by the same person, but the author of the *Odyssey* (composed before 620 B.C. at the latest) was intimately acquainted with the *Iliad* (composed before, about 700 B.C.).

For another opinion, see: A. G. Lehmann, "Sainte-Beuve and Romantic Scholarship," *Studies in Modern French Literature presented to P. Mansell Jones*, ed. L. J. Austin, Garnet Rees & Eugene Vinaver (Manchester: University Press, 1961), pp. 220–32.
56. *Le Livre d'Or*, p. 9.
57. *Regard*, pp. 162–63.
58. *Scheel*, p. 145.
59. *Canat*, III, 79.
60. *C.g.*, IX, 452.
61. *N.L.*, IX, 288–90, n. 1. See especially the note added in the 1867 edition, which ends with the statement of simple difference: "Et puis, les meilleurs et les plus fins jugements du monde ne sont pas la même chose qu'un recours direct aux manuscrits et que l'établissement définitif d'un texte."
62. *Chat.*, I, 257–59.
63. *N.L.*, XI, 135 and 440.
64. *C.g.*, XII, 496.

65. *N.L.*, XI, 174 ff. It is interesting to note that Professor Canat (I, 129) reproached Sainte-Beuve almost 100 years after his death for his constant defense of German scholarship.
66. Professor Lehmann wrote, in "Sainte-Beuve and Romantic Scholarship," that Sainte-Beuve knew, sympathized with, but in the end rejected Romantic scholarship. I cannot agree completely with Professor Lehmann. Sainte-Beuve accepted the method, but not always the conclusion. He was not personally interested in the Middle Ages, as many Romantic scholars were; his remarks therefore attempt to curb the exaggerated enthusiasm of his time. Finally he did accept a modified multiple Homer theory when it became apparent that the theory was based on solid scientific thinking.
67. *C.L.*, XIII, 303.
68. *C.L.*, XV, 378. See also: *N.L.*, V, 371 and *N.L.*, I, 277–95 on the Madame de Sévigné text. This last reference has already been quoted.
69. *P.C.*, V, 455.
70. *C.g.*, XI, 65.
71. *N.L.*, IX, 280.
72. *C.L.*, VI, 267–68.
73. *P.C.*, III, 443 and 447. Sainte-Beuve did not always appreciate Leclerc, whom he called the "savant et pédant doyen à la voix aigre" (*N.L.*, IX, 440), because he had refused to support Dübner for the *Académie des Inscriptions*. Less personal, but more complementary to the article on *Des Journaux* . . . is a comment in a letter to his friend Charles Labitte, dated December 6, 1839, by Jean Bonnerot: "Cet article m'ennuie bien et à mon dégoût de cette solide érudition je vois bien que je n'aime que les bluettes."
74. *N.L.*, VI, 112.
75. His own *Port-Royal* is an excellent example of such a combination.

Chapter 3
The Greek Anthology and Translation

Sainte-Beuve's affection for the *Greek Anthology*, and for various writers of epigrams, was very different from the kind of veneration and scholarly interest he brought to Homer and the Homeric Question. The *Greek Anthology* was, after all, a collection of small pieces, admirable in themselves but on a more human scale than the ample Homeric epic poetry. Furthermore, as we have already noted, the French poets who most impressed Sainte-Beuve were themselves readers of the *Greek Anthology*. In his comprehensive study of *The Greek Anthology in France*, Professor Hutton pointed out Chénier's recognition of the supreme excellence of Homer, but Chénier, in the work that he was able to finish before his death on the guillotine, was most influenced by the bucolic poets and the *Palatine Anthology*.[1] Sainte-Beuve shared this Januslike view. For the Pléiade writers there was also a kind of dual influence from Pindar as well as from the *Planudean Anthol-*

ogy. Sainte-Beuve readily admitted Pindar's greatness as a poet, but also said, sadly, that he had tried, but could not really appreciate Pindar in Greek.

Perhaps it would not be amiss to follow the critic in his articles on the anthologies and to recall here briefly the salient dates and changes in the work we now usually call the *Greek Anthology*.[2] The first anthology of short elegiac poems was compiled by Meleager of Gadara in the first century before Christ, and was named *The Garland* (Στεφανος). This volume contained examples of the work of forty-six poets from Sappho's time to his own. His introductory poem (*A.P.* 41) lists his "contributors," with an appropriate flower for each to make the garland. A second collection was made during the time of the emperor Trajan by Philip of Thessalonica, who used Meleager's work as a nucleus. Then came the anthology called the *Sylloge*, or *Cycle*, compiled by the Byzantine poet Agathias Scholasticus in the sixth century during the reign of Justinian. Agathias eliminated much of the older poets' work that he found in the previous anthologies in order to make room for newer selections. He also began the custom of arranging the selections under subject headings. These three compilations served as the basis for the famous anthology made by Constantine Cephalas about 917 A.D., known as the *Palatine Anthology*. The name derives from the fact that it was discovered by the famous French seventeenth-century scholar Saumaise in the Palatine Library of Heidelberg. This collection includes poems by 320 authors.[3] After the discovery of the *Palatine Anthology*, the *Planudean Anthology*, which the Renaissance writers had used, was superseded. It was, in fact, the *Palatine Anthology* which the Alsatian-French scholar Richard François Philippe Brunck used for his selections from the *Anthology* poets in editing his three-volume *Analecta* for the Greek poets in 1776.[4]

But to return to Cephalas. In 1401 another anthology was completed at Constantinople by a monk named Maximus Planudes. This work was essentially an abridgement of Cephalas's work into seven books, although it did contain a few new selections. Planudes was an intelligent scholar, and edited his text as well as rearranging Cephalas's selections. We may, however, regret that he eliminated some fine poems on moral grounds. After the appearance of this so-called *Planudean Appendix*, Cephalas's work disappeared from view as a unit. The only anthology known by Renaissance scholars, therefore, was the *Planudean Anthology*, printed by John Lascaris in Florence in 1484.

The modern *Greek Anthology* is composed of the *Palatine Anthology*, with additional poems from the *Planudean Anthology*. There are also some epigrams and inscriptions from elsewhere. The *Greek Anthology* contains over 6,000 epigrams and encompasses over seventeen centuries, from the seventh century B.C. to the twelfth century A.D. The range of subjects is broad, including dedicatory poems, epitaphs, reflections on life, death and fate, love poems, and poems on poets and their works as well as on artists. There are even some humorous and mildly satiric poems on athletes, rhetoricians, doctors, and other professionals. The short elegiac poems are usually from one to four distichs in length.

The publication of Brunck's *Analecta* gave a new popularity and impetus to the reading of the *Palatine Anthology*. Sainte-Beuve owned a copy of Brunck, and was fond of making written translations of the epigrams in it. The general revival of interest in the *Anthology* after 1750, noted by Professor Hutton, seemed to contain the seeds of a concrete and growing popularity, but Professor Hutton also recorded that a complete modern translation was not published until 1863, when Sainte-Beuve's old friend Frédéric Dehèque published his complete and new translation. Sainte-Beuve's preoccupation with the *Greek Anthology*, evidenced by his five articles on the subject, undoubtedly reflected the sympathetic atmosphere described by Professor Hutton, but it is equally evident that Sainte-Beuve played his own role in creating that atmosphere between 1827 and 1864. Certainly his personal predilection was more than a mere reflection of the Romantic vogue for the *Greek Anthology* in orienting the critic's continual reading of the work.

The first formal article dated from 1827 and was occasioned by the Veissier-Descombes translation of Anacreon. It is quite natural to find that the young critic devoted approximately one third of his article to sixteenth-century poetry in the Anacreontic vein. In fact, Rémy Belleau's mediocre translation of Anacreon introduced the second point of discussion in this article, namely, the problems peculiar to the translation of lyric poetry. In such translations, the critic stated, the feeling and the movement of the original are essential—even at the expense of exactness in detail. Paraphrase and free imitation frequently only encumber the original concision and grace. In poetry like that of Anacreon there is not an intermediary step between "the paltry and the exquisite." If Veissier-Descombes put behind him the elegant epithets of Saint-Victor's translation to attain a more Greek naturalness, his versification nevertheless left something to be desired.[5]

This very short youthful article needs to be complemented by another called "Anacréon au seizième siècle," which appeared in the 1842 edition of the *Tableau*.[6] This article is somewhat misnamed, for the Anacreon under consideration is the Anacreon translated by Henri Estienne in 1554, and most of these poems have been proved to be Anacreontic verse of a much later period rather than authentic poems of Anacreon. "L'Anacréon primitif avait l'*enthousiasme* proprement dit," while these Anacreontics are from "le dix-huitieme siècle de la Grèce," a period when *le joli* has replaced *le beau*.[7] The reader will recall that these are the same key words used by the critic in his attempts to refine his definition of genius in reference to Homer. In fact, Sainte-Beuve went as far in this 1842 article as to suggest, half seriously and half in jest, that Anacreon was the Homer ("un Homère aviné") of the *Greek Anthology*. The point toward which the critic was moving was that around every great poet there is a school of disciples, who have the charm without the force of the greater poet, but whose charm is more easily imitated, and, particularly, more easily translated into another language. The sixteenth-century French poets succeeded better, therefore, in seizing the spirit of the Anacreontics when they composed free imitations than when they attempted close translations. They could "anacréontiser sans trop y songer," and indeed did, thus forming a poetic tradition in France that has remained unbroken.[8] Chénier was not Anacreontic, however, according to Sainte-Beuve, for his inspiration stemmed directly from Theocritus and Anacreon rather than from their later disciples.

The critic provided an answer to the questions and the doubts he raised in his first article on Anacreon about the translation of lyric poetry. In this second article he made quite clear that free inspiration and imitation among poets creates a more fertile and authentic tradition than heavy, abortive translations. He also stated quite clearly the reasons for his own predilection for the *Anthology*. Quite simply, the *Greek Anthology* provided an easy and direct manner of approaching Greek poetry.[9] Already, in this 1842 article, Sainte-Beuve was implicitly following his as yet unwritten concept of families of minds, for Anacreon is surrounded by the whole *Greek Anthology* which, in turn, is enlarged to include spiritually Moschus, Bion, and Theocritus, about whom he said he hoped to write some day. It was in fact little more than four years later (November and December 1846) that Sainte-Beuve wrote three articles on Theocritus. Although he had tried, in 1842, to attach the *Greek Anthology* to Theocritus, he clearly divorced Theocritus from the *Anthology* in these articles of 1846. Theocritus stands as the last of the heroic tradition begun with Homer, while the *Greek Anthology* is "la lie de la littérature grecque," wrote the critic, quoting Joubert.[10]

Meanwhile, a year before the articles on Theocritus, Sainte-Beuve singled out Meleager from the *Anthology* poets for a full-length study. This 1845 article on Meleager was a major article, for it introduced a new series on ancient authors, attempting explicitly to motivate young scholars in the direction of writing about the new rediscovery of Greek literature for a broader public than that of university specialists. This article, moreover, presented for the first time a sizeable amount of personal translation by the critic himself. The relatively long introduction emphasized the necessity in France for information to move from the university to the cultivated public in order to become meaningful in the culture. Despite the superiority of Greek culture over its Latin derivative, real familiarity with Greek culture has always been less prevalent in France, and hence a less powerful civilizing force. Furthermore, one quality of Greek art, the ideal, the pure, has been emphasized over the equally important qualities of simplicity and truth which are fundamental to the Greek artistic ideal.

Sainte-Beuve chose a *poeta minor*, as he explained, because the cultivated but non-erudite French public judged Greece only on the very great names that recur constantly. As we have observed, however, in Sainte-Beuve's opinion one only really knows a country by knowing the bypaths as well as the major highways. The *Anthology* is a collection of just such bypaths.[11] Meleager, as a *poeta minor*, has, nevertheless, notes of "cette touchante simplicité" which, in Sainte-Beuve's opinion, characterized Greek literature. Horace, for the modern, represents a synthesis of the whole of Greek lyric poetry, but fine as his poetry is, it is not the fruit taken directly from the tree. The juxtaposition of Meleager's verses with a line of Lamartine, and the suggestion that Meleager's subtleties resemble images of the Petrarchian kind, perhaps through Ovid, Ausonius, and the Provençal poets, indicate the critic's continued preoccupation with the history of lyric expression, and with the spontaneous recurrence of certain feelings along with the reinvention of the images to express these feelings. In the particular case cited here Sainte-Beuve rejected historic filiation or even "influence" in favor of spontaneous reinvention. From this essay alone it is clear that Sainte-Beuve recognized the need for popularization and translation for the broad French public, but was also working out in his own mind the problem of lyric inspiration from a historic point of view, a question very closely related to the definition of "original genius," with Homer as the prototype.

Greek poetry, wrote the critic, could well serve as an example in the contemporary discussion of art and poetic language. This poetry has been variously read since the Renaissance, and adjusted to French taste, but Sainte-Beuve could not accept more than very general similarities to Northern and Shakespearean poetry: an abyss separates two races, two civilizations which are confused only by inexperienced minds which have not fully understood either culture. Greek poetry can, however, be penetrated more deeply than it has been or than has been supposed possible, by means of translations faithful to the spirit as well as to the letter of the text.[12]

154 • Implications for Criticism

The point here is delicate and of the utmost importance. A superficial reading would seem to reveal a sly attack on certain Romantics of the tradition of Madame de Staël, and hence tempt the reader to construe it as further evidence in 1845 of Sainte-Beuve's "return to neoclassicism." But the critic's point is somewhat different: he is saying that Greek *originality* has not been adequately rendered into French because of what he called the Scaliger-Fénelon influence, but that it can now be translated adequately *because of* the Romantics, that Greece and France have analogous civilizations, and that, if outside sources are to be sought at all by the poet, "l'Ida était dit, par excellence, *fertile en sources.*" Sainte-Beuve was still consistent to his own conception of the Romantic renewal of poetry with Chénier as the leader. Adequate translations, therefore, became of prime importance to the continuation of this renewal.

Sainte-Beuve returned once more to the *Greek Anthology* with two articles in 1864. These articles were prompted by Frédéric Dehèque's translation of the complete *Anthology*, edited by Jacob, but the subtitle to the articles proves to be of great significance: "De la question des Anciens et des Modernes." The short introduction to these articles stemmed quite naturally from the 1845 insistence on the necessity for adequate modern translations. It also crystallized one of Sainte-Beuve's major concepts about antiquity, namely, its precarious position as a dynamic force in nineteenth-century French culture. After a brief discussion, with examples of the Greek epigram as one of the continuing forms of Greek poetry rather than merely a decadent genre, Sainte-Beuve confined himself to one of the great but too little known *Anthology* authors: Leonidas of Tarentum. Leonidas was known by many readers only as the source of some of Chénier's charming Greek imitations. Sainte-Beuve analyzed various types of epigrams by

Leonidas as well as his pastoral pieces, comparing closely Chénier's imitation in his well-known "Mnaïs." Chénier adapted the poem gracefully to his own country and time, for "en France la poésie toute seule, dans sa simplicité et son charme nu, ne nous touche que médiocrement."[13]

It is evident that Sainte-Beuve intended to continue the discussion of poetry in the second article with a consideration of Agathias Scholasticus and Paul the Silentiary. He had frequently asked Boissonade to edit these poets separately, and now he recommended the work to Dezeimeris, outlining the kind of study, text translation, and notes he would like to see. From his own notes it is apparent that Sainte-Beuve himself had been working on just such an article, and many of his translations of Agathias have survived in his Greek notebook. Instead of writing the article he had planned, Sainte-Beuve felt he must explain one of his sentences, for which he had been reproached, from the Meleager article of almost twenty years before. This sentence was to the effect that the Ancients would some day, sooner or later, lose at least a part of the battle.[14] The rest of the article is devoted to the nineteenth-century chapter in the eternal Quarrel of the Ancients and Moderns; it need not detain us here at the moment.

One reason for following this particular series of articles is that it exemplifies so clearly one side of Sainte-Beuve's interest in Greco-Roman antiquity. It is very possible that the critic's attention was first called to Anacreon by his study of the Pléiade and further strengthened by his work on Chénier. The general atmosphere of the time, which made possible an appreciation of the *Anthology*, must also not be ignored, but in each case the point of departure led on to serious study, reading in Greek, consultation with friends, and finally, a carefully worked out article based on solid erudition but written with the general public in mind. What began with Anacreon continued with Meleager and ended with the whole *Greek Anthology,* which the critic read in Greek and considered as a part of the French poetic tradition. If Sainte-Beuve added nothing to classical erudition by his articles, he did, as Des Guerrois wrote at the end of the century, create a picture of antiquity: "C'est l'Antiquité mise à la portée des lecteurs de journaux, public, même quand il est choisi, plus exigeant pour son plaisir que pour la science approfondie."[15] Sainte-Beuve's work served as Des Guerrois's own avowed point of departure, and Des Guerrois praised Sainte-Beuve's objective admiration for "la grandeur et la puissance inventive" of these poets. Sainte-Beuve was a humanist, in the sense of a sophisticated amateur, during a new age of scientific specialization. The fact itself is important since professionally, as a critic, Sainte-Beuve might be called a scientific specialist. He knew and appreciated what the title meant; he never pretended to be a professional in classical studies, but he believed that he had a function, nevertheless, as a popularizer and as one active and informed in the field. This belief also led him on in two different but related directions. First, it led him to frequent criticism of classical translations as they appeared, with the result that a veritable theory of translation can be disengaged from his writings. Secondly, he also set himself the task frequently of translating the Greek poets that he read closely.

Translation was a literary exercise often practised by Sainte-Beuve, but almost wholly as an amateur. There are a number of poetic translations in his *Poésies complètes,* and the *Revue contemporain* noted that all the translations in the *Etude sur Virgile* were new ones, done by the critic.[16] In his critical essays he often gave a personal translation, sometimes to make an exact point, at other times to bring out his text.[17] A point of some importance, which he repeated many times, is that literary criticism based on a translation cannot be effective. Perrault attempted to judge the ancients without reading the original, and hence was unjust; Lamotte and Pons worked from a translation of Homer; Racan missed Horace's irony because he used a translation rather than the text.[18] The point may seem elementary to some, but the examples cited show egregious errors of judgment. Sainte-Beuve did not succeed, though, in ending the unfortunate practice. Of no little interest, then, are the translations from the *Greek Anthology* found in his *Cahier de notes grecques*, for these show the translator at work, with his hesitations, corrections, and changes. Sainte-Beuve's value as a translator can best be judged, however, only after consideration of his theory and practical criticism of translations by "professional" translators.

Sainte-Beuve clearly distinguished prose and verse translation as two distinct problems. Unquestionably they had common requirements in certain areas, but verse translation intensified a kind of creativity found in all good translation and thereby presented risks and requirements beyond those of prose. As early as 1827 Sainte-Beuve described lyric poetry as an "impromptu de volupté," and hence practically impossible to translate. At any rate, there is no mediocrity in poetic translation: it results in either success or failure.[19] Somewhat later, as his own poetic vein became more literary, Sainte-Beuve declared that the question of poetic translation, so much discussed by his contemporaries, was, in his mind, no real problem: a true and great poet who set out to translate Homer or Dante would, with time and effort, succeed in his task, if not literarily, "du moins par le sentiment et la couleur."[20] But, he added, such a poet would not long harness his talent to that of another poet, he would use it for his own ends. In fact, therefore, the critic merely shifted the problem from being one of philosophic impossibility to being one of practical improbability. The importance of the difference is undeniable, but is not pragmatically effective. The question also raises, by implication, the problem of imitation, and to a twentieth-century reader the statement evokes immediately Paul Valéry's position that translation provides the opportunity for the purest form of creation.[21] These points are not unimportant in Sainte-Beuve's thinking, either on the subject of translation or the question of poetic theory.

In verse, as in all translation, the poet begins with a text, which becomes the antagonist in a literal personal combat between the translator and the text. To avoid this total combat means, simply, final defeat, no matter what the success in individual lines, according to Sainte-Beuve.[22] The French linguistic tradition, particularly in verse, further complicated this "battle," for, as the critic pointed out, Racine and even nineteenth-century authors recoiled from their text "par pudeur de goût."[23] A recurrent adjective in this connection is *élégant*, which, as we shall see, is a commentary on style, used by the critic in passing as a compliment. When, for example, Sainte-Beuve wrote that Saint-Victor's translation of Anacreon's poetry was "instruit et élégant," or that Halévy's translations of the Greek dramatists were "élégantes et harmonieuses,"[24] he was not at all judging the fidelity of the translation. Elegant translations were, in general, neoclassic literary works, and translation, like every other art, is subject to changes of style, as Sainte-Beuve pointed out in 1867.[25] This kind of verse translation was no longer held in esteem as art. But these changes are due not solely to changes in public taste; there is also an inherent quality in each good translation which makes it temporary (*"provisoire"*). It must have meaning for a particular audience, the public of a specific age or cultural group.

Daru's translation of Horace left much to be desired, for example, in lyric movement, rhythm, imagery, and concrete detail; yet Daru had forceful passages and easy-flowing verse. He communicated the Horatian spirit to Empire audiences, he rendered the past accessible to the French public of his own age.[26] For his own generation, however, Sainte-Beuve preferred Janin's translation of the Roman poet, which succeeded in rendering Horace "dans tout son vif et comme s'il était français."[27] The critic was normally generous toward the Empire verse translations, but one of his more severe youthful articles was on Pongerville's translation of Lucretius. This translator had discovered in Lucretius "le premier parmi les poètes qui ait chanté l'unité de Dieu." Such manifest misinterpretation of the poet's thought resulted in a translation which was "une contrefaçon pâle et fade, vernissée d'une plate et monotone élégance où l'on ne retrouve bien du nerf logique ni de la poésie étincelante du maître. C'est un *faux sens* perpétuel, promené sur un alexandrin symétrique et bercé d'épithètes sonores." The young critic continued with chapter and verse for his statement. The severity of this review arose, as Sainte-Beuve himself later explained, from a kind of literary politics which made the critic express his thought bluntly rather than with his usual tact and delicacy.[28] These circumstances do not, however, change the evaluation or the criteria for a good translation: thorough understanding of the author and his text, which was to be couched in a language producing a similar effect upon the reader as the original. Another example of this last point might be Geoffroy, who understood antiquity well, but travestied Theocritus with high-flown rhetoric and "une fausse élégance."[29] Occasionally, too, the critic went so far as to correct errors in translation, as in the chorus of Sophocles' *Antigone*, newly translated by A. Vaquerie and

P. Meurice, or in a translation of Aristophanes' *The Clouds*.[30] More frequently, however, Sainte-Beuve merely noted inaccuracies and modestly disclaimed his ability to do such detailed work. These modest statements obviously result from the time involved in such work rather than from any real lack of ability.

In an effort to stimulate a new wave of verse translation as a healthy means of national poetic regeneration, Sainte-Beuve presented his article on Meleager in 1845. Sketching briefly the history of French verse translation since the sixteenth century, the critic pointed to its weakness as a result of the neoclassic concept of a noble language. He made clear, nevertheless, that he had no intention of identifying Greek poetry with the more violent northern Shakespearian vein. New translations should be faithful to the spirit as well as to the letter of the text, "et légèrement combinées avec les ressources de notre propre langue." Such translations would be innovations, and history had already proven, with Luther's Bible and Amyot's Plutarch, that such innovations have a profound influence on an evolving language like that of nineteenth-century French. Translations from Greek would be particularly helpful because of the delicate structural possibilities to be rendered into French: "arroser le languáge, le vivifier avec fraîcheur, cela demande des sources perpétuelles et pures."[31] It is not, however, the Greek ideal of pure beauty that the critic wanted to emphasize, but rather the simplicity, inseparable from truth, which is its base, that naïveté in feeling and expression, intermingled with grace, that adds to the poignant value and to the grandeur. In other terms, Sainte-Beuve was proposing a regeneration of French poetry of the sort seen in the lyric poetry of the Pléiade, that would stem from a new view of Greek literature, with its emphasis on simply stated human feeling. Once again it is clear that for Sainte-

Beuve poetic translation was an act of poetic creation, a challenge to real talent. By 1867, however, he had lost his optimism, for he admitted the inadequacy of translation as a means of aiding the evolution of a language: imitation, even "ces imitations détournées et savantes qui sont proprement l'invention des classiques,"[32] are necessary to such an evolution.

Homeric translation posed a special problem which was much discussed in the nineteenth century. Sainte-Beuve never really came to grips with this problem in the same way as did his colleague at the Mazarin Library, Philarète Chasles. In 1847 Chasles published his *Etudes sur l'Antiquité*, which contained an essay on "Des traductions d'Homère et de l'impuissance des traductions." Chasles's pessimism about such translations was based on the vast difference between the civilizations involved, as well as on an equally great difference between the poetic languages of Greece and France. He further compared in detail five famous translations of the poet: those of Pope, Cowper, Monti, Voss, and Bignan. Sainte-Beuve did not ever allude directly to reading this essay, though both men were at the Mazarin in 1847; he did, however, make quite clear in 1861 his reading and appreciation of Matthew Arnold's essay "On Translating Homer."[33] In fact, one result of his reading Arnold was that he defended Pope's understanding of Homer rather than repeating the usual phrases about Pope's "travesty" of the poems.[34]

The sympathetic double article on Madame Dacier, two years before the review of Rigault's *Querelle des Anciens et des Modernes*, underlined the importance, in Sainte-Beuve's opinion, of the Dacier translation, which tried honestly, and with some success, to bridge the gap between Homeric poetry and the elegant French society of the eighteenth century. The result was what Sainte-Beuve once called "a bourgeois Homer."[35] Such a Homer was infinitely better adapted to nineteenth-century taste, however, than the elegant, completely false Lamotte, but even Dacier was no longer adequate. At the end of his 1843 articles on Homer Sainte-Beuve made a few but important remarks on Homeric translation. He praised that of Dugas-Montbel as justly the most highly considered; Bignan's was an honorable attempt at verse translation. Bareste, in his new prose translation, had attempted to "rendre la *couleur* plus exactement que Dugas-Montbel et ses prédécesseurs ne l'avaient fait."[36] The critic then suggested an attempt analogous to that made by Chateaubriand in his translation of Milton, but admitted that it would require a great writer to combine a literal translation with readability in the second language. Bareste had tried this method and, despite some inadequacies had also had real success and pointed in the right direction. It is worthy of note that Sainte-Beuve never wrote about Leconte de Lisle's translation of Homer, but we may conjecture, since he evidently invited his friend Dübner to do an article on it, that Sainte-Beuve recognized its ineptness as well as its blatant inaccuracies, but had wisely invited a professional Hellenist to say so. Dübner's refusal letter to Sainte-Beuve minced no words, for he wrote that, despite the poet's vigorous love of Homer and the French public's esteem for the poet, "je déplore cette publication et je suis convaincu qu'elle fera beaucoup de mal à Homère dans le public contemporain, si elle doit se répandre."[37]

Prose translations, on the whole, claimed the critic's attention more frequently than those in verse, as much because of their sheer numerical superiority as for any other reason. The revolution in scholarly studies inspired much discussion of translation and produced rather generally accepted norms. Accuracy to the text became a *sine qua non* for nineteenth-century translators, with the result that prose was generally agreed upon as an expression which permitted the desired accuracy in a way verse could not, except under the pen of a genius. The problem of tone, or what the nineteenth-century translators frequently called *couleur*, continued to be discussed, and these discussions resulted in various compromises between the tone of the original work and a tone acceptable to a nineteenth-century cultivated public. Reduced to its most concrete terms, tone results from the vocabulary chosen to translate specific words, in particular, realistic terms which had been consciously eliminated from accepted usage in French under the influence of seventeenth-century neoclassicism. Marie Delcourt quoted, in this connection, from the theory of Charles Loyson, published in 1813, "Loyson voudrait qu'en traduisant on entrât dans l'esprit de celui qu'on traduit, sans aller jusqu'à donner à l'original le ton et la manière qu'il aurait pris s'il eût vécu dans le siècle de son traducteur: principe faux qui tend à effacer en partie l'originalité des ouvrages anciens, en les confondant tous dans la physionomie moderne."[38]

Sainte-Beuve never tired of citing Amyot's Plutarch as the French literary monument of translation comparable to Luther's Bible in German or the King James version in English. The article on Amyot, however, was not one of Sainte-Beuve's best. It was occasioned by Blignière's *Essai sur Amyot* and contained little personal estimate of Plutarch, no personal confrontation of texts. It began and ended with a judgment by Joubert that for France Amyot's translation had become an original work of art. This point was, indeed, the source of Sainte-Beuve's interest. Admitting readily all the inaccuracies and infidelities in translation according to modern standards, Sainte-Beuve underscored nevertheless Amyot's popularity both in his own century and since his death. He further insisted that Amyot be judged as an original writer, the creator of French prose, even though his style was outstanding only when he was translating. But Amyot's very inaccuracies and oversimplified style, according to the critic, *created* a French Plutarch.[39] Sainte-Beuve was once again drawn to the problem of defining the delicate line between a work of erudition and a creative work.

When Paul Courrier found the Venice manuscript of *Daphnis and Chloé* he added the new sections to Amyot's translation of the incomplete text of the work. In making these additions, he also corrected Amyot's errors and adapted his own style to that of the earlier translation. Sainte-Beuve found the result a real masterpiece of translation: "C'est peut-être la seule traduction dont on ait le droit de déclarer sans flatterie qu'elle est mieux que l'original et qu'elle le supplée avantageusement sans rien lui dérober."[40] Late in life Courrier undertook a vast project to translate Herodotus, and he did indeed publish one section. According to Courrier, all translations into French were marred by the omnipresent influence of court and Academy language. To translate Herodotus, he believed, one must blend certain qualities of science and simplicity, so as to arrive at "a somewhat self-conscious peasant prose." But what La Fontaine did naturally, what succeeded under the wing of Amyot, even, was less effective as a version of Herodotus for Courrier's contemporaries. Despite the accuracy of the translation the style, "vieilli après coup," appeared more like parody in the end, wrote Sainte-Beuve. The tone affected by Courrier to give color did not ring true any more. The style may have been faithful to Herodotus's own Greek style, but it did not transmit its characteristics sympathetically to the nineteenth-century French reader.[41]

More generally, however, Sainte-Beuve wanted to see in a prose translation accuracy with some form of equivalent style. The choice of words should be adjusted to the requirement of the French language without harming either the original expression or the effect on the reader of the translation. This last implied that some effective compromise was to be sought which would give the reader the same sort of impression, within the limitations of French, that the original Greek gives to a reader completely at home in the Greek cultural context.

In approaching this ideal there were, according to Sainte-Beuve, three major pitfalls for the good translator. Some evidence of these pitfalls is probably never absolutely absent even from the best translation. First, there was the pitfall of sheer mistranslation, as in Patru's futile attempts to translate the first four lines of Cicero's *Pro Archias*,[42] or Pongerville's Lucretius, which Sainte-Beuve had termed "un faux sens perpétuel" because the translator did not really understand his text. Sainte-Beuve also pointed out that seventeenth-century translators like Maucroix were inclined without scruple to "retrancher ou de l'adoucir," for, the critic added, the ideal translation in the seventeenth century was very different.[43] Denne-Baron in more recent times went too far in sheer textual manipulation, and Sainte-Beuve refused him even the title of translator.[44] The critic also reproached Racan for working only from previous translations without checking his work against the original text.[45] The poet Delille may have translated accurately, but he did not seize the significance, the art of his text.[46]

Textual problems were not due solely to the varying competence of translators. Style, as we shall see, often affected the textual accuracy of a passage. In translations from the classical languages, our main concern in this study, there was, according to Sainte-Beuve, the further probem of the textual reading itself. Benoist, whose translations of Virgil Sainte-Beuve generally admired, offered a new translation of a difficult passage, but the interpretation and translation depended on a different punctuation and, in this particular case, Sainte-Beuve rejected Benoist's interpretation.[47]

The second pitfall for the translator, in Sainte-Beuve's opinion, was that of being arbitrary in the interpretation of the author. Although the review of Nisard's *Etudes de moeurs et de critique sur les poètes latins de la décadence* contained a degree of personal animosity, the principles of translation set forth in the article are valid and characteristic of Sainte-Beuve's thought generally. He reproached Nisard forcibly with several types of arbitrariness, such as voluntarily choosing the wrong shade of meaning for a word, translating in such a way as to be "onéreux" to the author, or even of being arbitrary in the treatment of the text itself. Clearly, Nisard had imposed his intellect and will on his text rather than using his talent to bring out the intent of the original author.

Such arbitrary handling of a text led quite naturally to the third pitfall: lack of sympathy with and/or understanding of the original author. The two most negative reviews Sainte-Beuve wrote on translations charge the translator in each case with exactly this kind of obtuseness.[48] Rivarol's translation of Dante many have been bad in many ways, but it was the first in French to appreciate "avec élévation la nature et la qualité de Dante."[49] An important quality in any writing, sympathetic understanding is the foundation stone of the translator, according to the critic.

These three pitfalls (mistranslation, arbitrariness and lack of sympathy) are undoubtedly important, but are nevertheless negative. Sainte-Beuve also wanted to find the positive qualities of good translations. The first quality of a good translation was that of sustained competence, which Sainte-Beuve normally equated with the amount of time and care given by the translator. In one place he likened a translation to a battle, in which the translator "a lutté avec la beauté antique."⁵⁰ He also complimented Littré on his translation and study of Hippocrates, saying that Littré devoted twenty-three years to bring his work to such a felicitous end. Delille had real faults as a translator, but he had the quality of sustained work. Amyot also had "la constance d'un si long travail."⁵¹ On the other hand, Sainte-Beuve made perfectly clear that Marolles, whom he pictured as the epitome of a bad translator, produced an enormous quantity of lines and, what was more, knew exactly the total.⁵² Time alone, nevertheless, did not guarantee success, for Pongerville worked fifteen years on Lucretius and made only "une contrefaçon fade et pâle."⁵³

The second quality was termed *sentiment*, which is perhaps best explained as the positive counterpart of the pitfall of lack of sympathy. *Sentiment* and the adjectival form *sentimental* mean not only understanding but also sympathy, as well as an intimate acquaintance with the work. Sainte-Beuve described the process leading to the quality of *sentiment*, and defined it when he wrote in the article on Terence:

> . . . c'était de remettre sans cesse la traduction elle-même en question, de comparer et de confronter les textes, la copie avec l'original, et, s'il y avait plusieurs traductions rivales, comme c'était le cas pour Virgile, de mettre aux prises ces traductions entre elles. Dans ces jeux de l'érudition et du goût, l'original sans cesse relu, manié et remanié à plaisir, devenait chose familière, facile, non apprise, mais sue de tout temps et comme passée en nous; on ne l'oubliait plus . . . il ne suffit pas de les comprendre, de les [the ancient poets] lire purement et simplement comme on consulterait un texte, et de passer outre; il faut avoir vécu avec eux d'un commerce aisé continuel et de tous les instants; *Nocturna versate manu*.⁵⁴

The third quality of a good translation is much more complex despite the apparently simple title of "style." Style, in translation, is a complex adjustment of the original author's style, interpreted by that of the translator for sympathetic reception by an audience which may or may not share the author's concept of style. During the seventeenth and eighteenth centuries, translation into French of almost any ancient author, but particularly of Homer, was subjected to some sort of compromise about diction and the proprieties. For this reason, Sainte-Beuve's comments on style are normally limited to the flowing quality of the French prose, to the question of whether any awkwardness resulted from an imperfect conversion of the original idiom. This flowing quality of style was quite different from simple accuracy of translation, for a work might be accurate and still not have style, or it might have an easy style despite real inaccuracies.[55] "Elégant" is used to describe a translation style that not only produces good, easy French but also a happy equivalent of the original mode of expression. Sainte-Beuve wrote of Pope's translation of Homer that it was "d'une suprême élégance, ce qui est déjà une infidélité." Halévy's translations were considered "élégantes, harmonieuses, les plus belles pièces du théâtre grec." Bétolaud's translation of Apuleius was "élégante."[56] The critic's remarks on the style of Madame Dacier's translation of Homer are quite amusing, for "élégant" was hardly an appropriate compliment. He said of her early translations that they were "utiles, agréables à leur heure et . . . étaient d'une élégance relative," but that she really did better with the strength and abundance of Homer. When he came to judge her Homer, however, he called it "une traduction *généreuse et noble*," which rendered the spirit of the original beauty and had a certain Homeric effect; "il y a une certaine naïveté et *magniloquence* qui se retrouve dans la langue naturelle plus qu'élégante."⁵⁷ Such lack of resolute judgment probably indicated an unresolved conflict between the critic's own taste in style and what he intellectually knew to be appropriate for a translation of Homer in the late eighteenth century.

It would probably be an exaggeration to say that Sainte-Beuve answered fully the question of who should become a translator, since his views were most frequently expressed in terms of his practical criticism of a work already completed and before him. With the exception of Amyot, however, who wrote more firmly and more gracefully when he based his writing on the work of another author than when he was writing from his own talent, the translators generally considered by Sainte-Beuve were men of more than one talent and reputation. According to the critic, translation of scholarly work required a scholar familiar with the material. As a translator of imaginative literature Sainte-Beuve envisaged, on the other hand, the young creative writer, learning his trade somewhat as a young painter who copies the masters. Such an exercise would benefit both the translator and his public. The public would receive a work of art otherwise closed to it; the writer would not be slavishly imitating another author, he would rather be taking up a challenge to re-create style, diction, and sentiment in his own language, and the process might well re-create the poetic language of his native tongue. Innovation, so popular in France in 1840, would thus result from a good translation "de la manière . . . le plus exemplaire." These strictures of age and stage of creative development, used to describe the ideal translator, stemmed partially from observation and partially from the recognition of the fact, as he said, that such a talent would not long harness itself to that of another creator.⁵⁸

The critic's own evolution as a translator presents an interesting and revelatory reversal of the pattern he enunciated theoretically. We have already seen that it was the later volumes of poetry which contained more translations. At this point, however, the theoretical question of the relationship between translation and innovation is less appropriate than a simple description of his own method of translation, seen in the light of his critical principles on the subject. Examples are not lacking of both verse and prose translations, although Sainte-Beuve more readily published his prose translations in his critical articles. The verse translations found in the *Poésies complètes* illustrate well, however, his technique in this medium of expression. On the point of accuracy in translation, we have already seen that he asked Pantasidès, Loudierre, or other specialist friends to check the translations before he published them. Style, tone, and equivalent effects provide better measure of the critic's procedure and value as a translator. The poem entitled "Au Sommeil" with the note "traduit de Stace" may serve as a typical example despite its very limited form.

Au Sommeil
Traduit de Stace

Par quel crime, si jeune, ô des Dieux plus doux,
Par quel sort, ai-je pu perdre tes dons jaloux,
O Sommeil?—Tu me fuis.—Tout dort dans la nature,
Les troupeaux au bercail, l'oiseau dans la verdure;
5 Les fleuves mugissants, et de jour aux cent bruits,
Assoupissent au loin leurs murmures des nuits;
Les cîmes des grands bois penchent sous les rosées,
Et les mers au rivage expirent apaisées.
Moi, je veille! sept fois Phébé m'a regardé
10 De son char le plus haut où déjà retardé;
Sept fois j'ai répondu, debout, plus pâle qu'elle!
Autant de fois Vesper, de sa tendre étincelle,
M'a surpris, dès le soir, attendant vainement;
Et la fraîcheur d'Aurore aiguise mon tourment

15 Que faire? Argus lui-même et ses mille paupières
    Gardant pour Jupiter les beautés prisonnières,
    Ne veillaient qu'à demi: chaque oeil avait son tour.
    En ces nuits, ô Sommeil, trop courtes pour l'amour,
    Amères et sans fin pour ma veille pâlie,
20 Peut-être, au moment même où ma voix te supplie,
    Un autre, un plus heureux, dans son embrassement,
    Pressant un sein aimé, t'éloigne doucement . . .
    Sommeil! oh! laisse-les, viens à moi; viens, à peine,
    C'est assez, c'est beaucoup: à d'autres ta main pleine
25 De tes plus lourds pavots! à moi, doux Passager,
    Rien qu'un toucher humide, un coup d'aile léger![59]

Somnus

Crimine quo merui, iuuenis placidissime diuum,
quoue errore miser, donis ut solus egerem,
Somne, tuis? Tracet omne pecus uolucresque feraeque
et simulant fessos curuata cacumina somnos,
5 nec trucibus fluuiis idem sonus, occidit horror
aequoris et terris maria adclinata quiescunt.
Septima iam rediens Phoebe mihi respicit aegras
stare genas; totidem Oetaeae Paphiaeque reuisunt
lampades et totiens nostros Tithonia questus
10 praeterit et gelido spargit miserata flagello.
Vnde ego sufficiam? non si mihi lumina mille,
quae sacer alterna tantum statione tenebat,
Argus et hund umquam uigilavat corpore toto.
At nunc heu! si aliquis longa sub nocte puellae
15 brachia nexa tenens ultro te, Somne, repellit,
inde ueni, nec te totas infundere pennas
luminibus compello meis—hoc turba precatur
laetior—: extremo me tange cacumine uirgae,
sufficit, aut leuiter suspenso poplite transi.[60]

A comparison of the original poems with the translation

indicates clearly Sainte-Beuve's technique in verse translation. The simple fact that Sainte-Beuve's translation is twenty-six lines long, compared with Statius's nineteen lines, makes one suspect, even before reading the texts, some sort of addition either by way of explanation or of increased poetic development. Deviations in translation are few in number and are of some interest since they denote sensitivity rather than lack of knowledge. Sainte-Beuve construed *iuuenis* in line 1 with *merui*, whereas modern translators tend to read it with *placidissime diuum*. In line 2, Sainte-Beuve translated *quoue errore* as *quel sort* thus shifting an idea of guilt away from individual fault to an external fate. In line 3, the translator added the dynamic *Tu me fuis* to an otherwise poetically placid line. The next five lines contain a picture equivalent to the three Statius lines, but certain elements are omitted (*feraeque* in line 3); the order is changed (rivers before mountain tops); the image, in one case, is completely changed:

> et simulant fessos curuata cacumina somnos

became

> Les cîmes des grands bois penchent sous les rosées.

In the following series of images, the focal point in Sainte-Beuve's interpretation is clearly indicated by the active *Moi, je veille!*, not found in Statius's text, where Phoebe is the actor and in parallel construction, Vesper and Aurora. In the French,

> Et la fraîcheur d'Aurore aiguise mon tourment

is more abstract and dense than the concretely active

> [Tithonia] praeterit et gelido spargit miserata flagello.

The comparison with Argus moves from explicit to implicit in the translation as the sense of insufficient power is altered to utter helplessness. The wing of sleep (Statius, line 16) is transposed to the end of the poem by Sainte-Beuve as a final image. In its place at this point has been inserted *tes plus lourds pavots*.

It would be a mistake to read Sainte-Beuve's manner of translating in this one poem in any absolute sense, but it is not wrong to consider it representative of his poetic procedure. He stayed very close to his text, essentially, without being a slave to it. His changes and additions are interpretative of his own reading of the text, and serve to bring out a particular reading, like the change of focus in the images of lines 3–8 of the Latin poem. Some critics would perhaps argue that Sainte-Beuve was no longer translating accurately with such changes. The unhesitating response would be that it was this very matter which fascinated the critic, namely, the line of demarcation between translation and creation on a chosen theme. This particular poem can hardly be called a new creation, for at most there are only changes from the images of the original to related ones, or in matters of detail, and the overall impression of the translation is quite clearly analogous to that of the original poem.

The Moschus translations evidence a similar procedure: rhythm and accent analogous to that of the Greek, and a generally accurate textual translation with variations arising in the handling of detail. The translation of Moschus's sixth idyll, beginning "Pan aimait Echo sa voisine,"[61] has a charming concision which even surpasses that of the Greek text at the expense, however, of concrete repetitive parallels which have poetic value in the Greek. The tone and mood are eminently well rendered, nevertheless, in a poem which might truly be termed an "impromptu de volupté."

Sainte-Beuve more willingly inserted his prose translations into his various critical articles. His method of translating is further visible in the work sheets found in the *Cahier de notes grecques*, where an exceedingly literal translation is often accompanied by a freer, but smoother or more evocative, rendering of the passage. The critic's preoccupation with the mot juste is particularly evident with adjectives or epithets, as in a translation from Agathias which presents numerous alternates translations: "le verrou (les gonds, les barres)"; or "o Cypris, chargée de trophées (victorieuse, *Venus victrix*.)"[62] One particular passage from Meleager's *Proemia* merits close attention, for it brought sharp criticism from Bernard Jullien. In the "Factum contre André Chénier" Sainte-Beuve compared Chénier to the *Anthology*, and then translated in abbreviated form the *Proemia* of Meleager. The translation parallels the Greek quite closely, except at the point of mentioning Anacreon and Archilochus. Sainte-Beuve reversed the order, and in doing so condensed the description to the point that Jullien charged the translator with allowing his imagination to dictate what is not in the text. Despite Sainte-Beuve's ample protestations to the contrary, Jullien accused him of at least temporary voluntary suspension of his critical acumen, as well as of a sentimental nostalgia for an ideal literary past since lost.[63] Jullien's own erudite explanation, called forth by the phrase "brins d'élégie," of the difference between the French elegy and the Anacreon distich of the *Greek Anthology*, is impressive more as the kind of pedantry that Sainte-Beuve disliked in university people than as an example of any comprehension of the critic's admirable and, on the whole, accurate efforts to make *Proemia* meaningful to the cultivated French public. Such, after all, was Sainte-Beuve's fundamental theory of translation as he practised it: an accurate rendering of the text, accurate particularly with regard to the effect the original sought to convey, without undue rhetorical embellishment or dull pedantry, and easily comprehensible to a cultivated nineteenth-century French audience.

Jullien's article has a special importance by its malevolence. Seizing upon a statement by Sainte-Beuve that antiquity was better studied in the 1840s, Jullien remarked acidly that this "better studied" antiquity was factitious, "créée par chacun sur des lectures superficielles et en vue des journaux où il devait déposer le fruit de ses prétendues études."[64] He went even farther to say that antiquity was and, by implication, should remain the province of an intellectual elite. These charges could be supported only by the first thesis, namely, that Sainte-Beuve translated badly. The accuracy or inaccuracy of the critic's translation thus became the key to the validity of the total article, and, as we have seen, Jullien's pedantic corrections are not entirely convincing or conclusive. Nor do they reflect the general high regard in which Sainte-Beuve's translations were held by other readers.

Paul Saint-Victor esteemed Sainte-Beuve's translations of the same poet, Meleager, highly enough to borrow some of them, which he thought "exquises," for his own study of the poet.[65] Boissonade, the eminent professor of Greek at the Collège de France, wrote to Sainte-Beuve a long and helpful letter on his system of translation after reading the article on the *Medea* of Apollonius Rhodius. Boissonade raised an extremely important point in translation according to the critic's own theory. He recognized Sainte-Beuve's attempt to render Apollonius faithfully, imitating his tone (*"couleur"*), but added, "vos teintes ne sont pas à tous deux les mêmes." Apollonius's poetic simplicity is erudite; the translation is prosaic and popular. Greek and Latin translations into French need a poetic prose. Boissonade continued with numerous examples of what in one place he called "anti-poetic" translations. In his answer to this long letter, Sainte-Beuve expressed his gratitude for Boissonade's attention, adding that he would not have attempted the translation without the help of Pantasidès. Sainte-Beuve also restated the problem in his own terms: "C'est le caractère à la fois *artificiel* et *naturel* de la poésie grecque; d'une part, elle ne ressemblait *nullement* à la prose, et de l'autre, elle osait rendre la nature avec des traits vifs, *réels*": in other words, Greek poetry had a sort of composite language, somewhat comparable to that of Montaigne in French prose. Sainte-Beuve added, however, that he hoped to rectify his errors of interpretation by conversation with the learned Boissonade.[66] This sympathetic exchange of letters between specialist and critic brings out their agreement on a theory of translation, even as it points up the incomplete success in practice by Sainte-Beuve, even with Pantasidès to aid him.

A less erudite critic, Nicolas Martin, in discussing Sainte-Beuve's return to classical studies, termed the critic's translations "des essais pleins de couleur et de vivacité expressive." He further stated that these attempts show us "quelles excellentes traductions un vrai poète, conduit par un sentiment critique supérieur, pourrait nous donner des maîtres antiques."[67] It is clear, then, that for his nonspecialized contemporaries Sainte-Beuve's translations "rang true," communicated some kind of poetic or literary tone which they deemed to be "authentic." For the specialist in Greek studies, however, inaccuracies existed. Such inaccuracies sprang not from ignorance of the text or the language, but rather from the choice of means to express it in French. Sainte-Beuve understood cerebrally very well what he was about, but, just as he was not a poet of genius, so he lacked any "divine" gift for translation. Yet, with all that, he still accomplished the task he set out to perform: to bring certain pieces of Greek writing into the reach of a cultivated French public that would find pleasure in reading them.

Notes

1. Hutton, p. 74.
2. Most of the material in the following account of the *Greek Anthology* is taken from the following sources: Moses Hadas, *Ancilla to Classical Reading* (New York: Columbia University Press, 1956), pp. 302–4; A. S. F. Gow and D. L. Page, eds., *The Greek Anthology: Hellenistic Epigrams* (Cambridge: University Press, 1965), 2 vols., I, xvi–xxxix.
3. Saumaise copied from the manuscript and circulated a certain number of hitherto unknown epigrams, but he did not edit the work. In 1623 Maximilian of Bavaria gave the manuscript to Pope Gregory XV. It was rebound in two volumes in Rome. In 1797 when Napoleon and the Pope made peace, the volumes were removed to Paris. After Waterloo, Volume I was restored to Heidelberg, but Volume II was overlooked and remained in Paris, where it is still to be found in the Bibliothèque Nationale, separated from Volume I.
4. Sandys, II, 395.
5. *Pr.L.*, I, 194.
6. This article first appeared in the *Revue des Deux Mondes*, April 15, 1842. See also: Sainte-Beuve's letter to Professor Rossignol, dated February 15, 1842, in which he asked "or, où en est la *question Anacréontique?* pourriez-vous m'indiquer quelque édition ou dissertation ou volume, où soit traitée l'authenticité d'Anacréon, et où se trouve l'opinion des critiques sur la qualité de la publication d'Henri Estienne?"

7. *Tab.*, p. 442. The underlining is Sainte-Beuve's.
8. *Tab.*, p. 445. See also *C.g.*, VI, 525. In response to N. Martin's reservations about Sainte-Beuve's view of Anacreon, Sainte-Beuve replied late in 1846 by explaining and defending his position to the critic.
9. *Tab.*, p. 442. "L'agréable et le fin se gagnent encore plus aisément que le grand; on commence surtout très-volontiers par le mignard et le subtil."
10. *P.L.*, III, 3. One should not be misled by the word *lie* for Sainte-Beuve continued his quotation from Joubert by saying "La lie même de la littérature des Grecs dans sa vieillesse offre un résidu délicat. . . . "
11. *P.C.*, V, 444. This image deserves attention apart from the present context, because critics have been fond of denigrating Sainte-Beuve's interest in secondary writers as indicative of a second-rate mind. It is clear in this statement that there is no preference indicated by the critic for the "bypaths," but, rather, additional knowledge required for real familiarity.
12. *P.C.*, V, 410.
13. *N.L.*, VII, 27. Chénier had substituted, as a major change, a shepherdess Mnaïs for Leonidas's shepherd, Clitagoras.
14. *N.L.*, VII, 30. The sentence was: "Les Anciens, je le crains, perdront tôt ou tard une partie de la bataille."
15. Charles Des Guerrois, *Etude sur l'Anthologie grecque* (Troyes: Dufour-Bouquot, 1896), p. 3.
16. 31 octobre et 15 novembre, 1856.
17. *C.L.*, XI, 175. Normally he had these translations verified by a specialist before publication. See: Troubat, *Souvenirs*, pp. 137–138. Troubat says, "C'est à M. Loudierre que M. Sainte-Beuve demandait toujours la vérification des traductions qu'il faisait d'auteurs anciens dans ses articles. . . . "
18. *C.L.*, V, 270; *C.L.*, XIII, 154; *P.L.*, I, 85.
19. *Pr.L.*, I, 192–94. See also: Guyot, p. 344: "Une petite pièce de poésie s'évapore à la traduction comme une essence qu'on change de façon."
20. *P.L.*, II, 75.

21. Paul Valéry, *Oeuvres*, ed. Jean Hytier, Bibliothèque de la Pléiade (Paris: Gallimard, 1957), 2 vols., I, 216.
22. *C.L.*, X, 387.
23. *P.L.*, I, 85.
24. *N.L.*, X, 412.
25. *N.L.*, XIII, 307.
26. *C.L.*, IX, 431–32. See also *C.L.*, XI, 131 for a similar estimate of Delille's *Georgics*.
27. *C.g.*, XI, 555.
28. *N.L.*, XII, 440–49.
29. *C.L.*, I, 383.
30. *C.g.*, V, 660 and 707.
31. *P.C.*, V, 410–11.
32. *N.L.*, XIII, 303.
33. *C.g.*, XII, 146 and *N.L.*, VIII, 117.
34. *N.L.*, VIII, 116–117 (1864). See also: *C.L.*, XI, 214 (1854).
35. *P.C.*, V, 356. This is not to be construed as a "slur" on the critic's part. See the articles on Madame Dacier and her translation: *C.L.*, IX, 473–514.
36. *P.C.*, V, 356. The underlining is Sainte-Beuve's.
37. Ms. D. 601, Collection Spoelberch de Lovenjoul, p. 74.
38. Marie Delcourt, *Etude sur les traductions des tragiques grecs et latins en France depuis la Renaissance* (Bruxelles: Lamartin, 1925), p. 210, n. 2.
39. *C.L.*, IV, 467–69.
40. *N.L.*, IV, 106.
41. *C.L.*, VI, 357.
42. *C.L.*, V, 283.
43. *C.L.*, X, 232.
44. *C.L.*, X, 387.
45. *C.L.*, VIII, 77–78.
46. *P.L.*, II, 74–75.
47. *N.L.*, XI, 190.
48. *P.C.*, III, 328–57 and *N.L.*, XII, 445–53.
49. *C.L.*, XI, 262.
50. *N.L.*, I, 400.

51. *N.L.*, V, 218; *P.L.*, II, 76; *C.L.*, IV, 452.
52. *C.L.*, XIV, 126 and 133.
53. *N.L.*, XII, 449.
54. *N.L.*, V, 333.
55. *N.L.*, VIII, 116.
56. *N.L.*, I, 400; *N.L.*, II, 426; *C.L.*, IX, 484.
57. *C.L.*, IX, 490. The underlining is Sainte-Beuve's.
58. *P.C.*, V, 410.
59. *Poésies complètes* I, 322–23.
60. Stace, *Silves*. Texte établi par Henri Frère et traduit par H. J. Izaac (Paris: Les Belles Lettres, 1944), 2 vols., II, 205–6.
61. *Poésies complètes* I, 324.
62. *Cahier de notes grecques*, pp. 170–71. No. 176.
63. Bernard Jullien, *Thèses supplémentaires de métrique et de musique anciennes, de grammaire et de littérature* (Paris: Hachette, 1861), p. 435.
64. *Ibid.*, p. 436. Sainte-Beuve's letter to Dübner on Jullien's article sheds a good deal of light on the critic's private reactions.
65. Paul Saint-Victor, *Hommes et Dieux Etudes d'histoire et de littérature* (Paris: Michel Lévy, 1867), p. 47, n. 1.
66. *C.g.*, VI, 507–9.
67. Nicolas Martin, "Sainte-Beuve," *l'Artiste* (15 décembre 1848), p. 122.

Chapter 4

The Bucolic Poets and Poetic Theory

From the *Greek Anthology* to Greek and Latin lyric poetry is no distance at all. "Lyric," to use the word momentarily in its broadest modern sense, describes most of the themes treated in the *Greek Anthology* as well as the work of certain poets we shall treat as a group, simply because Sainte-Beuve dealt with them most often collectively. Lyric poetry, in the strictly Greek sense of poetry to be accompanied by a lyre, was never a category utilized by the critic. His differentiations were either by verse form, as between epigrams and elegies, or by general thematic type, as between elegiac and bucolic poets. Elegiac and bucolic poetry were, moreover, so closely related in the critic's mind that he frequently used the terms together. The immediately distinguishing feature of this group of poets is the predominance in numbers of the Roman poets, who had learned their craft from their Greek counterparts, of course, but who had learned well and brought their own personal note or original art to the form.[1]

The poetic description of nature is one of the themes that presented itself quite naturally enough to any nineteenth-century literary critic. Sainte-Beuve treated the subject more than once from a comparative point of view and, curiously enough, chose his examples from among the "didactic" poets. He chose for his three contrastive talents Hesiod, Lucretius, and Virgil. Hesiod was the poet of practical wisdom about the country and the economy of farming. Devoid of illusions about human nature and the natural world around him, he has nevertheless charm and sincerity, a feeling of good faith: "Il y a des rayons de miel dans le creux du vieux chêne."[2] Lucretius, on the other hand, was not earthbound like Hesiod; he sought out the "génie de la nature" at its source in all its grandeur and power. He swept away all the ancient nature gods of superstition, satisfying himself with a natural generative force. Lucretius did not describe nature in particular, but in his picture of the first ages of human society he painted a rural epoch with ample strokes and language: "on croit sentir la fraîcheur qui circule, on voit le pré peint de fleurs qui rit et verdoie." Virgil combined and softened these two talents in his *Georgics*. Detailed and technical like Hesiod, he "embrasse la pensée des mondes comme Lucrèce" though by choice he remained more practical, more in accord with the needs and desires of humble mortals. He is rural but not rustic. He knew evil but softened it, and "[il] veut être pour tous un consolateur."[3] Horace had still another manner of describing nature, as we shall see, but it was Tibullus whom Sainte-Beuve called "le plus affectueux après Virgile, et le plus doux des Romains."[4] He appreciated "le sentiment large et naïf de la nature champêtre" in Tibullus. In fact Sainte-Beuve wrote in his notebook, as a dream of happiness: "lire Tibulle à la campagne avec une femme qu'on aime."[5] A poem of Malherbe reminded the critic momentarily of Tibullus, but he quickly explained that Malherbe was a royal poet, and neither bucolic nor elegiac.[6]

Propertius, Catullus, and sometimes Ovid are frequently mentioned by the critic in a group with Tibullus as careful artists in a personal vein, the Romantics of antiquity, as it were. The Virgil of the *Georgics*, who described so well the virile, practical Roman love of nature, struck a different note in the *Eclogues* where he took Theocritus as his guide and teacher.[7] In reviewing Professor Rossignol's book *Virgil et Constantin le Grand*, Sainte-Beuve was most impressed by the results of Professor Rossignol's detailed study of Theocritus's pastoral hexameter, which he called "l'âme de la poésie bucolique" and whose light, happy movement Sainte-Beuve exemplified by a line from Virgil,

Huc ades, o Meliboee! caper tibi salvus et hoedi.[8]

Sainte-Beuve also followed Professor Rossignol in defining exactly the difference between Theocritus and Virgil in the *Eclogues*, which are magnificent poetic artistry, but much more abstract and literary than realistic. These remarks were followed by the more normal and opposite comment based on a comparison between Tibullus and Theocritus. The Roman poet was more earthly and did not have the poetic phrase which opened a vision to the imagination. Before we turn to Theocritus, however, we should glance at another of Virgil's teachers, the Greek poet Euphorion.

In September 1843, Sainte-Beuve reviewed the *Analecta Alexandrina*, by August Meineke, in an article entitled "Euphorion ou De l'Injure du Temps." The introduction is at first sight another panegyric of German erudition, but is somewhat ambiguous, and the concluding sentences to the article allow another interpretation. At any rate, Sainte-Beuve chose Euphorion of Chalcis to exemplify the ancient poets whose works have been lost. In Euphorion's case we have titles of long epic poems, and knowledge of epigrams and of elegies celebrated for their tenderness. The irony of Euphorion's fate is double, since Virgil's friend the poet Gallus chose him as teacher or master, and Gallus's poetry is now also lost. "Bizarrerie de la gloire!" exclaimed Sainte-Beuve. It is only too easy to find consolation in judging these lost works inferior, but, asked the critic, would the resignation be so easy if the modern Alexandrians, Southey and Wordsworth, were wiped out? Or, taking an example in the other direction, a certain kind of everyday, realistic description in poetry seemed completely modern until Meineke's volume appeared with a poem by Parthenius of Nicea, of which Virgil's *Moretum* is a translation. At this point the critic recounts a nightmarish dream of being overwhelmed by the volumes of literature in the Bibliothèque Royale. He concludes his essay by saying that perspective on the past, a sense of proportion, is gained through such losses. If they are not sustained in modern times, contemporary authors will indeed survive, but almost *ex aequo,* undifferentiated by posterity and lost in the mass.[9] If the tender, graceful Euphorion had to be sacificed, however, in order to have Theocritus, it would not be difficult to guess that Sainte-Beuve would have made the sacrifice.

Theocritus was the first Greek writer that Sainte-Beuve read with his tutor when he began his study again in 1840.[10] Theocritus was also the subject of one of the first full-length articles he wrote on ancient authors. This article is well known and often quoted among classical scholars.[11] Maxime Leroy was inclined, however, to see Sainte-Beuve drawing the Greek poet toward himself and he quoted a note from *Mes Poisons* to the effect that all of the portraits are in some measure a portrait of Sainte-Beuve.[12] Two or three other comments in the same intimate notebook are even more explicit, both on the significance of Theocritus for Sainte-Beuve and, indeed, in crystallizing the explanation for the abundant refer-

The Bucolic Poets and Poetic Theory • 185

ences to this whole loosely related group of poets we have thus far termed "lyric." The first comment seems, at first reading, to be simply an objective observation, delightfully tempting to anyone with literary imagination as well as characteristic of Sainte-Beuve's later expressed thought on "la faculté maîtresse." He wrote:

> Toutes les âmes dignes d'être appelées des âmes ont en elles un sentiment dominant qui peut se représenter par un poète. ... Les autres ont le fond de l'âme élégiaque; Tibulle, Properce, Ovide les retiennent longtemps et leur suffisent: méfiez-vous pour eux de la langueur et des plaisirs.[13]

The two categories remain puzzling, for certainly the critic was not implying that elegiac souls belonged to an inferior category. Furthermore, what is general here became specific and explicit in another observation in the same notebook. The poet commented that Vauvenargues had an historical imagination, and added, "Moi, j'ai l'imagination élégiaque: mon idéal est le tableau de Tibulle:

> Quam juvat immites . . .

ou le tableau de Théocrite. . . ."[14]

One other notation in this notebook presents us with the logical conclusion to this line of thinking and the critic-poet's self-revelation:

> Une gloire poétique comme celle de Goldsmith ou Cowper serait la couronne de mes rêves.
> Goldsmith ou Cowper chez les modernes, Catulle ou Théocrite chez les anciens.[15]

Clearly, the whole climate of bucolic and elegiac poetry which Sainte-Beuve found in all these ancient poets concerned him much more directly and intimately than can be explained by simple literary taste and Alexandrianism. These were the poets whose literary expression most closely paralleled his own talent. He might admire and appreciate, even adore, Homer as a greater poet, but it was the elegiac poets that helped him develop his own talent and expression. In such circumstances, the portrait of Theocritus, quite naturally, is both sensitive and personal.

Sainte-Beuve began the long triple article by situating the great age of Greek poetry between Homer and Theocritus, "encadrée entre la grandeur et la grâce." Theocritus maintained his favor continuously with posterity and even merited an attack by Fontenelle at the time that Perrault was attacking Homer. But such an attack only proved a surprising fact, namely, that Fontenelle little understood the "verte et agréable beauté de la muse pastorale." Furthermore, Fontenelle had to admit that he was powerless against Theocritus's admirers. Turning to Theocritus's poetry, Sainte-Beuve pointed out that the idyll, by its mixture of ingenuousness and art, requires rather special conditions in order to thrive. Theocritus, born in Sicily, knew at first hand both the natural setting and the artless folk singing of the shepherds. At the same time, he was a man of great education and refinement, highly cultivated in Greek literature. In this exact combination, according to Sainte-Beuve, lay the source of his imagination: "cette condition de demi-vérité est peut-être la plus favorable."[16] He had imitators, to be sure, including Virgil himself in the *Georgics*, but Roman culture, on the whole, was not pastoral. In France the pastoral form had always been something factitious rather than the spontaneous outgrowth of a mode of life, for the French had never had a really pastoral civilization any more than the Romans had had. It is also interesting that the critic raised some question about the authenticity of some of the last of the thirty idylls, as well as the epigrams, for two

The Bucolic Poets and Poetic Theory • 187

reasons: first, only about the first half of the collection of poems is truly bucolic and justifies the poet's reputation for originality; secondly, the scholia, or ancient commentaries, do not go beyond about the midpoint of the work, as if the commentators believed that only some of it was by Theocritus.[17] But, Sainte-Beuve concluded, only the discovery of a new manuscript could resolve this problem, and meanwhile the last selections are not unworthy of Theocritus.

The critic divided the poems into three groups: the purely pastoral, in which Theocritus was the incomparable master; several selections, more elegiac than idyllic, in which Theocritus showed himself a first-rank portrayer of passion; and miscellaneous pieces from diverse genres, heroic, epic, and satiric, in which Theocritus seemed less original to his contemporaries. Throughout the essay Sainte-Beuve used his own translations of Theocritus in order to emphasize the points he was making. Frequently he was forced to observe that the translator was powerless to transmit a rhythm or a word relationship. The critic compensated for the shortcomings of translation by comparisons between Theocritus and other authors. He often juxtaposed Virgil's use of a line or image with Theocritus in the original.[18] Once he categorized a description as Homeric, then added, "on se rappelle irrésistiblement, à l'aspect de cette riche peinture, Rabelais et Rubens; mais ici on a de plus la pureté des lignes et la sérénité des couleurs." By translation, by comparison, the critic was attempting to define and make clear to his French public the particular characteristics of Theocritus's poetic talent.

The Sicilian poet's treatment of love was vastly inferior to that of Ovid who, in turn, was of little worth compared to Honoré d'Urfé, in Lamotte's opinion. Pointing first to the fact that the nineteenth century was freer to appreciate the simple unadorned energy of artistic portrayals of love than were the contemporaries of Lamotte and Fontenelle, Sainte-Beuve argued his own point of view, nevertheless, only by a brilliant analysis of the passionate Simaetha in Idyll II, sometimes called "The Magician." To this picture the critic added a short portrait of the pure and chaste Theugenis as an example of Theocritus's range. The concluding part of the long articles is a brief treatment of the theme of the power and worth of the poet. It is done almost entirely by evocative allusions to Horace, Sappho, Pindar, Lamartine, or Chateaubriand. The sympathetic tone of the entire article was summed up: "C'est, après tant de siècles, un honneur en même temps qu'un charme de l'aborder de près et de venir s'occuper de lui." The repeated references to Lamotte and Fontenelle underline the relativity of taste as well as the need to reread ancient poets at the source. The other theme implicit in this first one is, of course, the Quarrel of the Ancients and Moderns, the issue of imitation and originality argued so bitterly and so badly by the seventeenth and eighteenth centuries. Theocritus exemplified for Sainte-Beuve the truly original but nonprimitive poet, the poet who could combine artistic imagination, literary culture, and natural inspiration into a harmonious and original work of art.

The allusion to Pindar is interesting, for the nineteenth century brought something of a vogue for Pindar. His popularity seems to have stemmed, at least in part, from the renewed interest in "divine poetic fury," and Sainte-Beuve's occasional allusions or quotations of this sort might seem to indicate some positive reaction to, even a participation in, this vogue. The *Cahier de notes grecques* indicates that the critic made several attempts to read Pindar in Greek, but his real attitude toward the *Odes* was quite clearly stated in a letter to Aimé Camp in 1862. Pantasidès had evidently encouraged and helped the critic with the difficult Greek; as long as Pantasidès translated,

Sainte-Beuve recognized the beauty, the special elevation, and the "merveilleux éclat" of this genius, but "de moi-même je ne me sentais pas de force à recommencer le voyage et je revins vite me reposer avec le grand et le bon Homère dans les plaines d'Ionie."[19] Clearly it was not Sainte-Beuve who could explain Pindar's great poetry to the general French public. Nor did he try. The allusions are those of a person familiar with the poetry, but contain no special perception.

To Theocritus should be added, of course, the Latin elegiac poets, whom Sainte-Beuve knew well and loved to quote, as we have already seen. The whole range of Latin lyric poetry was familiar to the critic and came frequently to his mind to provide an enriching comparison, an apt allusion, a clarifying analogy for some modern or less well-known poet. Tibullus, Ovid, Catullus, and also the late Latin lyricists like Ausonius or Sidonius Apollinarius are frequently mentioned. One Latin poet, however, may be singled out from all the rest, as an object of the critic's predilection and even affinity. Indeed, the link between Horace and Sainte-Beuve is less one of literary appreciation or imitation than one of affinity of mind. Horace fulfilled the role of companion, friend, and frequent inspiration. Many a critic has said with M. Regard, "Cet Ancien si curieusement semblable à lui."[20] In his long career, however, Sainte-Beuve wrote only one short article on Horace in which, after a brief sketch of the poet's fortunate life, he pointed out that Horace's great original work among the Roman and modern poets was as a lyric poet. It was Horace who adapted the Greek lyric meter to Latin, and it was also Horace who first wrote great Latin satire, using as his vehicle the free epistle form. But, above all, continued Sainte-Beuve, "c'est cette qualité raisonnable toute fois, ce bon sens qui fait d'Horace un lyrique d'ordre à part."[21]

Clearly Sainte-Beuve had no wish to denigrate in any fashion Horace's poetic talent, but for him, the distinguishing feature, the real originality of his poetic talent, rested on a particular view of life.[22]

In 1855, when he wrote this slight article, Sainte-Beuve had long been preoccupied by the encroachments of the modern scientific and industrial world on the aristocratic, humanistic culture of France. The note is muted and in a major key here: as antiquity gradually fades from the modern education and culture, Horace may well stand as a single symbol of the civilization of antiquity as a whole. The measured poet provides an easy access to the grace of antiquity, and this fact may well explain why he has been held in even greater esteem by modern readers than by his own contemporaries, who were a part of the culture he represents for us. In Horace we do not deviate from our own habits, and yet we grasp antiquity through him: "on revient à lui en vieillissant et en redevenant soi-même plus faible et aussi plus sensible." The critic then traced, in a brief but concretely allusive fashion the history of Horace's reputation among French literary men from the Renaissance to his own day. On arriving at the nineteenth century he was forced to note the disdain for Horace among the Romantics generally and by Lamartine in particular. But, he reasoned, men who sought elevation and the heroic view of life in their poetry would react in this fashion to Horace. "D'autres poètes de nos jours," continued the mature critic, "plus fidèles à la mesure humaine et à notre limite d'horizon, se sont moins éloignés d'Horace, et quelques-uns même ont essayé de traduire en vers, ou, qui plus est, de produire à la scene telle de ses odes gracieuses, étincelantes."

Making an allusion to Musset's plays, Sainte-Beuve seems also to be remembering his own *Joseph Delorme*, which bears certain external resemblances to Horatian poetry. The humble anti-heroic landscape of *Joseph Delorme*, set against the pomp of Restoration society, is somewhat analogous to the Horatian ideal of the simple life in contrast to the brilliance of the Augustan court. One major difference, nevertheless, resulted in a totally different poetic effect: Joseph Delorme aspired to something beyond his present reality and was morbidly unhappy in his dull scenery, while Horace's note may be ironic or without illusion, but it is essentially positive, and often openly happy. The peaceful urbanity that is responsible for much of the Horatian charm is lacking with Joseph Delorme. Sainte-Beuve, not Joseph Delorme, wrote a sonnet in 1829, under the protection of a Horatian epigraph, which expressed a very Horatian preference for a peaceful, middle-of-the-road life. The poem "Mes livres" in *Joseph Delorme*, humanist in inspiration and Horatian-humanist in form, led Gerald Antoine to note "un fond permanent de classicisme, de délicatesse de goût"[23] which might be more strictly defined as a permanent affinity for the Horatian view of life. The least favored of Sainte-Beuve's poetic volumes, both by contemporary and subsequent critics, has been *Les Pensées d'août*, which has been summarily dismissed as "prosaic" and "lacking in inspiration,"[24] and which evoked from J. J. Ampère the comparison with Horace's Letters "par un lien de parenté poétique sans ombre d'imitation."[25] Ampère seems to have had in mind a similar lack of clarity or precision in the two volumes. One could also add, as a quality reminiscent of Horace, the frequency of the epistle form in the *Pensées*, but the tone is really quite different from the gentle urbanity of Horace. The "whine"[26] of Joseph Delorme is still present, and, indeed, the nonacceptance of reality is a unifying note in all of Sainte-Beuve's poetry. The letter to Villemain covers over the poet's dissatisfaction with his friend by a rather thin veneer of Roman urbanity, and the allusion to "Ad Pisones" makes Sainte-Beuve's poem seem only more of a pastiche of the Roman poet. Sainte-Beuve felt things too strongly to have the real Horatian tone. His affinity for Horace can hardly be considered poetic, and even less as an example of poetic imitation. Sainte-Beuve's poetry simply is not Horatian except in a very few superficial details.

The affinity arises rather from the *aurea mediocritas* view on life, Sainte-Beuve's tendency toward taking a position between two extremes. He was Romantic but not as frenetic as Hugo; he was an artist, but certainly not to the logical conclusion of Théophile Gautier or the Goncourts. Late in life Sainte-Beuve said as much in a letter to M. Louis Dépret: "Je suis resté malgré tout, de l'école classique, de celle d'Horace, du chantre de la forêt de Windsor, et même en n'y mettant plus tant de passion, je reste obstiné par ce côté de mon esprit et dans ce for intérieur de mon sentiment."[27]

Starting from this sentence, Professor MacClintock has studied carefully the relationship of Sainte-Beuve and Pope,[28] noting also, at the outset of his article, Sainte-Beuve's "native kinship with Horace." Professor MacClintock's study is illuminating on this point, however, in his conclusion that Horace, Boileau, and Pope represent for Sainte-Beuve the "common-sense" school of criticism, and he further notes that even in the early period Sainte-Beuve had constantly made reservations and concessions in the direction of this common-sense literature.[29] The major point of Classic versus Romantic must be put aside for the moment, however, in order to focus our attention more clearly on questions of identification, influence, and poetic theory. What Maxime Leroy saw as unconscious identification with Theocritus certainly rose to the conscious level with Horace, and yet there are only scattered, if consistent, concrete points of contact where the influence of Horace's poetic technique or philosophy is clearly evident. The poet-critic's interpretation of poetic inspiration is obviously important to a clearer understanding of Sainte-Beuve's real relationship with the ancient bucolic poets.

Pinpointing Sainte-Beuve's exact position in the evolution of the concept of poetry from the neoclassic Horatian concept of *ut pictura poesis* to the Baudelairian Symbolist concept is difficult, to say the least, yet is highly important to the present study. The problem has, in the past, been complicated by the natural tendency of critics to draw Sainte-Beuve in either direction according to the conception under discussion. Baudelaire's statement of indebtedness to Sainte-Beuve and "Les Rayons jaunes" have made Sainte-Beuve a kind of proto-Symbolist for some, while his own statement about Boileau and Pope, quoted above, frequently appears as evidence of an essential, if tardy, neoclassicism.

Although the *Pensées de Joseph Delorme* are too fragmentary to compose a developed essay on poetic theory, they do make clear the orientation of the poet's thought. Madame de Staël's insistence on emotion as the source of true poetic inspiration appeared to him too evident to need further discussion. He differentiated between what he termed the de Staël school of prose writers and the Chénier poetic school only on the point of preoccupation with technical facture—versification—rather than on the basis of theory of inspiration.[30] In commenting on versification, "on ne prétend pas contester la prééminence des sentiments et des conceptions." In a later comment (VII) Sainte-Beuve characterized Lamartine's poetry as "exprimant ce qu'il y a de plus rêveur et de plus inexprimable en l'âme humaine . . . " with no care for form. The end of this same thought, however, clarified somewhat obliquely Sainte-Beuve's own preoccupation with verse technique:

> C'est précisément à mesure que la poésie se rapproche davantage de la vie réelle et des choses d'ici-bas, qu'elle

doit se surveiller avec plus de rigueur, se souvenir plus fermement de ses religieux précepts, et tout en abordant le vrai sans scrupule ni fausse honte, se poser à elle-même aux limites de l'art, une sauvegarde incorruptible contre le prosaïque et le trivial.[31]

Such a statement does not imply a dichotomy between the poetic idea and its expression (external ornament), but rather refers to the magic ability of poetry to evoke emotion, which must be a part of poetry even while the formal subject matter loses this magic quality by proximity to daily reality.

In Pensées XIII and XIV, Sainte-Beuve compared Delille's neoclassical descriptive poetry with that of Chénier and his followers. His praise for Chénier springs from the fact that the poet combines realistic, picturesque language with more indefinite, suggestive terms. Concluding Pensée XIV, Sainte-Beuve characterizes Chénier's style in a metaphor of a great verdant forest full of new flowers, fruits and leafage, grasses of all colors and song birds of diverse plumage "et çà et là de soudaines échappées de vue, de larges clairières *ouvrant des perspectives mystérieuses et montrant à nu le ciel.*"[32] Such picturesque, descriptive poetry is not an end in itself, but, rather, a means to an expanded vision beyond the confines of earthly nature. This metaphor became fully explicit and the central point of the last Pensée (XVIII), so frequently quoted by Baudelaire critics for its conception of a symbolic poetry. M. Antoine has pointed out that the idea is not original with Sainte-Beuve, that it follows closely the beginning of the preface to Hugo's *Odes et Ballades* published some six years earlier. Priority is of no importance in the present discussion, however, for the question is only to define Sainte-Beuve's conception of poetry and the function of the poet. The pertinent issue is that despite the confused discussion about local color and the use of concrete words, which seems to imply a fundamentally Aristotelian-Horatian mimetic concept of poetry, Sainte-Beuve's thought has evolved beyond both Aristotle and the Staël-Chénier concept of emotional reaction to the external world as the source of poetry to a concept rooted in the poet's imagination, in which the external world serves to open unseen visions. Perhaps his clearest definition from this same period can be found in the *Tableau*, where he completely united matter and form: "Le vers, en effet, selon l'idée que nous en avons, ne se fabrique pas de pièces plus ou moins étroitement adaptées entre elles mais il s'engendre au sein du génie par une création intime et obscure."[33] His own success in *Joseph Delorme* from this point of view was almost completely lost to his contemporaries.

Equally important with this early expression of a conception of poetry resulting from creative imagination, which is inherent in the last Pensée of the *Joseph Delorme*, was the obviously personal description of the poet, overwhelmed rather than inspired by life, who hunts distraction in technical details, in formal and stylistic analysis, which will one day strengthen and free his inspiration " . . . et par degrés à propos de la manière d'exprimer les choses il se sentira bientôt rendu au sentiment des choses exprimées."[34]

Now, it is commonplace to comment on Sainte-Beuve's fragile poetic talent, which quickly dried at the source, and M. Antoine sees the text above as evidence of the critic showing through the poet. But what is more important to our discussion is that the poet, lacking inspiration, turned to analysis, form, the poetry of others, as a means of filling his time and, hopefully, of touching off new inspiration. We have already seen in our discussion of translation that Sainte-Beuve's verse translations are characterized by changes, and frequently by additions to the original. The poet-translator takes off on his own to create his personal version of the poem he is translating. It is little wonder that after the *Joseph Delorme* the thin new volumes of poetry contain more translations and more apparently imitative verse. Professor Lehmann aptly remarked, in discussing the very real originality of the *Joseph Delorme*, that "Sainte-Beuve as a poet was—paradoxically—stifled by the Cénacle."[35] When, in the *Tableau*, therefore, the young critic divided poets into two categories: "les poètes primitifs et les poètes studieux," he was reflecting a train of thought very much in the air at the time and following Herder's definition of *Nature-Genius*, as Madame de Staël and the Schlegel brothers introduced it in France. In the article on Racine, where he opposed the two types of poets, he not only followed this train of thought, but also, half unconsciously, gave a personal interpretation to the difference between two different kinds of genius. The personal interpretation was to crystallize gradually and remain with him to the end of his life. But it is important, from the beginning, to keep clearly in mind that Sainte-Beuve is distinguishing between two kinds of *genius*, not between genius and talent in the eighteenth-century tradition.[36] In the 1829 article on Racine, then, Sainte-Beuve contrasted the two types of genius quite apart from any question of genre. There are first the "poètes primitifs, fondateurs, originaux sans mélange, nés d'eux-mêmes et fils de leurs oeuvres": Homer, Pindar, Aeschylus, Dante, Shakespeare. Then there is a second type of genius, "studieux, polis, dociles, essentiellement éducables et perfectibles des époques moyennes": Horace, Virgil, Tasso. The latter group is more accessible and appreciated, despite their not attaining the heights of the first group whose members, by the fecundity and god-given quality of their genius, spend it prodigally, fully, without fatigue or calculation. They create their sublime monuments by internal law and a powerful original gift, whereas the second group needs favorable surroundings, study, reflection, silence, and revision to bring forth a finished, harmonious, lucid masterpiece.[37]

Six years later, in another major article on a seventeenth-century classic author, Sainte-Beuve came back to this definition of "le poète primitif" to refine it and make it considerably more precise. In this article on Molière, he put aside the "poète studieux" to consider only the natural, or primitive, poet. The true, original genius, according to Sainte-Beuve, is a very rare occurrence; there are perhaps five or six in all of western literature. The new, further distinguishing characteristics of the small group begin with "l'universalité, l'humanité éternelle intimement mêlée à la peinture des moeurs ou des passions d'une époque." In Greek literature Homer is assured of a place, of course, but Sophocles, despite his fecund and human genius, remains too narrowly Greek, as does Aristophanes. Menander, on the other hand, belonged to the small group of universal geniuses. Among the Roman writers, only Plautus would qualify as truly original. The Renaissance, however, brought a flowering of this special kind of genius in Shakespeare, Cervantes, Rabelais, and Molière.[38] Sainte-Beuve continued by making a formal distinction between this group and other fertile, facile geniuses who remain secondary to the universal group. The works of the truly universal natural poet "sont encore combinées, fortes, nouées quand il le faut, achevées maintes fois et sublimes." But this achievement is never for them "le souci quelque fois excessif, la prudence constamment châtiée des poètes de l'école studieuse et polie des Gray, des Pope, des Despréaux." They have in their perfection a quality—something freer and bolder, something "qui se joue, qui étonne et déconcerte par sa ressource inventive les poètes distingués d'entre les contemporains." In short, there is, according to Sainte-Beuve, a kind of "natural form," which the great genius creates for himself and his expression, that provides a formal beauty but one inherent in the work itself rather than being prescribed from the outside.

The critic further nuanced the whole definition by pointing out explicitly that such poets are not truly primitive in the folklore sense; rather, they occupy a median position between the Homeric and Alexandrian epochs. They read, compare, imitate, like their contemporaries; "cela ne les empêchent pas de créer comme aux âges naissants." Within the main classification of "poètes primitifs," as opposed to "poètes studieux," there are then several categories in the former class: first of all, the true *primitif* of the Homeric epochs, secondly, the *primitif* who possesses universality in addition to fecundity and facility, and form that is spontaneous or unconscious in its creation, and thirdly, *primitifs* who are fecund and facile but lack the consummate qualities of the previous groups. This definition of primitive genius marks a noticeable refinement in meaning for the term which was so commonly and loosely used by the critic's contemporaries. He continued to use the term in his critical writings without any significant deviation from this meaning. Toward the end of his life, however, he did make explicit one point that is implicit in the Molière article and which is of some importance to the present discussion of poetic inspiration. In 1865 he wrote, "Je suis bien certain qu'Homère imitait déjà un autre Homère plus vieux que lui." This statement, postulating Homeric predecessors, implies not only that Homer is *primitif*, by internal evidence to be noted in his work, but also that *historically* no predecessor can be found. Quite apart from the Homeric aspect of this statement, Sainte-Beuve has arrived at a positive statement of disbelief in spontaneous natural genius outside a cultural tradition. Whatever temporal value may have been implied in the 1835 categories differentiating the first two groups was gone by 1865.[39] The first two categories have fallen together. What remains is a difference in quality of originality. Homer, Dante, Shakespeare, Molière, all belong to the category by the originality of their genius, which created its form of expression as well as its vision of the universe. What is more important to the clear understanding of Sainte-Beuve's thought is that the 1865 statement merely makes explicit and unequivocal a point of view that lends itself to possible confusion in 1835. From his earliest period Sainte-Beuve found it illogical for modern cultured writers to pretend to a primitive ideal. He tended to see the Romantic school in historic perspective and, as Miss Gilman noted, saw revival where Hugo saw revolt.[40] He also tended to interpret his own period, in Hegelian terms, as a synthesis of the Renaissance and the age of Louis XIV and, as he preferred to call it, Alexandrian. This pronounced strain of historicity led him to interpret natural genius as a matter of innate character rather than of either historic period or cultural level of the society.

Personally, Sainte-Beuve recognized that his own poetic gift was not at all that of natural genius. Just a few months after the Molière article he wrote to his friend Victor Pavie almost nostalgically: "Le plus grand des plaisirs pour quiconque est un peu artiste, c'est la fertilité et la fréquence de la création."[41] Such moments were no longer frequent for Sainte-Beuve. He could hardly help but recognize that he belonged with that other group of poets, "les poètes studieux," Virgil, Racine, the writers who were *consciously* aware of maintaining a literary tradition. The affinity for Pope and Horace now becomes clearer. The important point is that when Sainte-Beuve divided poetic genius into "primitif" and "studieux" he was not opposing creative imagination to neoclassic imitation, as it would first appear. Rather, he was classifying two different types of poetic imagination: one, stimulated by the external world, created a new vision of that external world in a personal form; the other received at least part of its impulse from an existing literary or artistic tradition. However, the magnitude of success of poets of this second type results, in Sainte-Beuve's judgment, not from the perfection of their art, as in neoclassic doctrine, but rather from the original authenticity of the vision.[42] From this point forward, the critic's major interest was to be concentrated on a problem logically resulting from his dual form of classification and his self-knowledge, that of originality in humanistic writers. What, in essence, distinguishes a Virgil or a Racine as a creative poet? Where does his *originality* lie? For, even among the "poètes studieux," originality or the personal vision is, as we have seen, the measure of success and art.

In Sainte-Beuve's articles on humanistic authors the principle of creation is an ever-present theme. Racan's imitation of Horace's "Beatus ille qui procul" fails as an imitation because the French poet did not comprehend the irony in the Latin poem. It succeeds, however, as a French poem through its uniformly rustic and naïve tone, which gives the poetic theme a new and original expression. In this change Racan "a retrouvé par ce côté non la supériorité, mais une originalité en face d'Horace."[43] Barthélemy's *Télémaque* is a re-creation rather than an imitation of antiquity, but even as re-creation it is not scientific or intense; it is, rather, "naïf et naturel, libre transformé et refait insensiblement . . . adoucie et non altérée . . . fontaine abondante et facile, une fontaine toujours sacrée."[44] Remembering the definition of natural given in the 1835 article on Vigny, we note particularly the consistent use of the adjectives "naïf" and "naturel" to describe the originality of the French poems. The poet Parny is, in Sainte-Beuve's opinion, a good example of a less successful poet whose efforts result in mere imitation. His "Fragment from Alcaeus" is "transparently Greek." Parny lacks Chénier's assiduousness to combine taste, erudition, and the lessons of the masters of the Eolian lyre.[45] Incidentally, Sainte-Beuve says clearly elsewhere that Chénier, like Chateaubriand, adored antiquity but was not dominated by it. Mérimée too attained "quelques accents des Anciens" in *Colomba*,[46] which could hardly be viewed as neoclassic. Apropos of *Télémaque*, again, the critic pointed out that a pure ancient style in modern times would inevitably be artificial and something of a pastiche. In other words, perfect imitation would not be poetically effective.

The most elaborate, most detailed development of this line of thought in Sainte-Beuve criticism found its expression in the *Etude sur Virgile*. From the very first lecture, when he outlined his proposed point of view for considering the work of the great Latin poet, he explicitly said that he intended to recall the procedures of Virgil's genius, and to give an account of the principles of Virgil's inspiration as seen in his most monumental and carefully-composed work, the *Aeneid*. Sainte-Beuve notes, specifically, that Virgil borrowed from, imitated, and, to a certain extent, even in his creation, merely "transplanted" Homer, but that in him, apart from all that, lay "l'inspiration romaine profonde et l'à-propos national," which should never be forgotten and which is one of the major original creative qualities of the poem.[47] In short, Virgil wrote a poem in the fullest sense of the word, "quelque chose de libre et d'inspiré, de combiné en vertu d'éléments secrets dont nul ne sait tout à fait ni les proportions ni les mystères."[48] He was not only more than an imitator of his literary ancestors, but also more than a mere imitator of the external world around him. He created by an inspiration containing secret and mysterious elements; his work is a product of genius as truly as the *Iliad* or the *Odyssey*. In a curiously delicate passage in the fourth chapter, where he concretized further the constituent elements of Virgil's genius, Sainte-

Beuve defined unequivocally his concept of creative genius in the humanistic poet:

> Cette imitation des livres et des auteurs, à ce degré de sentiment et avec une si vive reflexion des beautés, est *encore une manière de naturel; c'est le sang qui parle;* ce ne sont pas des auteurs qui se copient, *ce sont des parents qui se reconnaissent et se retrouvent.*[49]

This language is vastly different from the rationalistic imitation theory of the neoclassicists. Implicit in Sainte-Beuve's statement is the unconscious "blood-call" of a *mythos*. The sentence following, nevertheless, returns to a principle of pure intellectual pleasure on the part of the reader, quite external to the deeply mysterious affinities of the creator.[50]

What our study of Homer has already shown, namely, the marked predilection for the Greek poet, has not changed. In the *Etude* Sainte-Beuve again made explicit his personal preference for the Homeric genius, but he also stated his critical opinion that the nineteenth century needed a corrective to the cult of the spontaneous, undisciplined genius. He did this by repeatedly insisting on the artistic qualities of another type of poetic genius, that of the humanistic poet, such as Virgil. The central point of importance in this whole discussion is that, in Sainte-Beuve's opinion, the mysterious action of genius is essential to the creation of a true work of art, but that there are at least two major types of temperament among such creators. Exaggeration in favor of either type by the public or the critics will inevitably stultify the other creative temperament. Through a long and seemingly digressive discussion we have come back to an essentially Horatian concept—an *aurea mediocritas* in literary taste—but we are far from any concrete Horatian concept of literature. The ordinary nineteenth-century idea of genius as something always spontaneous is revised to include those poets who find their best inspiration in the reading and study of other poets.[51]

The Bucolic Poets and Poetic Theory • 203

In an earlier article on l'Abbé Barthélemy (1852), Sainte-Beuve had already expressed this same idea in a simpler form. He had traced the history of the French idea of Greece and imitation, noting the emphasis of different generations of humanistic poets and their varying degrees of success. His conclusion was concise and revelatory: one literature can not be transported into another any more than the characteristic genius of a people and its language can be transplanted. Much reading of Greek literature will bring understanding, but "pour en tirer quelque chose dans l'usage courant et moderne, le plus sûr encore est d'avoir du talent et de l'imagination en français."[52] A full decade after the *Etude sur Virgile*, his statement was again unequivocal and even more far-reaching in its implications. He expressed his pleasure in rereading the ancients, who add humanity to art, but said in the same sentence that one cannot always "s'inquiéter à tout jamais des Anciens. Aussi-voudrais-je que l'artiste ne s'en souvînt que de loin, pour lui-même et pour sa gouverne; sans le laisser paraître."[53]

Before leaving the subject of Sainte-Beuve's special interest in Greek and Latin poetry, which led to the central idea of his concept of poetic creation and originality, it is pertinent to look for a moment at his reading of ancient rhetoricians. The quality of his critical thought, practical rather than systematic, is evident in the paucity of his attention to the conceptual thought of the ancient rhetoricians. Sainte-Beuve tended, rather, to regard them as critics of literature, who could provide him, on the one hand, with factual information about ancient authors or, on the other hand, as critics whose procedure was worth noting for what he may gain for his own procedures.

There can be little doubt that Sainte-Beuve was quite familiar with the Platonic conception of art; he refers several times to the position of the poet in the Platonic scheme, and he quotes Plato directly several times, but he had probably read parts of Cousin's translation, for there is no evidence of any Greek reading, and there is none, likewise, that Sainte-Beuve had any part in, or even taste for, the Platonic vogue that resulted from Cousin's translation and teaching. It was Aristotle, rather, who provided the kind of scientific rational basis for criticism which Sainte-Beuve sought. Aristotle was "un génie directement observateur et original, critiquant l'objet de ses expériences ou de ses lectures, et aspirant à découvrir les vraies lois."[54] The rationalism of Aristotle was cited in contrast and in preference to the Christian spiritualist bias in literature. When this rationalist spirit was overwhelmed by second-century credulity, the loss necessitated the long slow rediscovery of "cette méthode d'examen et d'analyse, la seule vraie, la seule capable de mener à bien l'esprit humain dans la voie du progrès et des connaissances positives."[55] Here and there Sainte-Beuve found this kind of erudition and criticism among his contemporaries. Fauriel, "né d'une école philosophique, d'une école déjà plus psychologique qu'idéologique, c'est un critique au vrai sens d'Aristote, qui parle chez nous pour la première fois."[56] Littré, too, had Aristotle's high view and Gandar possessed "du sérieux et de l'affection en tout, de cet approfondissement attentif et pénétré, quelque peu étranger à la nature française et que les Allemands qui se l'arrogent expriment très bien par le mot Gründlichkeit, réalisant encore l'idée du σπουδαῖος d'Aristote, l'homme vertueux et non léger."[57] For Sainte-Beuve, then, it was Aristotle's method of attack, his solid rationalism, and his penetrating observation which were the continuing motivations for reading his work rather than the systematization of his observations on literature which had so attracted Sainte-Beuve's predecessors.

Longinus, Quintilian, and Cicero were frequently quoted,

but as critics rather than as theorists of poetry. Sainte-Beuve frequently linked together these three names into a group which he called the "admirative critics," whose emotion and eloquence has its place in criticism. Their admiration was, however, based on completely personal, direct impression "qu'ils confondent d'ailleurs avec la donnée traditionnelle." Sainte-Beuve contrasted in this same passage the historic and rationally inductive method of Egger as being more appropriate to modern literary criticism.[58] In a clever, brief history of ancient criticism, done as a pastiche of Saint-Marc Girardin's method, Sainte-Beuve delineated both his respect but also his essentially different concept of criticism from that of the Rhetoricians, however meticulous, attentive, and serious they were.[59] He made this distinction clear in a more positive fashion when he outlined his own critical procedures and said, "Je ne renonce pas à Quintilien, je le circonscris." Baconian rationalism seemed to Sainte-Beuve the foundation for surer judgment and taste.

Despite the differences in concept of criticism on both a practical and philosophic level, Sainte-Beuve took special care to read the ancient commentary on Homer, the *Greek Anthology*, Theocritus, and others of his favorite poets. We have already seen that he particularly appreciated Plutarch as "une mine féconde"; it is not surprising, therefore, to have him quote Aristarchus, Dionysius of Halicarnassus, or Dion of Chrysostome on Homer. In similar fashion he quoted Calpurnius on Theocritus. Such reading frequently provided him with helpful suggestions about ancient interpretations of the text in question and hints about its cultural context. Both of these points, as well as the careful search for information about the poem and author, were important to his own critical procedure. One looks in vain, nevertheless, for discussion of the ancient ideas on poetic inspiration, divine fury, or creation. For these concepts Sainte-Beuve never really went farther back in history than the Renaissance.

Sainte-Beuve's admiration for the theory and aspirations of the Pléiade poets, with their doctrine of poetic creativity enriched by study and "innutrition" from other literatures, never faltered. At the same time as he admired this theory, however, he realized the shortcomings of their literary products, and in 1827 warned his fellow Romantics against the pitfalls of overclose imitation. In the last series of articles on Du Bellay Sainte-Beuve returned again to admire, nostalgically this time, as a characteristic of a past era, the Pléiade humanistic theory, or what he called "true classic imitation," practised by poets up through Racine.[60] This consistent admiration should not be confused, however, with complete acceptance of the results. What Sainte-Beuve put forth as Romantic theory in 1827 had not been generally accepted and followed; hence, the nostalgia of 1867. At both moments, however, the affinity for the Pléiade stemmed from a basic agreement on the assumption of poetic creation. Sainte-Beuve deviated less in the evolution of his own thought from 1827 to 1867 than did the world around him. From his youth he had conceived of Romanticism as a rich new spirit, venturesome but not wholly cut off from the literary tradition of the past. The critic's enthusiasm for Baudelaire was not a return to Romanticism but a recognition of the fulfillment of his own conception of Romanticism: Art is creation, not merely the formless effusion of emotion. In his maturity he was trying to evolve a synthesis of the best of French literary tradition without regard for terms like Romantic and Classic. His practical criticism became inevitably a variety of literary eclecticism, from a theoretical point of view. The recurring opposites in his synthesis were innovation and tradition.

Notes

1. Sainte-Beuve once suggested the possibility that a Greek poet learned from a Roman counterpart: "Je crois entrovoir du Properce à travers les flammes amoureuses de Paul le Silentiaire." *P.C.*, V, 422.
2. *N.L.*, II, 272–76.
3. *N.L.*, II, 278.
4. *P.L.*, III, 51.
5. *Mes Poisons*, p. 134.
6. *N.L.*, XIII, 393.
7. *P.L.*, III, 50.
8. *P.L.*, III, 49. Sainte-Beuve was quoting here *Eclogues*, VII, 9.
9. *P.C.*, V, 455.
10. *C.g.*, IV, 150.
11. See e.g.: W. C. Wright, *A Short History of Greek Literature* (New York: American Book Co., 1907), pp. 430 and 436.
12. *Oeuvres*, II, 1456, n. 9.
13. *Mes Poisons*, pp. 26–27.
14. *Mes Poisons*, p. 10.
15. *Mes Poisons*, p. 124.
16. *P.L.*, III, 5.
17. See: Albin Lesky, *A History of Greek Literature,* trans. James Willis and Cornelius de Heer (New York: Thos. Crowell Co., 1966). Mr. Lesky wrote (p. 721): "It still remains to be demonstrated that the body of tradition contains much that is spurious."

18. *P.L.*, II, 20-21. On pp. 22-23, Sainte-Beuve also suggested a parallel between the Comatas legend (Idyll V) and more than one medieval fabliau.
19. *C.g.*, XII, 360. See also: *C.g.*, XV, 411.
20. *Regard*, p. 154.
21. *EsV*, p. 435.
22. See: Jean Marmier, *La Survie d'Horace à l'époque romantique* (Paris: Didier, 1965). Professor Marmier set Sainte-Beuve apart from his Romantic friends because of his "sympathie inaltérable" (p. 47) for Horace. He also synthesized the results of his study of Sainte-Beuve and Horace. "Ainsi le double enrichissement dû à ses réflexions esthétiques et à ses expériences intellectuelles bénéficie à Horace" (p. 51). Professor Marmier's excellent and penetrating study unfortunately appeared after my paragraphs were written. The two accounts are taken from different vantage points but are in essential agreement I believe.
23. *Antoine*, p. 191.
24. See e.g.: André Bellessort, *Sainte-Beuve et le dix-neuvième siècle* (Paris: Perrin, 1954), pp. 90-96. See also: M. Allem, *Portrait de Sainte-Beuve* (Paris: Albin Michel, 1954), p. 318. "Les réserves traditionnelles faites sur les *Pensées d'août.*"
25. *C.g.*, II, 281.
26. Lehmann, *Sainte-Beuve*, p. 69.
27. (29 mars 1867). *Nouvelle Correspondance de C-A Sainte-Beuve, avec des notes de son dernier secrétaire* (Paris: Calmann-Lévy, 1880), p. 235. This very important sentence needs to be set beside the conclusion to the article on Taine's *Histoire de la littérature anglaise* (30 mai 1964) where Sainte-Beuve contrasted Balzac and Pope in regard to their kind of genius and creative imagination. He wrote in part:

> Vous nous invitez, vous nous obligez, à force de talent, à marcher avec vous vers le grand, le fort, le difficile, vers ce que nous n'aurions pas abordé à ce degré sans vous; mais aussi ne nous supprimez pas nos points de vue

habituels et agréables, nos paysages de Windsor et nos jardins de Twickenham. Agrandissons-nous du côté des hautes vallées et des hautes terres, mais gardons aussi nos riants domaines.

En un mot, n'allez pas donner raison à ce pessimiste qui me disait pas plus tard qu'hier encore: "le moment n'est pas bon pour Pope, et il commence à devenir mauvais pour Horace." [*N.L.*, VIII, 112-13].

Sainte-Beuve's concept of creative imagination was not exclusive; literary tradition contains many different kinds of genius, each to be appreciated in his own way.

28. Lander MacClintock, "Sainte-Beuve and Pope," *Publications of the Modern Language Association*, XLI (1926), pp. 442-52.
29. Ibid., p. 446. Professor MacClintock also says (p. 449): "Indeed, it would be an interesting and illuminating task to disengage the threads of this psychological and critical tangle in Sainte-Beuve's mind—his deprecatory, often patronizing tone toward certain writers whom he constantly and stoutly declared to be his own favorites." Professor MacClintock had earlier defined this opposition as between Romantic and classical authors. It is, indeed, important to try to disengage the threads to some extent. It seems important as a first step to differentiate quite clearly between Sainte-Beuve's reflections on critics and criticism and his remarks on poets and poetry.
30. Antoine, pp. 131-34. Pensée III.
31. *Ibid.*, p. 143.
32. Antoine, p. 147. The underlining is mine.
33. *Tab.*, p. 157.
34. Antoine, p. 151.
35. Lehmann, *Sainte-Beuve*, p. 73.
36. See: *Tab.*, p. 157 where Sainte-Beuve distinguished between genius and talent by saying "Ceux-ci [poets of talent] ne créent pas mais fabriquent, et tout leur main d'oeuvre se dépense à l'extérieur. Malherbe est de droit leur chef. . . ."
37. *P.L.*, I, 69-72. It is not totally irrelevant to note that Sainte-Beuve interprets Racine in this article as a lyric poet who

wrote tragedy because of his environment; that he was "déplacé dans le temps."
38. *P.L.*, II, 13. Dante was omitted in this list.
39. See: Carl A. Viggiani, "Sainte-Beuve (1824–1830): Critic and Creator," *Romanic Review*, XLIV, No. 4 (December 1953), pp. 263–72.
40. Margaret Gilman, *The Idea of Poetry in France; from Houdar de la Motte to Baudelaire* (Cambridge: Harvard University Press, 1958), p. 204.
41. *C.g.*, I, 528.
42. See *C.L.*, V, 145–67. Sainte-Beuve began his article on Le Brun-Pindare: "Ce poète *original* et incomplèt n'est pas indigne d'un souvenir." The critic used originality as his criterion throughout the article. See the conclusion (p. 166) where he again spoke of imagination.
43. *C.L.*, VIII, 79.
44. *C.L.*, II, 20.
45. *C.L.*, XV, 292.
46. *P.C.*, II, 496 ff. and *P.C.*, III, 492.
47. *EsV*, p. 64.
48. *EsV*, (See also: pp. 79, 82, 95–96.) This is the conclusion to a discussion to the effect that Virgil did not transfer Augustus Caesar and others into his poem as thinly veiled actors.
49. *EsV*, p. 95. The underlining is mine. See also the poetics of T. S. Eliot and Ezra Pound in the twentieth century.
50. See also: *EsV*, p. 85. "Et à leur tour les gens instruits sont heureux de retrouver dans une seule lecture le souvenir et le résumé de toutes leurs belles lectures."
51. The terms Romantic–Classic become quite impossible for exact use in this particular context, for either term draws in one direction and hence destroys the delicate balance of Sainte-Beuve's thought.
52. *C.L.*, VII, 218.
53. *N.L.*, X, 409.
54. *C.L.*, II, 47.
55. *N.L.*, IV, 401.

56. *P.C.*, IV, 196.
57. *N.L.*, XII, 372.
58. *N.L.*, VII, 44–45. Villemain was, in Sainte-Beuve's opinion, the outstanding modern example of the admirative type of criticism.
59. *C.L.*, I, 13–15.
60. *N.L.*, XIII, 295–301. See also the epilogue to the 1866 article on Racine, where Sainte-Beuve clearly defined the distance between seventeenth and nineteenth-century concepts of poetry, associating himself with his own century despite his almost exaggerated irony toward the end of his statements. *N.L.*, X, 390–92.

Chapter 5
The Active Campaign for Tradition

From each individual study attempted thus far there has repeatedly come into focus the portrait of a mind deeply interested in contemporary questions, in innovations, yet viewing them always in a historic context, not deterministically as affairs of cause and effect, but rather as elements in a natural continuity, a normal juxtaposition. Professor Levin, in his essay "Notes on Convention," has recently redefined the natural balance that exists in the arts between continuity and innovation: "If genius is distinguished by originality, convention is what originality is distinguished from . . . and we may well agree that convention without invention would be undesirable, but we seldom realize that the converse is unthinkable . . . . Whereas new movements are propelled by individual talents, the vehicle of convention is tradition."[1] As early as 1836 Sainte-Beuve created the striking visual image of the lame man whose good leg was restless and adventurous, whose lame leg was sturdier and more dependable, but each unable to walk alone, only in harmony with the other. These two legs are innovation and tradition.[2] Poetic creation, originality, innovation, must necessarily, therefore, entail a consideration of tradition. The critic's use of this latter word, moreover, was quite precise within any given context, although its meaning was not rigidly identical in all circumstances. Confusion has come into the understanding of Sainte-Beuve's interpretation of the idea through a tendency to make specious substitutions of synonyms.

When Ezra Pound wrote, "The tradition is a beauty which we preserve and not a set of fetters to bind us,"[3] he was perhaps not aware that he was echoing in an oversimplified form what Sainte-Beuve had written so many times. Pound's national literary heritage did not, moreover, include an overt intellectual battle on the very terms of his beautifully expressed antithesis. The usual chronology for the Quarrel of the Ancients and Moderns sets it in the late seventeenth and early eighteenth centuries. In 1866, however, Sainte-Beuve wrote that the question "est loin d'être épuisée et elle recommence toujours";[4] specifically, he cited the Goncourt brothers as resolutely modern, even antitraditional. The critic had earlier reviewed Rigault's great history of the Quarrel, treated Charles Perrault in two articles, and studied carefully the role of Madame Dacier. With Rigault, Sainte-Beuve agreed that a necessary condition for such a quarrel was a high point in modern civilization, which could reasonably compare itself with the great civilizations of antiquity. Sainte-Beuve also saw the quarrel as a constant of all ages, and wrote that each new generation has at least one advantage over its predecessors in that it is alive.[5] For Sainte-Beuve, nevertheless, the perennial Quarrel was essentially a false one, which could never be completely resolved because the discussions always turned on accidental rather than on essential points. Even Madame Dacier, whom Sainte-Beuve admired on the whole, had tried to defend Homer in the neoclassic terms of Lamotte's criticism with the result that each side misread or misinterpreted Homer in its own way.[6]

In two articles on Perrault, written just ten years apart (1851 and 1861), may be seen the complexity of Sainte-Beuve's own position and the confusion of issues in the Quarrel. Perrault's impelling force in the discussion at all times was the idea of "l'émancipation et . . . l'égalité moderne." His great weakness was that he did not understand poetry, and hence his reasoning was frequently inappropriate to the subject, but his objectivity and lack of emotional involvement permitted him to manoeuvre more cleverly against Boileau's heavy seriousness. The two men wrote without communicating; there were skirmishes, said Sainte-Beuve, but no confrontation, and he concluded finally that the Quarrel was false. "Dans ces assertions hardies de Perrault et dans les réponses que lui fit Boileau, ce qui me frappe, c'est à quel point ils ont raison l'un et l'autre, mais incomplètement et sans se répondre, sans presque se rencontrer."[7]

Ten years later Sainte-Beuve came back to the same antagonists, and this time he began by drawing parallel portraits of his authors. Each had his own indisputable genius, but they were opposite: Boileau, narrow and literary; Perrault, curious and open. Sainte-Beuve himself accepted Fontenelle's and Perrault's position on all but one point, that of Greek poetry. He accepted also their simile of organic civilizations as evolving like man through childhood, adolescence, youth, and maturity. In fact, it is only the Moderns' lack of indulgence, a certain vengeance they took in finding "errors" in ancient writers, that separated Sainte-Beuve from the earlier Moderns. In this same article, he gave his own instructions for reading the ancients:

> La vraie et juste disposition à leur égard est un premier fonds de respect, et tout au moins beaucoup

de sérieux, de circonspection, d'attention, une patiente et longue étude de la société, de la langue, un grand compte à tenir des jugements des Anciens les uns sur les autres, ce qui nous est un avertissement de ne pas aller à l'étourdie, de ne pas procéder à leur égard avec un esprit tout neuf en partant de nos idées d'aujourd'hui.[8]

Despite this counsel of long and patient preparation, however, the critic rejected categorically any idea of pretense in the matter of taste for the ancients, for, as he said, "ce serait donner de gaîté de coeur dans la superstition et l'idolâtrie."

The conclusion to his article on the *Anthologie grecque* in 1864 returned to the same subject, pointing out that if there were no longer open hostilities there were still two camps. The critic continued on a note of real confidence that historically, antiquity did not lose; Greece as the golden link in the chain of time was better classified and coordinated. He was less confident about direct sentiment and true familiarity with the sources, but he could only blame the circumstances of modern life for the change. One must learn to read the ancient authors early in life when memorizing is facile. Later on, life is too full of everyday problems to allow a true appreciation of the ancients. Sainte-Beuve concluded by quoting Dr. Thomas Arnold, to the effect that faith and humility are the prime requisites for a true appreciation of great art. To those who would point to the ever-expanding knowledge of modern society, the critic answered that modern preeminence in science, industry, and even in human ethics was only a further reason to keep alive the admiration for "cette beauté première, cette excellence parfaite dans son cadre et en ses contours limités." This was not to be done with a credulous enthusiasm, "mais un enthousiasme léger, clairvoyant, intelligent, divinateur et réparateur, qui n'est que l'émotion la plus délicate et la plus vive en face de tant de belles choses; accomplies une fois en leur juste cercle et à jamais disparues."[9] Here, as elsewhere, Sainte-Beuve's fundamental attitude is clear: respect for the ancients is fitting, but firsthand practice and knowledge of their works is even more important. The artist must maintain a complete independence of spirit, nevertheless, for the creation of his own art. It is in this context that Sainte-Beuve's estimate of the importance of tradition for the modern literary world must be understood. The Quarrel thus became specious and false. It was not, in Sainte-Beuve's mind, a question of choice; instead, there is a necessary but separate independent function of each side which must work in harmony together. Innovation and tradition are not antagonistic; Ancients and Moderns need to be fused.

A second interpretation of the meaning of tradition has brought confusing results by an equally unhappy equation of terms, innovation with Romanticism, tradition with Classicism. A number of studies in the last fifty years on various phases of the classicism of the Romantics, augmented by nineteenth-century interpretations of the great seventeenth-century literature in Romantic terms, have done much to nuance the bald, oversimplified opposition of the terms "Classic" and "Romantic." Individual critics, however, continue to apply the opposition to Sainte-Beuve and to see a marked break in his own thinking and career between an early Romanticism, before 1840, and a "classicisme élargi" in his maturity, particularly after the famous essay "Qu'est-ce qu'un classique?"[10] Nor did Ernst-Robert Curtius solve this problem, essentially because he maintained the historic opposition of the terms, but he did shed much light on the immediate matter of Sainte-Beuve by setting the whole question into the context of the special history of French literary criticism. He pointed out that French literature is the only modern literature in which the scholastic Classic-Romantic antithesis has any meaning, and that its meaningfulness in France is due to a historic national will to *systematic* regulation. According to Curtius, this will to systematic regulation was in full evidence at the beginning of the nineteenth century and was still being discussed in the twentieth century. He cited Paul Valéry as an example of a modern French mind which ran to this conformism, despite the relativism prevailing in his time as a result of the nineteenth-century discovery of other literatures. "The concept of a world literature," added Curtius, "could not but shatter French canon. Sainte-Beuve sensed the dilemma. He did not solve it."[11] Here would seem to be the crux of the whole problem and the source of confusion. The concept of a "dilemma" to be resolved obscures the true objective, that of a balance to be sought and maintained.

An awareness of this particular tendency to confusion is so important to the proper understanding of Sainte-Beuve's concept of tradition that a momentary digression in order to quote the critic's own remarks on the point will help to minimize specious contradictions later; it is evident that even many of the critic's contemporaries thought they saw an essential change in his position. His clearest and most explicit statement appeared in 1861, when he wrote that he had not become a classicist at his election to the French Academy.[12] His own redefinition of a classic, made in 1850, hardly needs mention here except to note that he rejected completely the idea of prescriptive regulation based on models as a means of attaining an original and lasting work of art, and added, "avant tout je voudrais n'exclure personne entre les dignes et que chacun y fût à sa place."[13] The neoclassical concept of a classic had been rejected in favor of simple consecration by time as a condition for awarding the term.

It is also important to set beside this famous essay a lesser-known one on Théodore Banville which was published in 1857. The publication of Banville's complete works gave Sainte-Beuve the occasion, which he had evidently been awaiting for two years, to respond to some remarks about the Romantics in Sacy's reception speech at the French Academy in 1855. Sacy had said in essence that Jay, whose chair he was taking, had not converted the Romantics, but that they, by their own talent and good sense, had seen the errors of their ways. Sainte-Beuve took exception to this historic conclusion on his own generation, and in the essay on Banville summarized in a penetrating, concise fashion the various definitions of Romanticism, and the diverse currents of its development, insisting, nevertheless, that however the group may have grown apart and apparently reconsidered their early enthusiasms, "ce signe persiste; il peut se dissimuler par instants et se recouvrir, il ne s'efface pas." At a moment of crisis or combat, at a moment of veritable choice, the members spontaneously realign themselves on the same side, whatever their present apparent groupings. "Voilà que vous vous retranchez dans le beau convenu et dans le noble, fût-il ennuyeux, et moi je me déclare pour la vérité à tous risques, fût-elle même la réalité."[14] Reduced to this final essence, Romanticism has many faces, some barely distinguishable from true classic art, but the similarities are accidental, according to Sainte-Beuve, while the difference is essential. In such terms the critic maintained his essential Romanticism, explicitly in 1857, and implicitly to the end of his life.

It would appear that we have come back to Curtius's opposition only to agree with it, but the conclusion is not quite so simple. The essential opposition established by Sainte-Beuve was also a reductio ad absurdum. In his own criticism he had always admired the poetic and moral truth in the works of Racine and Molière; in the very essay he was writing he admired the poetry of a Romantic, Banville, for its delicate renewal of Greek art. The key lies in the critic's definition of classicism in a passage in which he plainly described the late Neoclassic ideal prevailing during his youth, and the work that resulted. That ideal was based on an artistic system, and was indeed frequently tedious, but the Romantic school had rediscovered a Hellenic civilization whose regulated art expressed real and observed truth. From that moment on such an opposition of terms became hopelessly confusing, and in fact, any real opposition in aesthetic between "true" Classic and Romantic is only relative.

It is time to consider directly Sainte-Beuve's concept of tradition, which is one of the few terms that he took the pains to explain personally. His axiomatic premise, the existence of a tradition, was self-evident. His definition is quite typical, starting from a very broad concept, which by gradual refinement becomes more limited and precise, normally without cutting off any possible ramification. Tradition, according to Sainte-Beuve, is more than just the body of works assembled in libraries; it is also to be found in laws, institutions, customs, in all the hereditary and unconscious culture of a people; "elle consiste en un certain principe de raison et de culture qui a pénétré à la longue, pour le modifier, dans le caractère même de cette nation gauloise, et qui est entré dès longtemps jusqu'à la trempe des esprits."[15] So defined, Sainte-Beuve added, tradition is altered only at a nation's peril. This last point is equivocal, however, and must be balanced by a later clarification (1862) that the logical conclusion to passive fidelity to tradition is sterility.[16] Tradition, then, is the total accretion of the intellectual past, but is primarily characterized by a dynamic, living quality. Sainte-Beuve had once written that much serious thought about the past, with true comprehension, was, in point of fact, the proper way to think about the future.[17] Tradition is not identical with history, moreover, for tradition implies both an ideal and a choice, as well as a variety in its expression.[18] If the Renaissance poets had not chosen to close their eyes to Tristan, Lancelot, etc., as epic heroes "la tradition vive était retrouvée."[19] Here appears the practical, historic stricture to the critic's broad definition.

The total continuity of the intellectual heritage from Greece through Rome and Christianity to France, as outlined in "De la Tradition," oversimplified the literary history of France. A nation could turn its back on a part of its tradition, as sixteenth-century France had done and as Sainte-Beuve feared his own century was in peril of doing. The critic's note of urgency about the positive choice for the complete tradition sprang from a deep conviction expressed in one of his rare categorical statements:

> C'est une loi de l'esprit de l'homme que le passé doit profiter à qui vient ensuite et que le génie n'entre dans toute sa plénitude, dans l'entière possession de lui-même, que quand il ajoute l'héritage antérieur au sien, l'expérience des prédécesseurs à sa propre faculté inventive. Dans cette rencontre de la tradition et de l'originalité est le secret des grandes époques littéraires.[20]

What at first sight seems to be a direct contradiction of the all-encompassing definition of tradition by a narrow limitation to conditions appropriate to masterpieces found a parallel development in the essay on tradition, when on the one hand Sainte-Beuve granted primacy to Shakespeare, but at the same time managed to bring him into the Greco-Roman-Christian tradition. The essay on the Latin poets underlined Racine's poetic originality in his imitations, and Molière's in his Latin borowings independently of his own century's taste. Clearly,

The Active Campaign for Tradition · 221

for Sainte-Beuve the necessity of a continuous, dynamic tradition was broader than the Classic-Romantic opposition, for both of these latter groups belong to tradition and merely evolve from one to the other in an organic fashion.[21]

Sainte-Beuve had long been aware of the historic relativity of taste; he was equally aware that his own century had thus far established only one criterion, originality, as a means of judging literature. Tradition, then, was the counterbalance, and a whole canon resulted from the varying proportions of each. According to such a canon the very highest rank was allotted to a perfect balance of tradition and originality. Such a balance, he noted further, results from an inner and outer equilibrium between the poet and his society. Tradition, in this sense, then touches the cultural *mythos* of a nation freely accepted by the individual poet, even cultivated by him, to the end of fertilizing his own originality, of protecting it from frenetic aberration. Tradition alone, however, is totally unable to produce any great work of art without the vital creative force of genius.

Quite naturally Sainte-Beuve, in his criticism, tended to categorize authors by their attitude toward tradition. Nisard, for example, represented strict tradition, and Charles Magnin knew how to combine the new and the old. At times the term seems almost equivalent to knowledge in general, as when he wrote, "Gramer de Cassagnac n'a pas la tradition des choses dont il parle."[22] Rigault, on the other hand, "possède la tradition." The young generation of Taine "n'a pas reçu . . . la tradition successive," and hence its work becomes bookish and scientific. Finally, the portrait drawn by Sainte-Beuve of an ideal secretary for the Academy of Fine Arts included the quality that he be a man of tradition, ready to recognize change.[23]

In our attempt to reach the critic's concrete definition of

tradition we have been continuously hampered by his constant tendency to orient any discussion of the concept toward its function for the artist and for the nineteenth century. The fact that his major essays on the subject were directed, not to his general newspaper public, but to a select group of students, whose professional role in life Sainte-Beuve defined as "guardians of tradition," is an important but an insufficient explanation for the note of urgency in his defense of tradition. Quite beyond his role as a teacher, Sainte-Beuve viewed tradition, and particularly the Greco-Roman tradition which was, in his mind, at the source of all of French culture, as clearly in peril during the period of his maturity as a critic. The peril was further complicated by its multiplicity, for what no single enemy could do might be accomplished by simultaneous attacks from several sides.

As early as 1839 Sainte-Beuve had been seriously disturbed by the effects of modern industrialization upon literature and art in general. The sheer speed of production threatened to create an industrial society, devoid of any art or reflection, a civilization which had no time to consider its cultural tradition. "De la littérature industrielle" (1839) and "Dix ans après en littérature" (1840) are usually read as part of a final break with Romanticism, with the critic's Romantic friends, in particular Victor Hugo. The break with the Hugo is certainly clear, but Sainte-Beuve's mature position on Romanticism always had a distinct "girondin" quality.[24] The critic's argument in these articles, however, was not primarily for or against literary liberalism; it was against the industrialization of literature, the control of art by elements interested in monetary profit. After deploring the industrialization of literature itself, Sainte-Beuve proceeded to make a positive appeal to his Romantic friends to close their ranks against a common foe: facile, industrialized art of all kinds.

The critic did, however, declare two types of contemporary literature free from the encroachments of "big business" popularization, but quickly added that, although they formed an integral part of literary studies, they were not literature of the imagination. These two were critical studies fostered by the Académie des Inscriptions and university theses later developed into mature volumes. This literature had "dès longtemps sortie de la routine *sans perdre la tradition.*"[25] The second article, "Dix ans après en littérature," provided the constructive program for literature after the condemnation of its industrialization. It was a call to the quadragenarians who had been "le jeune siècle" to unite, without losing their individuality, in a "union conservatrice" to guarantee the fulfillment of the promise of their generation. Although he did not speak in his own name, Sainte-Beuve went on to propose "une critique nouvelle, et sans prétention de l'être, faisant digue au mal, refaisant appui aux monuments." The "call," as Sainte-Beuve termed it, was not a renunciation of his youthful ideas, but an appeal to the friends of his youth to unite against a peril to the tradition of French culture in a modern industrial world.

The picture of this active campaign against industrialized literature in the name of a cultural tradition would seem at first sight to lead the critic toward a concept of "art for art's sake," and, indeed, some critics have attempted to interpret some of Sainte-Beuve's earlier writings (ca. 1831) in this way.[26] Although Sainte-Beuve would perhaps have considered such a philosophy less of a fatal error than industrialization, he could not be long satisfied with so static and limited a concept of literature. His own campaign was carried on in periodical literature with a broad literate public and never included any sort of withdrawal from the problems of the world at hand.

A second major threat to tradition, in the critic's eyes, evolved from the exaggeration of a typically Romantic line of thought, the cult of primitivism, with the resulting confusion in literary taste and judgment. He recognized that although for his own century Greece was in style after the travel accounts of the 1820s, the developing interest in national tradition and folk literature, resulting in large measure from German erudition, led more directly to medieval studies than to Greco-Roman anitiquity. In 1862 Paulin Paris took Sainte-Beuve to task for judging the medieval mystery plays without reading them carefully. The critic answered with a jibe about a difference of opinion between the brothers Paris; the remark resulted a long letter of recrimination and explanation from Paulin Paris. Although Sainte-Beuve's answer was personal and particular, it stated clearly his attitude as a critic toward this newly rediscovered literature: "Je ne fais pas la guerre au moyen âge, je l'étudie. . . . Ce que j'ai imprimé depuis quinze ans est plein de ces témoignages d'attention . . . vous verriez que je tâche de me mettre au pas et de me tenir au courant."[27] For Sainte-Beuve the Middle Ages had created a form of art acknowledged by him to be a true manifestation of the human soul, not without beauty, but not comparable in "grandeur ou flamme du sentiment, éclat de l'expression et . . . harmonie de composition et d'ensemble" with that of Homer, Sophocles, or Euripides.[28] The critic's open, tolerant attitude avoided any judgments; the new enthusiasms were welcome, and enriching to tradition. He could even view them in a kind of absolute sense: "Je ne demande pas mieux que d'oublier la Grèce quand on me parle du moyen âge,"[29] but when enthusiastic scholars forced a comparison between Homer and the chanson de geste, his own critical acumen led him to make explicit his value judgments. It was in this same line of thought that Sainte-Beuve pointed out that

Fauriel's enthusiasm over Greek folk songs and early Provençal poems logically led him to prefer them to fully developed works of art.[30] We have already seen that Sainte-Beuve, in defining primitive genius, felt little nostalgia for some simple primitive past. Part of the miracle of Hellenic civilization, for Sainte-Beuve, was exactly the apparent paradox between its chronological date and its civilized sophistication. He took Volney to task for comparing the American Indians to the Greeks, and for different reasons he distinguished carefully between Firdousi and the Homeric epic. Other traditions, mythologies from the North, have played their part in forming modern man, but, insisted Sainte-Beuve, Greece is unique, not only for France, but for humanity. Rome was touched by Greece, the Christian Dante had Virgil as his guide, and in the century of Louis XIV Biblical grandeur and Hellenic beauty mingled in high simplicity. No great writer has been produced completely outside this tradition. Even Shakespeare, the great creative imagination, the "primitive genius," had been affected by this Greco-Roman-Christian tradition through Montaigne and Plutarch. Goethe, the greatest of the critics in Sainte-Beuve's opinion, was open and sympathetic, curious about all the varieties of beauty without losing himself in the indeterminate, because Olympus was his measure.[31] The necessity of determination in literary taste was broader in both its causes and its results than the single question of primitivism.

Sainte-Beuve frequently referred to his own generation as inadequately trained in antiquity, and this crisis in traditional education constituted the third threat to the national heritage. The same generation in both England and Germany had been more thoroughly grounded in ancient literatures ("la tradition"), but the French literary men had to get to the source by other means.[32] Though the critic never went as far as to see cause and effect between their education and their revolt against literary tradition, he did acknowledge in 1855 a break, and hence an uncertainty in judgment, because of "la nouvelle [tradition] n'ayant pris ni le temps ni le soin de s'établir."[33] In 1868, just before his death, Sainte-Beuve went even farther, and asked, "Qu'est-ce qu'elle est devenue cette tradition nouvelle; élargie, féconde, qui une fois nouée, devait se perpétuer et grandir pour l'honneur de la civilisation et de la libre intelligence?"[34] The threat that Sainte-Beuve had seen, almost thirty years before, in the opposition of two traditions, that of Greco-Roman civilization and the new ideal of various northern primitive cultures, ended in an almost complete negation of the value of both, as a result of the attempt to encompass too much too quickly.[35] The critic's increasing concern about the new trends in literature, and particularly about a valid critical concept by which to judge them, led him to make distinctions with regard to tradition.[36]

In his opening lecture at Liège he distinguished clearly between the critical and pedagogical functions in the maintenance of tradition. The teacher's position as guide, which permitted no truancy, required of him that he light up the principal monuments without prejudice, as far as possible, so that his students might enter into their cultural heritage. The critic, on the other hand, was free to follow his own instincts and diverse tastes. The critic, gifted with curiosity and an inclination to research, might at times revise severe judgments, correct inequitable preferences, bring about clarifications: "En un mot, on pourra par moments avoir l'air de harceler la tradition afin de la forcer à devenir plus complète et plus fidèle." Tradition formed a part of the education of every cultivated person, nevertheless, and at this level tradition was interpreted in the narrow sense. Once this Greco-Roman-Christian tradition was solidly grasped, new grafts could be made to enrich and render it dynamic, but the threat of a complete rupture with the past by default or excessive zeal was never absent from the mature thinking of Sainte-Beuve.

The fourth and last major threat to the French cultural tradition again presents a complex picture, because of the critic's apparent ambivalence. The threat was closely related to that of education and was at the opposite pole from the industrialization and democratization of literary production. It consisted in the whole new area of cultural research under the leadership of the German philologists. Sainte-Beuve never wavered on the principle of welcoming the new science of literary erudition, but he was also quite well aware of "les inconvénients aussi de ces nouveaux procédés, à une époque où il y a trop peu de haute critique surveillante et judicieuse."[37] The divorce between erudition and the cultivated reader was, in Sainte-Beuve's opinion, a serious threat to the maintenance of the national tradition.

Erudition was undergoing its own "industrial revolution," creating new specialities and specialists to the point that these latter spoke only to each other within their group. Sainte-Beuve had said as early as 1839, "L'érudition a bien peu de juges au soleil. . . . Les érudits restent entre eux, se dénigrant, se combattant, se louant, et se citant. Le public même éclairé, ne sait trop sur eux à quoi s'en tenir."[38] Almost twenty years later he reminded Taine "que le savant doit être artiste." Zeller merited the critic's praise, because "il a de bonne heure uni les deux esprits, celui de la recherche approfondie et de la science et, celui de l'exposition nette, claire et précise." And Rollin, completely outmoded in his criticism, still merited admiration for his ability to open a window between the university and the world. The problem of communication with a broader public was by no means restricted to classical scholarship, and Sainte-Beuve spoke even more sharply about it in reference to French literary history,[39] but since a true understanding of the Greco-Roman tradition was particularly threatened, the need for communication on the part of its adepts was singularly vital.

Sainte-Beuve had not renewed his series of articles on ancient authors after 1850, explaining publicly that such articles required a preparation and specialized knowledge which he did not have.[40] The problem was, moreover, not merely the limitation of his own knowledge, but also the fact that the literary scientists had developed "le culte des vieux papiers," even in modern literature. This mystique of the *inédit* tended to give inordinate value to minor rediscoveries, thus dislocating, temporarily at least, the focus for any real critical judgment of literature. Sainte-Beuve saw himself, as a result, being frustrated in his critical function as the intermediate interpreter between the erudites and the general public. The gap between the two groups continued to widen. In 1863 the critic closed his long and appreciative article on Boissonade, the eminent Hellenist of an earlier generation, with a plea to the new generation of Hellenists to abandon Boissonade's methods, to defend and revitalize antiquity "en rattachant les anciens le plus possible au train moderne . . . au progrès de l'esprit humain et de la civilisation elle-même."[41] The danger, according to Sainte-Beuve, was not positivist scholarship in itself; it was rather that, through lack of contact with the mainstream of nineteenth-century thought, classical scholarship might lose itself and finally dry up entirely, taking with it the rich French cultural tradition of over two thousand years.

Sainte-Beuve was, above all other things, a functional critic, an active journalist, and it is only normal that seeing so clearly the threats to the French cultural tradition he do something about it. For over twenty-five years he carried on an active campaign, less for the "maintenance of tradition" than for the creation of a dynamic tradition. This campaign was conscious, explicit and intentional, for, as he wrote at the beginning, tradition, "chose essentielle et vraiment sacrée en littérature . . . serait en danger de se perdre chez nous, si quelques-uns, comme élus et fidèles, n'y veillaient sans cesse et ne s'appliquaient à la maintenir!"[42] In 1850, early in the series of the *lundis,* he expressed a more positive program, saying, "Je voudrais aider avant tout à maintenir, à renouer la tradition, sans laquelle rien n'est possible en bonne littérature; et dès lors quoi de plus simple que de tâcher de renouer cette tradition au dernier anneau."[43] His ideal would be to conciliate traditional interpretations and new facts into a harmonious whole, "mais cette sagesse est rare; la mesure n'est la qualité et le don que de quelques-uns."[44] Several years later, in 1864, in the introduction to an article on Catinat, he defined his concept of the defense of tradition. He protested against the custom of casting all previous interpretations aside to begin anew "on new evidence." "Pour mon compte," he wrote, "je respecte la tradition, et j'aime la nouveauté; je ne suis jamais plus heureux que quand je parviens à les accorder et réconcilier ensemble." Then, in the military language of a siege, Sainte-Beuve went on to say that if the new evidence succeeded in breaking a gaping hole in tradition's defenses, he examined the new evidence, took into account the new truth and, just when the new forces thought they had gained complete victory, he had rebuilt a new defense behind the first broken wall. This time he tried to make it more solid and impregnable. "C'est de cette façon, du moins, et en ce sens que je conçois la défense de la tradition en matière littéraire,—moyennant une vigilance de chaque jour et une réparation infatigable."[45] Whatever his success, there can be no doubt that Sainte-Beuve's mature criticism was consciously oriented in the direction of such a conciliation.

During the 1840s, as we have seen, he turned his attention directly to ancient authors and wrote the greater number of his articles on them: Homer, Meleager, Theocritus, Euphorion, Apollonius Rhodius, etc. This was also the same decade of Sainte-Beuve's activity in behalf of the French School for Classical Studies in Athens and his suggestion to Salvandy of a Chair for Homeric Studies at the Collège de France. He wrote "Des lectures publiques du soir" (January, 1850) in support of this practical method for educating the taste of the new democratic public, suggesting the desirability of reading such authors as Plutarch, Homer, Demosthenes. An intellectual dilemma for the critic was posed in 1857, however, by the projected Fortoul laws on educational reform. The old Latin-oriented education of the young aristocrat in the eighteenth century simply did not prepare young men of the nineteenth century for the commercial professions they would enter. With his usual lucidity and sense of reality Sainte-Beuve accepted the necessity for these changes and even complimented Fortoul on an effective compromise, but added that he hoped that the new education, in preparing the young people for the material world they must know and direct ("posséder"), would do it "en respectant le plus possible la partie délicate à côté de l'utile, et en laissant aussi debout que jamais ces antiques images du beau impérissables et toujours vivantes pour qui sait les adorer."[46] With this very article Sainte-Beuve brought to a temporary close the long series of *lundis* in order to prepare himself for the more direct and restricted teaching at the Ecole Normale.

It is into the context of concrete points of conflict between modern civilization and traditional cultural education, with the critic opting for a compromise between new reality and static tradition, that one must set the essay "De la Tradition," with emphasis on the particular audience for which it was first written: the *Normaliens* of 1858. The argument of the essay is that an intellectual elite of the country, charged specifically with the transmission of the cultural tradition, must know thoroughly and completely this national literary tradition. It must interpret and transmit this tradition to the rest of the citizens in terms they can understand. Some of this elite group should also be provided the oportunity for high-level research on the origins of French culture. The first step in effecting such research is the acceptance of modern scientific methodology, but this acceptance must be selective and reconciled with traditional French taste in interpretation. The dynamic tradition must be re-created by accepting the new where it is better without losing what was better in the old, and conciliating the two where there is conflict.[47]

According to Sainte-Beuve, the Academy, like the university, was an active force in the maintenance of tradition. Its function was and should remain distinct from that of the university, but like the university, it ran the risk of maintaining a sterile, dead tradition unless it acted energetically in the contemporary world to interpret tradition in terms comprehensible to the cultivated public.[48] Sainte-Beuve, himself, was meticulous and assiduous in fulfilling his obligations as an Academician.

The evidence cited here for Sainte-Beuve's active campaign in behalf of a dynamic tradition should not be construed, however, as the basis for a system or as the central point of a doctrine, either in criticism or in teaching. We have already seen Sainte-Beuve's lack of sympathy for the doctrinaire historians of his time and his reservations on Taine's critical method because of its rigidity. He judged that tradition was not better as a system for literary criticism. In 1865 Victor Duruy asked Sainte-Beuve to make a report on the state of literature within the past fifteen years. Sainte-Beuve had been

232 • *Implications for Criticism*

delighted with the originality of Duruy's idea, had accepted and had indicated Gautier, Champfleury, and Monselet as collaborators. Meanwhile, Duruy had modified his original idea under the influence of Victor Cousin. Sainte-Beuve's reaction was immediate and direct, as is shown in a letter dated December 9, 1865, in which he first pointed out his own fundamental disagreement on "le beau, le bien, le vrai." He then continued:

> Prétendre étudier la littérature actuelle au point de vue de la *tradition*, c'est l'éliminer presque tout entière. C'est en retrancher l'élément le plus actuel, le plus vital, celui qui lui fera peut-être le plus d'honneur dans l'avenir.
> Si j'avais un rapport à faire il me serait impossible sans me mentir à moi-même, de ne pas contredire une telle idée, que j'ai toujours soit directement, soit indirectement combattue.[49]

Saint-Beuve was repeating forcefully in this letter the same thought announced by the *Constitutionnel* in September 1849 as a preface to the first series of *lundis:* "Le temps des systèmes est passé même en littérature. . . . " The continuity of a dynamic tradition was of utmost importance to the mature critic, but it was neither a system nor a doctrine, nor even a point of departure for literary criticism. Professor Scheel has found a happy phrase which seems to note very well this restriction on Sainte-Beuve's active campaign for tradition. He called it "the sense of responsibility toward tradition [das Verantwortungs bewusst sein gegenüber der Tradition]," which is something quite different from a slavish imitation or unquestioning acceptance and continuation of antiquity.[50]

Although Sainte-Beuve's ideal of balance between originality and dynamic tradition seems clear and direct to careful twen-

The Active Campaign for Tradition · 233

tieth-century readers, his own contemporaries, and even Sainte-Beuve scholars of the generations immediately after his death, did not always see his work in a total perspective, and hence oriented their interpretation in one direction or the other. Furthermore, it is axiomatic that each reader brings his own "traditional" point of view to the interpretation of this fundamental principle in the critical work of Sainte-Beuve. For these reasons, then, a rapid survey of some of the interpretations of Sainte-Beuve's concept of tradition is in order before leaving the subject.

In one of the first full-length articles on the critic and his work, Nicolas Martin applauded Sainte-Beuve's return to the study and translation of Greek authors which, he added, had resulted in protests on the part of some of his public and friends. "Des plaintes étranges sont parfois élevées au sujet de cette prétendue trahison du poète critique. En le voyant dans le camp des Grecs, des fanatiques ont crié qu'il était passé à l'ennemi."[51] Although Martin defended the critic's intellectual independence and approved his study of Greek authors in the original language, he did not at all seize the importance of this study in a broader context and his defense acquiesced to the idea of redirection rather than seeing it as another facet of the same development.

We have already seen that Bernard Jullien, in 1861, attacked Sainte-Beuve for his article on Meleager in an article entitled "L'Idolâtrie de l'Antiquité." The second half of the same article posed the thesis that in Sainte-Beuve's eyes works are good only "à la condition d'être anciennes,"[52] and the rest of the article is devoted to a refutation of this supposed opinion by means of the same arguments used by all Moderns. Sainte-Beuve did not reply directly to this article, but his passing note of scorn in the *Constitutionnel* brought another attack by Jullien in March. Again the theme turned on the idea of progress in art and on Sainte-Beuve's mistaken idolatry of antiquity. It is evident that in the case of Bernard Jullien there is more than lack of perspective and literary misunderstanding. Sainte-Beuve was not more than a "straw-man" to an ambitious critic seeking notoriety, but the statements represent, nevertheless, the degree of distortion to which Sainte-Beuve's thought was subjected by his contemporaries.[53]

If the critic's contemporaries tended at times to confuse the issue of the role of tradition in his thought by not seeing the broader context or by voluntarily distorting the concept, critics after his death, at the turn of the twentieth century, did him no greater service in making him the champion of conservatism and/or a great but incomplete humanist. Louis Dimier called Sainte-Beuve one of the masters of nineteenth-century counterrevolution and pointed out that Charles Maurras "a pris le nom de Sainte-Beuve comme enseigne politique."[54] Meanwhile Irving Babbit and Paul Elmer More, in the United States, praised the critic's humanism although they were deeply troubled by his nontranscendental philosophy, since their context of humanism was opposed to the frank materialism of John Dewey.[55] Once again, Sainte-Beuve's subtle distinctions were drawn out of balance, resulting in a one-sided, distorted, and inadequate interpretation of his thought.

Professor Lander MacClintock was more objective in his discussion of tradition as the third "pierre de touche" in Sainte-Beuve's criticism, finding that even a Romantic writer may be classic in one of the senses normally given to the term by Sainte-Beuve.[56] Professor MacClintock also emphasized the humanistic-Romantic ("mesure-démesure") opposition as more meaningful in the nineteenth-century context than the Classic-Romantic-Realist progression by means of reaction to the previous orientation. He further saw the necessary link of French tradition through Rome to Greece, but limited his discussion to the French tradition, where the primacy of seventeenth-century literature "assumes the proportions of a 'fixed idea,' a state of mind quite unexpected in one who, in other things, invariably provided room for *'un certain contraire.'* " Professor MacClintock thus provided a more accurate definition than earlier critics without, however, providing the complete picture essential to the full understanding of Sainte-Beuve's concept. As a result, Professor MacClintock did not break away from the "Romantic become Classic" interpretation of the critic's thought. Sainte-Beuve's classicism led to a humanistic reaction against scientific naturalism at times, according to Professor MacClintock. "This brings us, by another path, to that irreconcilable contradiction in his thought . . . the contradiction of the humanist and the scientist, the devotee of tradition and the believer in progress, the apostle of the ancients and the champion of the moderns." The question which arises immediately is whether these are indeed true contradictions, or have perhaps become more rigid in the opinion of Professor MacClintock than they actually were in the critic's conception and in his functional criticism. Completing the picture of tradition as conceived by the critic by adding to the specifically national culture its antecedents does resolve "that irreconcilable contradiction," as we have seen, at least to the extent of putting two essential, vital forces into balance, creating a harmonious and delicate tension which provides a healthy positive action rather than the warring frustration of opposing factions.

One other approach to the role of Greco-Roman tradition in Sainte-Beuve's thought, common in recent years, deserves close attention. René Canat uses this approach. Under the general heading of "La tradition sacrée," Canat presents a discussion divided into three parts.[57] In the first part he quotes from the copious public commentary on the subject by the critic, as well as from some of his contemporaries, providing ample evidence of Sainte-Beuve's positive and recognized interest in Greco-Roman tradition during the decade 1840–50. Professor Canat finds Sainte-Beuve a critic of the French university, but at the same time the bridge between it and the general public, a role which brought out "du meilleur Sainte-Beuve." In the second section of his discussion Professor Canat undertakes to show how Sainte-Beuve saw Hellenism and what he expected from it in the rejuvenation of French poetry. The originality of Sainte-Beuve's view lay, not in the actual picture, but in his capacity to make it "une vérité sentie" by telling comparisons with modern literature. Professor Canat sees the key to the critic's view in his concept of Greek realism, which was related neither to worn-out neoclassicism nor to Romantic exaggeration. Sainte-Beuve's Alexandrianism, according to Professor Canat, was "un mélange exquis de naturel et d'élégance." The third section of the discussion deals with the problem of imitation. Sainte-Beuve saw Greece as the eternal source and fountain of fresh inspiration, both moral and linguistic, according to Professor Canat. He also saw the unity of Greco-Roman tradition and centered his view of Greece on the union of realism and beauty, not in the form of plastic art, but rather as ease and grace reconstituted.

In many ways Professor Canat's discussion complements and is the counterpart of Professor MacClintock's discussion, for it deals quite exclusively with the critic's knowledge and opinion of the Hellenic tradition. Professor Canat's context is, however, that of a broadly synthetic study of Romantic

Hellenism, in which category he classed Sainte-Beuve and Gautier as the "deux grands maîtres" of 1840-50. He could not, therefore, do more than isolate this facet of the critic's thought without giving to it the perspective it needs to have, which requires an exposition of its relationship to other expressions of the critic's thought. It is not at all surprising, therefore, to find that Professor Canat seems to have missed entirely the active, dynamic quality of the critic's work and for that reason to have come to apply to it the adjectives "charming" and "Alexandrian"; this same narrow view explains the static title of his exposition.

Within more recent years it has been fashionable among some Anglo-Saxon critics to dismiss Sainte-Beuve's critical talent as more suited to history or biography than literature, while they have preferred to emphasize the text with its formal structure. Sainte-Beuve's Greek notes, as well as his articles, provide ample evidence that he too considered textual analysis important.[58] After all, the *explication* method was already a French "tradition." In his profession as a daily working critic in the mid-nineteenth century, however, issues relating to literature, the terms of its survival, and the quality and character of its guardians were of immediate practical importance. His campaign for tradition may not always have been completely understood, but it was effective to a degree, nevertheless, and most certainly brought issues to the eyes of the public, usually in an urbane fashion. Obviously the delicate tension of the balance between innovation and tradition was not a single campaign to be won once, but the daily concept of a humanist of brilliant intelligence and practical spirit. Perhaps the twentieth century, as it evolves beyond uniquely textual considerations, is becoming aware of the fact that the problem is being posed once again very pressingly in this century, that Sainte-Beuve's nineteenth-century solution is perhaps no longer entirely adequate, but that it has, in addition to historic validity, an exemplary quality. Sainte-Beuve himself enjoyed tracing the changes in critical opinion about ancient authors, aware that each generation had to make its own synthesis of past and present and thus declare its own identity. In the tradition of Montaigne, one of his favorite authors, Sainte-Beuve looked backward in order to look ahead.

Notes

1. Harry Levin, "Notes on Convention," in: Walter Jackson Bates and others, *Perspectives on Criticism*, Harvard Studies in Comparative Literature 20 (Cambridge: Harvard University Press, 1950), p. 77.
2. *P.C.*, III, 336.
3. *Literary Essays of Ezra Pound*, ed. T. S. Eliot (New York: New Directions, 1954), p. 91.
4. *N.L.*, X, 396.
5. *C.L.*, XIII, 133–35.
6. *C.L.*, IX, 473–513.
7. *C.L.*, V, 271.
8. *N.L.*, I, 305–6.
9. *N.L.*, VII, 46–52. See also *N.L.*, IV, 401–2 on what misguided educational pronouncements can do to tradition in the name of tradition itself.
10. Michaut, *Sainte-Beuve*, p. 483.
11. Ernst-Robert Curtius, *European Literature and the Latin Middle Ages*, trans. Willard K. Trask (New York: Pantheon Books, 1953), p. 271. It is also important to note that Curtius continued, saying: "From his [Sainte-Beuve's] day to Van Tiegham's, France's tie to the Classicism of the seventeenth century has proved to be a tenaciously maintained attitude of opposition to Europeanism. But today it strikes one as a pure anachronism."
12. *N.L.*, I, 266.

13. *C.L.*, III, 50.
14. *C.L.*, XIV, 77.
15. *C.L.*, XV, 358.
16. *N.L.*, III, 73–74. See also: *N.L.*, VII, 50. "Ne nous figeons pas; tenons nos esprits vivants et fluides."
17. *P.L.*, III, 370–71.
18. See: *P.C.*, IV, 18. "La tradition populaire tend à imprimer un certain caractère de débonnaireté et de bonhomie."
19. *N.L.*, XIII, 315–16. See also: *EsV*, p. 79.
20. "De la lecture des poètes latins sous Louis XIV," présentation par Jean Bonnerot, *Mercure de France*, No. 1152 (août 1959), pp. 588–613.
21. *C.L.*, XV, 369–73.
22. *C.g.*, XI, 485.
23. *N.L.*, II, 245.
24. Michaut, *Sainte-Beuve*, pp. 205–8, and 228–31.
25. *P.C.*, II, 450. The underlining is mine.
26. See in particular: W. M. Frohock, "The Critic and the Cult of Art: Sainte-Beuve and the Esthetic Movement," and Edna C. Frederick, "The Critic and the Cult of Art: Further Observations."
27. *C.g.*, XII, 462. See also: *N.L.*, II, 384.
28. *N.L.*, III, 378.
29. *N.L.*, III, 396.
30. *P.C.*, IV, 230–31.
31. *C.L.*, XV, 368–69.
32. *C.L.*, XIII, 60. It is important to note that Sainte-Beuve explicitly stated here that he came to the study of ancient literatures through the Pléiade poets. See *N.L.*, VII, 39–41 and *N.L.*, XI, 198–202 on English classical education.
33. *C.L.*, XII, 428.
34. *N.L.*, XIII, 206.
35. It is important to note here an idea of rigid norm implicit in Sainte-Beuve's thinking. His relativism never reached a point of replacing entirely a standard of taste as a basis of critical judgment.

36. See *C.g.*, XIV, 45. Sainte-Beuve wrote to E. and J. Goncourt about their new book *Germinie Lacerteux* on January 15, 1865: "Mais déjà j'étais frappé d'une chose, c'est que pour bien juger cet ouvrage et en parler, il faudrait une poétique toute autre que l'ancienne, une poétique appropriée aux productions de l'art nouveau, d'une recherche nouvelle."
37. *C.L.*, XV, 376.
38. *P.C.*, III, 442–43.
39. See, e.g.: *C.L.*, XIII, 303.
40. *C.L.*, II, 44–45.
41. *N.L.*, VI, 112.
42. *P.L.*, III, 370. It is important to note that the direct allusion is to Charles Labitte, but I think that the value of the statement is not lost thereby. I go even farther in reading an implicit personal allusion in the group of *fidèles*.
43. *C.L.*, II, 266. See also: *C.L.*, XI, 260, n. 1., where he wrote, "je cherche . . . à établir . . . une filiation naturelle." See also: *N.L.*, IX, 326.
44. *N.L.*, X, 418.
45. *N.L.*, VIII, 390–91.
46. *C.L.*, XI, 283.
47. *N.L.*, X, 418. See also: *N.L.*, XI, 182.
48. *N.L.*, XII, 426 ff.
49. *C.g.*, XIV, 486.
50. Scheel, p. 150.
51. N. Martin, "Sainte-Beuve," *l'Artiste* (15 décembre 1848), pp. 120–23 and 142–44; p. 121.
52. Jullien, p. 438.
53. *C.g.*, XIV, 329–31.
54. Louis Dimier, *Les maîtres de la Contre-Révolution au dix-neuvième siècle* (Paris: Nouvelle Librairie Nationale, 1917), p. 138.
55. Irving Babbitt, *The Masters of Modern French Criticism* (Boston: Houghton Mifflin Co, 1930), chapters 5 and 6, pp. 97–188. Paul Elmer More, *Shelburne Essays: Third Series* (New

York: G. P. Putnam's Sons, 1909), "The Centenary of Sainte-Beuve," pp. 54–81. See especially pp. 79–81.
56. Lander MacClintock, *Sainte-Beuve's Critical Theory and Practice after 1849* (Chicago: University of Chicago Press, 1920), p. 57. I should like to thank Professor MacClintock for giving me a copy of his fine study which is no longer available in bookstores.
57. Canat, III, 151–80.
58. One of many times he said it explicitly is in *Chat.*, I, 19. There, he wrote: "Pourtant, connaître les hommes n'est pas assez quand il s'agit des oeuvres; et tout en s'appliquant à bien caractériser les productions de l'esprit comme l'expression d'un temps et d'un ordre de société, on ne saurait négliger d'y saisir ce qui n'est pas de la vie passagère, ce qui tient à la flamme immortelle et sacrée, au génie même des Lettres."

Appendix

List of Publications by Sainte-Beuve with Reference to Antiquity (by year of publication, and chronologically within the year)

1824	"Samos"	*Globe* II, 49
	L'Ile d'Ipsara	*Oeuvres* I, 55–56
	Chio	57–59
	Mitylène	62–64
1825	Candie	*Oeuvres* I, 75–78
1826	Bonaparte et les Grecs suivi d'un Tableau de la Grèce en 1825	*Pr.L.* I, 131–36
1827	Odes d'Anacréon	*Pr.L.* I, 189–96
	Oeuvres completes de Tacite	231–40
1828	*Tableau historique et critique de la Poésie française et du théâtre français au XVIe siècle* chez Sautelet, Johanneau et Mesmer 2 vol.	
1829	*Vie, Poésies et Pensées de Joseph Delorme* chez Delangle Frères	
	Mathurin Régnier et André Chénier	*P.L.* I, 159–75
1830	*Les Consolations* chez Urbain Canel, Levavasseur Lucrèce	*N.L.* XII, 445–53
	De la Grèce moderne et de ses rapports avec l'antiquité	*P.C.* II, 307–8, note
1831	———	

1832	De l'esprit et de la critique littéraires chez les peuples anciens et modernes	*Oeuvres* I, 394–95
1833	————————	
1834	Oeuvres d'André Chénier	P.C. II, 496–504
	Volupté chez Renduel	
1835	Molière	P.L. II, 1–61
	de Vigny	P.C. II, 52–77
	Du génie critique de Bayle	P.L. I, 364–87
1836	Villemain	P.C. II, 358–96
	Quinet	307–26
	Nisard	III, 328–57
1837	*Pensées d'août* chez Renduel	
1838	————————	
1839	Quelques documents inédits sur André Chénier	P.L. I, 176–208
	Notes et Sonnets	*Poésies complètes*, II, 378–405
	De la littérature industrielle	P.C. II, 444–71
	Eglogue napolitaine	*Poésies complètes*, I, 326–30
	Des Journaux chez les Romains	P.C. III, 442–69
1840	La Rochefoucauld	P.F. 288–321
	J-J Ampère	P.C. III, 358–86
	Dix ans après en littérature	472–94
	Un dernier Rêve	*Poésies complètes*, II, 413–423
1841	————————	
1842	Anacréon au seizième siècle	*Tab.*, (edit. 1843) 440–56
1843	Homère	P.C. V, 325–58
	Tableau historique et critique de la Poésie française et du théâtre français au XVIe siècle (augmenté) Charpentier	
	Quelques vérités sur la situation en littérature	P.C. III, 415–41

	Euphorion ou de l'injure du temps	V, 445–55
	Charles Magnin	III, 387–414
1844	Un Factum contre André Chénier	P.C. V, 300–24
	Daunou	IV, 273–359
1845	Fauriel	P.C. IV, 125–268
	De la Médée d'Apollonius de Rhodes	V, 359–406
	Méléagre	407–44
1846	Charles Labitte	P.L. III, 362–93
	Sur l'Ecole française d'Athènes	478–84
	Théocrite	3–45
1847	Virgile et Constantin le Grand	P.L. III, 46–55
1848	————————	
1849	Madame de Sévigné	C.L. I, 49–62
	Villemain et Cousin	108–20
	Thiers	138–58
1850	Des lectures publiques du soir	C.L. I, 275–93
	Firdousi	332–50
	Pline le Naturaliste	II, 22–43
1851	André Chénier, homme politique	C.L. IV, 144–64
	Essai sur Amyot	450–70
1852	De la Retraite de MM. Villemain et Cousin	C.L. VI, 146–64
	Paul-Louis Courrier	322–61
	l'Abbé Barthélemy	VII, 186–223
1853	Gibbon	C.L. VIII, 431–72
1854	Madame Dacier	C.L. IX, 473–514
1855	Instruction générale sur l'éxecution d'un plan d'études de lycées	C.L. XI, 271–88
	Thiers	157–72
1856	Histoire de la Querelle des Anciens et des Modernes	C.L. XIII, 132–71
1857	*Etude sur Virgile suivie d'une Etude sur Quintus de Smyrne* Garnier	
	Taine	C.L. XIII, 249–84
	Banville	XIV, 69–85

246 • *Appendix*

1858	Histoire de l'Académie française	C.L. XIV, 195–217
	De la Tradition en littérature	XV, 365–82
1859	———————	
1860	Thiers	
	Chateaubriand et son groupe littéraire sous l'empire Garnier	C.L. XIV, 338–54 2 vol.
1861	Oeuvres d'Hippolyte Rigault	N.L. I, 255–76
	Lettres de Mme de Sévigné	277–95
1862	Le Poème des champs	N.L. II, 247–89
	Histoire du roman dans l'Antiquité	422–45
1863	Charles Magnin	N.L. V, 440–78
	Emile Littré	200–56
	La Grèce en 1863	308–29
	Térence	330–70
	Boissonade	VI, 82–113
1864	Anthologie grecque	N.L. VII, 1–52
	Réponse à Taxile Delord	C.L. XI, 401–03
	Taine	N.L. VIII, 66–137
1865	Entretiens sur l'histoire	N.L. IX, 280–341
	Histoire de la Grèce–Grote	X, 46–69
1866	———————	
1867	Oeuvres de Virgile	N.L. XI, 174–202
	M. Viguier	420–32
	L'Académie française	XII, 402–38
1868	Dübner	N.L. XI, 433–44
	Eugene Gandar	XII, 337–401
	Jean-Jacques Ampère	XIII, 183–265
	Joachim Du Bellay	266–356
	———————	
	Ma Biographie	N.L. XIII, 1–48
	Début d'un article sur l'histoire de César	461–65
	De la lecture des poètes latins sous Louis XIV	Mercure de France No. 1152 (août, 1959), pp. 588–613

Bibliography of Works Cited

(See also Note on Abbreviations and Index Volumes, p. xiii)

Allem, Maurice. *Portrait de Sainte-Beuve* (Paris: Albin Michel, 1954).

Ampère, J-J. "Une Course dans l'Asie Mineure: Lettre à M. Sainte-Beuve," *Revue des Deux Mondes* 29, 4e série (1842), pp. 161–85.

Babbitt, Irving. *The Masters of Modern French Criticism* (Boston: Houghton Mifflin Co., 1930).

Babou, H. "Des Amitiés littéraires," *Revue française* XVI (20 février 1859), pp. 177–84.

Badolle, Maurice. *L'Abbé Barthélemy et l'hellénisme en France dans la seconde moitié du XVIIIe siècle* (Paris: Presses universitaires, 1928).

Bellesort, André. *Sainte-Beuve et le dix-neuvième siècle* (Paris: Perrin, 1954).

Bertrand, Louis. *La Fin du classicisme et le retour à l'antique* (Paris: Arthème Fayard et Cie., n.d.).

Boissier, Gaston. "L'Etude sur Virgile de Sainte-Beuve," *Le Livre d'or*, pp. 1–14.

―――― "Les Théories nouvelles du poème épique," *Revue des Deux Mondes* LXVII, 2de période, (15 février 1867), pp. 848–79.

Briod, Blaise. *L'Homérisme de Chateaubriand* (Paris: Anc. H. Champion, 1928).

Canat, René. *L'Hellénisme des Romantiques* (Paris: Didier, 1951–55), 3 vols.
The individual volume titles are:
I *La Grèce retrouvée*
II *Le Romantisme des Grecs 1826–1840*
III *L'Eveil du Parnasse 1840–1852*
Catalogue des livres composant la Bibliothèque de M. Sainte-Beuve dont la vente aura lieu le lundi 21 mars 1870 et les cinq jours suivants à sept heures du soir (Paris: L. Potier, 1870) 2 vols.
Chénier, André. *Oeuvres complètes*, ed. G. Walter. Editions de la Pléiade (Paris: Gallimard, 1958).
Curtius, Ernst-Robert. *European Literature and the Latin Middle Ages*, trans. Willard K. Trask (New York: Pantheon Books, 1953).
Delcourt, Marie. *Etude sur les traductions des tragiques grecs et latins en France depuis la Renaissance* (Brussels: Lamartin, 1925).
Des Guerrois, Charles. *Etude sur l'Anthologie grecque* (Troyes: Dufour-Bouquot, 1896).
Desonay, Fernand. *Le Rêve hellénique chez les poètes parnassiens* (Louvain: Librairie universitaire, 1928).
Dimier, Louis. *Les Maîtres de la Contre-Révolution au dix neuvième siècle* (Paris: Nouvelle Librairie Nationale, 1917).
Dupont-Ferrier, Gustave. *La Vie quotidienne d'un collège parisien pendant plus de trois cinquante ans. Du Collège de Clermond au Louis-le-Grand (1563–1920)* (Paris: E. de Boccard, 1921–25), 3 vols.
Duquesnil, Félix. *Souvenirs littéraires* (Paris: Plon, 1922).
Egger, Emile. *Mémoires de littérature ancienne* (Paris: Auguste Durand, 1862).
Eichoff, Frédéric G. *Etudes grecques sur Virgile, ou Recueil de tous les passages des poètes grecs imités dans les Bucoliques, les Géorgiques et l'Enéide avec le texte latin et les rapprochements littéraires* (Paris: Delalain, 1825), 3 vols.
Eliot, T. S., ed. *Literary Essays of Ezra Pound* (New York: New Directions, 1954).

Bibliography • 249

Faguet, Emile. "Montaigne annoté par Sainte-Beuve," *La Revue Latine* 5 (25 août 1906), pp. 449–76.

Falcucci, Clément. *L'Humanisme dans l'enseignement secondaire en France au 19e siècle* (Toulouse: Privat, 1939).

Faure, Gabriel. *Sainte-Beuve, Voyage en Italie, Notes inédites* (Paris: Variétés littéraires, 1922).

Frederick, Edna C. "The Critic and the Cult of Art: Further Observations," *Romanic Review* XXXIII (1942), pp. 385–87.

Frohock, W. M. "The Critic and the Cult of Art: Sainte-Beuve and the Esthetic Movement," *Romanic Review* XXXII (1941), pp. 379–88.

Gilman, Margaret. *The Idea of Poetry in France; from Houdar de La Motte to Baudelaire* (Cambridge: Harvard University Press, 1958).

Goncourt, Edmond and Goncourt, Jules. *Journal; mémoires de la vie littéraire* ed. R. Ricatte (Monaco: Imprimerie nationale, 1956–), 22 vols.

Gow, A. S. F. and Page, D. L., ed. *The Greek Anthology: Hellenistic Epigrams* (Cambridge: University Press, 1965), 2 vols.

Guillois, Antoine. "Notes inédites de Sainte-Beuve sur un exemplaire de la première édition des Oeuvres d'André Chénier," *Bulletin du Bibliophile* (1902), pp. 212–24. And also: (Paris: Leclerc, 1902).

Guyot, Charly. "Sainte-Beuve et les philosophes de l'histoire" *Revue de Suisse* (octobre, 1952), pp. 71–87.

Hadas, Moses. *Ancilla to Classical Reading* (New York: Columbia University Press, 1956).

Hutton, James. *The Greek Anthology in France and in the Latin Writers of the Netherlands to the year 1800* (Ithaca, New York: Cornell University Press, 1946).

Joubert, Léo. *Etudes de Critique et d'histoire* (Paris: Firmin Didot, 1863).

Jullien, Bernard. *Thèses supplémentaires de métrique et de musique ancienne, de grammaire et de littérature* (Paris: Hachette, 1861).

Lair, Adolphe. "Un Maître de Sainte-Beuve," *Le Correspondant* (23 avril 1900), pp. 317–26.
Lapauze, Henry. *Histoire de l'Académie de France à Rome* (Paris: Plon, 1924), 2 vols.
Lefranc, Abel. "Sainte-Beuve au Collège de France" *Le Livre d'or*, pp. 203–20.
Lehmann, A. G. *Sainte-Beuve: A Portrait of the Critic 1804–1842* (Oxford: Clarendon Press, 1962).
——— "Sainte-Beuve and Romantic Scholarship," *Studies in Modern French Literature presented to P. Mansall Jones*, ed. L. J. Austin, Garnet Rees and Eugene Vinaver (Manchester: University Press, 1961), pp. 220-31.
——— "Sainte-Beuve and the Historic Mind," *The French Mind: Studies in honor of Gustave Rudler*, Will Moore, Rhoda Sutherland, and Enid Starkie ed. (Oxford: Clarendon Press, 1952), pp. 256–73.
Lesky, Albin. *A History of Greek Literature*, trans. James Willis and Cornelius de Heer (New York: Thos. Crowell Co., 1966).
Levin, Harry. "Notes on Convention," in: Walter Jackson Bates and others, *Perspectives on Criticism*. Harvard Studies in Comparative Literature 20 (Cambridge: Harvard University Press, 1950), pp. 55–83.
Liard, Louis. *L'Enseignement supérieur en France 1789–1889* (Paris: Armand Colin, 1888), 2 vols.
Le Livre d'or de Sainte-Beuve publié à l'occasion du centenaire de sa naissance 1804–1904 (Paris: Fontemoing, 1904).
MacClintock, Lander. *Sainte-Beuve's Critical Theory and Practice after 1849* (Chicago: University of Chicago Press, 1920).
——— "Sainte-Beuve and Pope," *Publications of the Modern Language Association* XLI (1926), pp. 442–52.
Marmier, Jean. *La Survie d'Horace à l'époque romantique* (Paris: Didier, 1965).
Martin, Nicolas. "Sainte-Beuve," *l'Artiste* (15 décembre 1848), pp. 120–23, 142–44.
Mérimée, Prosper. *Mélanges littéraires* (Paris: Calmann Lévy, 1884).

Michaut, Gustave. *Quibus rationibus Sainte-Beuve opus suum de XVIe seculo iterum atque iterum retractaverit, cui dissertationi adjectus est ejusdem operis apparatus criticus* (Paris: Fontemoing, 1903).

—— *Sainte-Beuve avant les lundis* (Paris: Fontemoing, 1903).

—— "Le 'La Bruyère' de Sainte-Beuve," *Revue d'Histoire littéraire de France* XIII (1906), pp. 202–44 and 714–26.

Moore, Will; Sutherland, Rhoda; and Starkie, Enid, eds. *The French Mind: Studies in honor of Gustave Rudler* (Oxford: Clarendon Press, 1952).

More, Paul Elmer. *Shelburne Essays: Third Series* (New York: G. P. Putnam's Sons, 1909).

Moreau, Piere. "Sainte-Beuve latiniste," *Revue d'Histoire littéraire de France* 44 (1937), pp. 45–64.

—— "Sainte-Beuve poète latin," *Annales littéraires de la Franche-Comté* LV (1949), pp. 55–63.

Myres, Sir John L. *Homer and His Critics*, ed. Dorothea Gary (London: Routledge and Kegan Paul, 1958).

Nicolson, Harold. *Sainte-Beuve* (London: Constable, 1957).

Olivier, Juste. *Paris en 8130: Journal de Juste Olivier*, ed. André Delattre and Mark Denkinger (Chapel Hill: University of North Carolina Press, 1951).

Pailleron, M-L. *François Buloz et ses amis* (Paris: Calmann-Lévy, 1919).

—— "Les Petits Carnets de Sainte-Beuve," *Revue Hébdomadaire* n.s. 31 (29 juillet 1916), pp. 620–29.

—— *Sainte-Beuve à 16 ans* (Paris: Le Divan, 1927).

Pichois, Claude. *Philarète Chasles et la vie littéraire au temps du Romantisme* (Paris: Corti, 1965), 2 vols.

Pierrot, Charles. *Table générale et analytique des Causeries du lundi, Portraits de femmes et Portraits littéraires* (Paris: Garnier, 1881).

Radet, Georges. *L'Histoire et l'oeuvre de l'Ecole française d'Athènes* (Paris: Fontemoing, 1901).

Regard, Maurice. *Sainte-Beuve* (Paris: Hatier, 1959).

Rigault, Hippolyte. *Oeuvres complètes précédés d'une notice biographique et littéraire par M. S.-Marc Girardin* (Paris: Hachette, 1859), 4 vols.

Sainte-Beuve, Ch.-Aug. See also: Note on Abbreviations and Appendix.

———— *Cahier de notes grecques,* ed. Ruth Mulhauser (Chapel Hill: University of North Carolina Press, 1955).

———— "De la lecture des poètes latins sous Louis XIV," présentation par Jean Bonnerot, *Mercure de France* No. 1152 (août 1959), pp. 588–613.

———— *Mes Poisons: Cahiers intimes inédits,* ed. Victor Giraud (Paris: Plon, 1926).

———— *Notes inédites de Sainte-Beuve,* ed. Charly Guyot (Neufchatel: Secrétariat de l'Université, 1931).

———— *Vie, Poésies et Pensées de Joseph Delorme,* ed. G. Antoine, (Paris: Nouvelles Editions latines, 1956).

Saint-Victor, Paul. *Hommes et Dieux: Etudes d'histoire et de littérature* (Paris: Michel Lévy, 1867).

Sandys, John Edwin. *A History of Classical Scholarship* (Cambridge: University Press, 1903–8), 3 vols.

Scarfe, Francis. *André Chénier: His Life and Work 1762–1794* (Oxford: Clarendon Press, 1965).

Scheel, Hans Ludwig. *Die Ürteile Sainte-Beuves über das Verhaltnis der französischen Literatur zur Antike (1500–1800)* (Kiel: University Press, 1950).

Seznec, Jean. "L'Alain Chartier de Sainte-Beuve," *Romanic Review* XXXV (October, 1944), pp. 203–19.

Smith, Horatio. "Tommaso Fiore, *Studio su Virgilio Traduzione e Saggio introduttiva sul Sainte-Beuve,*" *Romanic Review* XXXI (1940), pp. 412–14.

Scarfe, Francis. *André Chénier: His Life and Work 1762–1794* Izaac (Budé edit.). (Paris: Les Belles Lettres, 1944), 2 vols.

Taine, Hipplyte A. *Essai sur Tite Live* (10e édition) (Paris: Hachette, n.d.).

Troubat, Jules. *La Salle à manger de Sainte-Beuve* (Paris: Mercure de France, 1910).

——— *Souvenirs et Indiscrétions* (Paris: Michel Lévy Frères, 1872).
Valéry, Paul. *Oeuvres,* éd. Jean Hytier. Bibliothèque de la Pléiade (Paris: Gallimard, 1957), 2 vols.
Vauther, Gabriel. "Une Lettre de Thouvenel sur l'Ecole française d'Athènes en 1848," *L'Acropole, revue du Monde hellénique* II (1927), pp. 251–56.
Viggiani, Carl A. "An Introduction to Sainte-Beuve's Critical Vocabulary" (Ann Arbor, Mich.: University Microfilms).
——— "Sainte-Beuve (1824–1830): Critic and Creator," *Romanic Review* XLIV, No. 4 (December, 1953), pp. 263–72.
Wright, W. C. *A Short History of Greek Literature* (New York: American Book Co., 1907).

Index

About, Edmond, F. V., 63
Adert, Jacques, 32
Aeneid, 60
Aeschylus, 118, 196
Agathias Scholasticus, 35, 148, 155, 174
Alexandre, 54
Alexandrian writers, 84, 85
Ampère, Jean-Jacques, 27, 47, 65, 117, 191
Amyot, Jacques, 57, 102, 103, 160, 163, 167, 169
Anacreon, 12, 31, 47, 48, 55, 150, 151, 155, 158, 174
Andrieux, François, G. F. S., 17
Antoine, Gerald, 191, 194, 195
Apollonius Rhodius, 55, 175
Apuleius, 79
Arbouville, Madame d', 53
Archilochus, 174
Aristarchus, 129, 130, 205
Aristophanes, 160, 197
Aristotle, 101, 125, 130, 195, 204
Arnold, Matthew, 161
Arnold, Thomas, 215
Atala (Chateaubriand), 56
Athens, 53

Augustus, 60
Ausonius, 189

Babbitt, Irving, 234
Babou, H., 64
Banville, Thédore, 218, 219
Bareste, 76, 127, 162
Barnes, Joshua, 75
Barthélemy, Jean Jacques, 4, 57, 97, 200, 203
Bast, 126
Becq de Fourquières, 65, 77
Belleau, Rémy, 12, 150
Belloc, Madame, 45
Benitez, Rubén, *xi*
Benoist, 65, 66, 136, 137, 165
Bertrand, Louis, 83
Bétolaud, 168
Bignan, 162
Bion, 152
Blignière, 163
Bliss, Francis, *xi*
Boileau-Despréaux, Nicolas, 48, 99, 192, 193, 214
Boissier, Gaston, 61, 63, 135
Boissonade, Jean François, 6, 13, 33, 55, 57, 65, 75, 83, 126, 131, 132, 139, 155, 175, 176, 228

Bonhomme, Honoré, 66
Bonnerot, Jean, *xi*, 51, 54
Bouteron, Marcel, *xi*
Brunck, Richard François Philippe, 148, 149
Bucolic poetry, 181–189
Buffon, 48
Burnouf, 6

Caesar, 48
Calpurnius, 205
Camp, Aimé, 188
Campaux, 134
Canat, René, 80, 83, 135, 236, 237
Cassagnac, 221
Catinot, 229
Cato, 106
Catullus, 183
Cephalas, Constantine, 148, 149
Cervantes, 197
Champfleury, 232
Champollion, Jean François, 43
Chardon de la Rochette, 6
Chasles, Michel, 20
Chasles, Philarète, 20, 161
Chassang, A., 63
Chateaubriand, François René de, 5, 7, 10, 11, 13, 16, 56, 82, 121, 162, 188, 201
Chénier, André, 7–13, 16, 24, 52, 56, 65, 77, 83, 118, 147, 151, 154, 155, 174, 193, 194, 200, 201
Choerilus of Samos, 25
Choiseul-Gouffier, Comte de, 129
Christianity, 82, 83
Cicero, 66, 106, 107, 165, 204

Clark-Ernesti, 75
Clouet, 22
Collection Lovenjoul, 78
College de France, 59, 123
Coray, Adamantios, 6, 47, 75
Corneille, Pierre, 48
Couriard, Adèle, 62, 82, 83
Courrier, Paul, 6, 57, 164
Cousin, Victor, 6, 18, 31, 53, 98, 123, 204, 232
Cowper, William, 185
Creuzer, Georg Friedrich, 43
Crinagoras, 32
Crocker, Lester G., *xi*
Curtius, Ernst-Robert, 216, 217, 218

Dacier, Madame, 57, 75, 124, 127, 132, 161, 162, 168, 213
Daguesseau, 19, 20
Dante, 118, 120, 131, 166, 196, 199, 225
Daru, 159
Daunou, 6, 49, 98, 109
Dehèque, Frédéric, 149, 154
De la littérature (Madame de Staël), 5
"De la littérature industrielle" (Sainte-Beuve), 222
"De la Tradition" (Sainte-Beuve), 62
Delcourt, Marie, 163
Delille, 165, 194
Delorme, 76
Demosthenes, 48
Denis d'Halicarnasse. See Dionysius of Halicarnassus.
Denne-Baron, 165
Dépret, Louis, 192

Desbordes-Valmore, Marcelline, 32
Descartes, 20
Deschanel, Emile, 131
Des Guerrois, Charles, 35, 156
Desonay, Fernand, 83
Despréaux, 197
Devine, Nancy, xi
Dewey, John, 234
Dezeimeris, 66, 155
Diderot, 118
Didot, Firmin, 6, 136
Dimier, Louis, 234
Dindorf, 76
Dion of Chrysostome, 205
Dionysius of Halicarnassus, 106, 205
"Dix ans après en littérature" (Sainte-Beuve), 52, 222, 223
Du Bellay, 12, 206
Dübner, Frederick, 65–67, 137, 162
Dubois, Paul, 23, 42, 44, 47
Dugas-Montbel, 75, 127, 162
Dupont-Ferrier, Gustave, 18
Duquesnil, Félix, 29
Duruy, Victor, 231
Duveyrier, 86

Ecole française d'Athènes, 53, 63
Egger, Emile, 32, 57, 58, 66, 104, 129, 134, 205
Eichoff, Frédéric, 44
Elegiac poetry, 181–189
Epictetus, 21
Estienne, Henri, 31, 82, 150
Etude sur Virgle (Sainte-Beuve), 61, 62, 64, 117, 123, 124, 156

Euphorion of Chalcis, 138, 183, 184
Euripides, 43
Eustathius, 76, 132
Eynard, 53, 54

Faure, Gabriel, 25
Fauriel, Claude, 43, 46, 117, 126, 137, 139, 204, 225
Fénelon, 57, 154
Firdousi, 57, 225
Flaubert, 65
Florian, 57
Fontenelle, 186, 188, 214
Fortoul, 60, 61, 230
France, Anatole, 83
Frémy, Arnould, 11, 12
French education, 16–19
Froissart, 110

Gaillard, Théodore, 22
Gallus, 184
Gandar, Eugène, 63, 65, 77, 116, 204
Garsonnet, 67
Gautier, Théophile, 192, 232, 237
Génie du Christianisme (Chateaubriand), 5, 56
Geoffroy, 159
German scholarship, 44, 61
Gibbon, 57
Gilman, Margaret, 199
Girardin, Saint-Marc, 110, 205
Globe, Le, 42–49
Goethe, 132, 225
Goldsmith, Oliver, 185
Goncourt, Edmond and Jules, 67, 192, 213

258 · *Index*

Gray, Thomas, 197
"Grèce en 1863, La" (Sainte-Beuve), 45, 64
Greek Anthology, 25, 36, 64, 66, 78, 79, 83, 88, 89, 147–153, 181, 205
Greek historians, 101
Gresset, 116
Grote, 64, 132, 133
Guérin, Maurice de, 86
Guigniaut, 43, 128
Guilford, Lord, 43
Guille, Frances, *xi*
Guizot, 18, 98, 103
Guyot, 99, 100

Halévy, 32, 158, 168
Hase, 6
Hausset, Madame, 48
Herder, 98, 118, 196
Herodotus, 101, 102, 164
Hesiod, 78, 182
Heyne, 75
Hippocrates, 81, 167
Homer, 5, 53, 55, 56, 63, 67, 75–77, 88, 102, 103, 108, 116–140, 151, 153, 161, 162, 168, 186, 187, 196–199, 205, 213, 224
Homeric Question, 124, 126, 128, 132, 134
Horace, 26, 48, 57, 64, 66, 118, 153, 157, 159, 182, 188–193, 196, 199, 200
Hugo, Victor, 7, 49, 67, 194, 199, 222
Hutton, James, 147, 149, 150

Iliad, 75, 76
Itinéraire (Chateaubriand), 56

Jacob, 154
Janin, 159
Jasmin, 126
Jay, 218
Joubert, Léo, 132, 152, 163
Jouffroy, 23, 43, 98
Jullien, Bernard, 64, 174, 175, 233, 234

Koechli, 125

Labitte, Charles, 46, 51, 65
La Bruyère, 77, 125
La Fontaine, 164
La Harpe, Jean François de, 4, 6, 13, 127
Lamartine, 7, 24, 105, 153, 188, 190, 193
Lamotte, 124, 157, 162, 188, 213
Lanfrey, 109, 110
La Rochefoucauld, 100
Lascaris, John, 149
Le Brun-Pindare, 57
Leclerc, Joseph-Victor, 51, 52, 66, 106, 138
Leconte de Lisle, 75, 162
Legrand, 53
Lehmann, A. G., 196
Lenormant, Charles, 27
Leonides of Tarentum, 154
Lermercier, 6
Lerminier, 65, 138
Lerous, Pierre, 42
Leroy, Maxime, 184, 192
Létronne, 139
Levin, Harry, 212
Littré, 57, 58, 167, 204
Livy, 105–108
Longinus, 119, 204
Longus, 79

Loudierre, 170
Loyson, Charles, 163
Lucian, 57
Lucretius, 34, 48, 49, 65, 165, 182
Luther, 160

MacClintock, Lander, xi, 192, 234, 235
Magnin, Charles, 44, 46, 65, 126, 221
Malherbe, 182
Marolles, 167
Marot, 48
Martin, Nicolas, 55, 176, 233
Martyrs, Les (Chateaubriand), 56
Maucroix, 165
Maurras, Charles, 234
Mazarin Library, 27, 34
Meineke, August, 183, 184
Meleager, 12, 64, 79, 85, 148, 152, 153, 155, 156, 160, 174, 175, 233
Menander, 197
Mérimée, Prosper, 27, 132, 201
Mes Poisons (Sainte-Beuve), 45
Meurice, P., 160
Michelet, 98, 99
Michelle, 62
Milton, 162
Molière, 120, 197, 199, 218, 220
Monselet, 232
Montaigne, 77, 103, 176, 225, 238
More, Paul Elmer, 234
Moschus, 152, 173
Mulhauser, Frederick, xi
Musset, 7, 190

Naples, 26
Napoleon I, 16, 104, 129
Napoleon III, 60
Niebuhr, Berthold, 44, 105, 106
Nisard, Désiré, 50, 51, 62, 166, 221
Numa, 105, 106

Olivier, Juste, 45, 84, 126
Ortigues, Madame d', 55
Osborn, Catherine Bill, xi
Ovid, 60, 66, 79, 183

Pantasidès, Jean, 28–30, 35, 53, 55, 67, 68, 116, 170, 188
Parallel Lives (Plutarch), 102, 103
Paris, Paulin, 224
Parny, 200
Parthenius of Nicea, 184
Pascal, 48
Pasquier, 57
Patin, Henri, 23, 43, 45, 46, 66
Patru, 165
Paul the Silentiary, 35, 155
Pavie, Victor, 32, 33, 199
Pecchio, Giuseppi, 43
Peerlkampf, 66
Pensées d'août, Les (Sainte-Beuve), 191
Péricaud, 32
Perrault, Charles, 57, 157, 186, 213, 214
Philip of Thessalonica, 148
Philodemus, 32
Piccolos, Nicolas, 6, 45, 47
Pierrot, Jules-Aimable, 22
Pindar, 12, 79, 118, 147, 148, 188, 189, 196
Piscatori, 53, 54

260 · *Index*

Pisistratus, 128, 129, 130, 133
Planche, Joseph, 22
Planudes, Maximus, 149
Plautus, 197
Plautus, 197
Pléiade, 12, 13, 147, 160, 206
Pliny the Elder, 57
Pliny the Younger, 58, 65, 110
Plutarch, 102, 103, 163, 205, 225
Polybius, 65, 101, 106, 110
Pommier, Jean, *xi*
Pompeii, 26
Pongerville, 49, 65, 159, 165, 167
Pons, 157
Ponsard, 122
Pontmartin, 66
Pope, Alexander, 168, 192, 193, 197, 199
Port-Royal (Sainte-Beuve), 52, 83, 134
Pound, Ezra, 213
Propertius, 12, 183, 185

Quarrel of the Ancients and Moderns, 213
"Qu'est-ce qu'un classique," 57
Quinet, 49, 50, 98, 117
Quintilian, 204, 205
Quintus of Smyrna, 64, 79

Rabelais, 197
Racan, 157, 165, 200
Racine, 43, 120, 121, 158, 196, 199, 200, 206, 218
Radet, Georges, 53
Raoul-Rochette, 23, 44
Ravaisson, 33
Raybaud, Maxime, 43

Récamier, Madame, 47
Regard, Maurice, 67, 135, 189
Régnier, Mathurin, 10, 12, 48
Renan, 63
Reymond, William, 135
Rigault, Hippolyte, 59, 63, 161, 213, 221
Rivarol, 166
Roland, Madame, 109
Rollin, 19, 20, 57, 97, 106, 227
"Roman dans l'antiquité et Apulee, Le" (Sainte-Beuve), 64
Romanticism, 216, 218, 219, 222
Ronsard, 12, 63
Rossignol, Professor, 31, 57, 66, 137, 183
Royer-Collard, 111
Ruhnkenius, 76

Sacy, 130, 218
Sainte-Beuve, Madame, 20
Saint-Pierre, Bernardin de, 122
Saint-Victor, Paul, 67, 150, 158, 175
Salel, Hugues, 76
Sallust, 105
Salvandy, 53, 54, 230
Sappho, 148, 188
Saumaise, 148
Scaliger, 154
Scheel, Hans, 87, 135, 232
Scherer, 116
Schiller, 118
Schlegel brothers, 196
Scott, Walter, 11
Sénécé, 65
Sévigné, Madame de, 130

Shakespeare, 103, 118, 120, 131, 160, 196, 197, 199, 220, 225
Sidonius Apollinarius, 189
Simonides, 102
Sismondi, 6
Sophocles, 120, 159, 197
Southey, 184
Staël, Madame de, 4, 5, 11, 13, 16, 99, 154, 193
"Stances et sonnets imités d'Ovide" (Saint-Beuve), 31
Statius, 51, 172
Suetonius, 48, 105

Tacitus, 21, 101, 105, 108–111
Taine, Hippolyte, 107, 108, 138, 221, 226, 231
Tasso, 118, 196
Terence, 64, 65, 78, 79, 137, 167
Theil, 76
Theocritus, 12, 25, 55, 78, 79, 89, 151, 152, 159, 183–189, 192, 205
Théry, 49
Thiers, 108–110
Thucydides, 104, 108, 137
Tibullus, 182, 185, 189
Tissot, 23
Translation, 153–176
Troplong, 101
Troubat, Jules, 28, 30, 67, 68, 103
Turgot, 86

Urfé, Honoré d', 187

Valéry, Paul, 158, 217
Valmore, Ondine, 32
Vaquerie, A., 159

Varro, 106
Vauvenargues, 185
Veissier-Descombes, 150
Vico, 84, 98, 99, 105, 128
Vie, Poésies et Pensées de Joseph Delorme (Sainte-Beuve), 9, 10, 11, 190, 191, 193, 195, 196
Viggiani, Carl, 118, 119
Vigny, Alfred de, 120, 121, 200
Viguier, 46, 63, 65
Villemain, Abel François, 6, 18, 43, 45, 46, 57, 60, 139, 191
Villoison, Anse de, 75, 126
Viollet-le-Duc, Eugène Emmanuel, 82
Virgil, 57, 60–66, 88, 108, 117, 118, 121, 123, 124, 165, 182, 184, 186, 187, 196, 199–202, 225
Vitet, 23
Voltaire, 124
Volney, 102, 225
Volupté, 19
Voss, 44

Walkenaer, 57
Walter, G., 7
Wolf, 44, 46, 75, 124, 125, 126, 128, 129, 131, 132, 134
Wood, 130
Wordsworth, 184
Wright, John, 44

Xenophon, 101, 104

Young, 118

Zeller, 136, 138, 227